D0411586

Enter the Dragon

THEO PAPHITIS

with Laurie Stone

Enter the Dragon

How I Transformed My Life and How You Can Too

This edition first published in Great Britain in 2008 by
Orion Books
an imprint of the Orion Publishing Group Ltd
Orion House, 5 Upper St Martin's Lane,
London WC2H 9EA
An Hachette Livre UK Company

1 3 5 7 9 10 8 6 4 2

A CIP catalogue record for this book is available
from the British Library.

ISBN: 978 0 7528 9097 5 (Hardback)
ISBN: 978 0 7528 9729 5 (Export Trade Paperback)

Printed in Great Britain by Clays Ltd, St Ives plc

The Orion Publishing Group's policy is to use papers that are natural, renewable and
recyclable and made from wood grown in sustainable forests. The logging and
manufacturing processes are expected to conform to the environmental regulations of
the country of origin.

Every effort has been made to fulfil requirements with regard to reproducing
copyright material. The author and publisher will be glad to rectify any omissions at
the earliest opportunity.

www.orionbooks.co.uk

Contents

Acknowledgements

I would like to thank the wonderful Mrs P, our five lovely children – Dominic, Zoe, Alex, Annabelle and Hollie – Mum, Dad, Kyriacou, Demitri, Marinos and Debbie's dad, Tony Stocker, and his wife, Betty, for all their support in what has turned out to be a most incredible journey.

No book would be complete without a mention of some of our closest and dearest friends who have shared our laughter and tears and enhanced our lives. Peter, Jo, Andrew and Chris Gowland, Ray, Jan, Claire and Mark Trowell, Ken Brown, Denise, Adam and Joy Thornton-Brown, Sean and Lynn O'Neill, Michael and Louisa Kesta, Howard, Rachel and Taylor MacPherson.

I would also like to extend my warmest thanks and appreciation to some people without whom this book would not have seen the light of day, namely Ian Marshall and his editorial team at Orion for their enormous help in the project, my literary agent, Robert Smith, and Laurie Stone and Stuart Brodkin for their help in writing this book.

My journey was also greatly enhanced by working with some marvellous people who unfortunately don't get a mention here, but that is not because I have forgotten you. I love you all lots and here's a name check: Richard Aquilina, Lisa Bond, Rick and Yvonne Bradbrook, Rachel Brain, Kato (Michael Brown), Pru Buckley, SAS Jim (Jim Carpenter), Ken Chapman, Ian Childs, Josephine Cocks, Chris Collison, Malcolm Cooke, Sheelagh Cooke, Bill Cooper, Sue Dover, Palvinder Dulai, Ces Edwards, Katie Evans, Mary Gilfillan (who is looking down on us all with her radiant smile), Vasco Gomes, Georgina Gray, Lesley Grayburn, Yvonne Haines, Debbie Johnson, Chris Jones, Laura Keane, Enda Kelly, Kypros Kyprianou, Richard Lewczynski, Dick Lidell, Mike Lilley, Ann Mantz, Tom Moore, Jenny Pearce, Lucy Pepper, Sean Pine, Roy Putt, Veronica Quinn, John Saunders, Colin Sayer, Mary Sheehan, Jane Smith, Deano Standing, Brian Tonks, Dick Towner, Jane Turner, John Varney, Anne Watkins, Mike Watkins, Beverley Williams, Caroline Williams, Karen Wilson and all the staff at Contessa, La Senza, Partners, Ryman and Red Letter Days who are too numerous to mention here.

Preface

When I was first approached to write this book, I wanted to run a mile. Why me? First of all, I'm dyslexic. Secondly, I left school with only one certificate – for colouring in maps. I think it's called geography now! But here I am, setting down my thoughts on paper, hopefully for posterity, and dispensing oodles of free business advice into the bargain.

In the end I was persuaded that my story might be worth telling – and more importantly, worth reading. But what I didn't want was the usual 'I was born on such and such a date'-type volume. I've started reading plenty of those and I'm usually fast asleep halfway through the first chapter.

Beginning my memoirs with 'My name is Theo Paphitis and I was born on 25 September' would have been as deadly dull as it would have been wholly inaccurate. In fact, for the record, I discovered when I applied for my first passport many moons ago that I was actually born on 24 September, and not a day later, as I had previously believed. It was quite a shock to the system, I can tell you.

But discovering that my name isn't Theo Paphitis was even more of a shock.

It all happened rather unexpectedly while I was halfway

through writing this book. I was having Sunday lunch with my father, Bambos, his wife, Kyriacou, my two brothers, Marinos and George, and my step-brother, Xanthos, and our respective families. During the conversation, it emerged that our family name is Charalambos.

My elder brother, Marinos, and I looked at each other in disbelief. I was then in my forty-seventh year, and my brother is two years older. We had lived all these years with the name of Paphitis, so being told that we were, in fact, the Charalambos family left us speechless.

My father continued to tuck into his Sunday roast as if nothing had happened and it took us a while to grab his attention and ask for an explanation. He looked up at us and said, 'It's nothing to do with you, innit,' and swallowed another mouthful of lamb. We had to stop him, almost forcibly, and insist that he tell us exactly what he meant. At first he said he had no intention of discussing it with us, that it was totally irrelevant, that it was his name and shouldn't bother us. He couldn't grasp that we had more than a passing interest in the bombshell he had just dropped!

Eventually his wife cajoled him into explaining how the confusion had come about. It seems that my granddad, Theo, after whom I was named, lived in a village called Lysos in the region of Paphos. But his parents died when he was young – both on the same day, apparently, although I never got to the bottom of that mystery – and my granddad was sent to live with a distant uncle in the capital, Nicosia. By the time he was nine he was working in his uncle's tailor's shop.

Part of his job was to help out with ironing clothes after they had been tailored or altered. In those days they used a great big metal iron, which was heated with hot coals. One day he had overfilled the iron with coal and was ironing some dignitary's Sunday finest when the coal spilled out on to the cloth and made a gaping hole in the garment. When his uncle saw what had happened, he beat my granddad. That was the final straw and Granddad decided that night that he had had enough and ran away.

He ended up in Limassol and was somehow befriended by British soldiers who saw him wandering homeless through the streets. They would give him little jobs, errands and the like, and he even learned to drive. By the time he was sixteen he was on the payroll as a British Army driver and he continued to work for the British, eventually joined by his son, my father, until the Brits left in the early sixties.

At that point Granddad was given a British passport as a sort of parting gift – and it seems that is when our name changed. The British in Cyprus by this time were far from popular and had to contend with the local resistance movement. People who worked for the British were not always popular either. By giving my grandfather a passport, the British were giving him the opportunity to come to England to escape the potential wrath of the locals.

Rather ungratefully, on receipt of his new passport, my grandfather pointed out that they'd got his name wrong. He told them, 'I am named as Theodoros Paphitis and my son as Bambos Paphitis. That's not our name – our name is Charalambos.' It wasn't surprising that the British had got it wrong. When my grandfather first arrived, he had told them that he was called Theo and came from Paphos – and people from Paphos were known as Paphitis. They refused to change the name. After all, they knew him as Paphitis. So that's how I came to be known – wrongly – as Paphitis. But I suppose I'm stuck with it now. It's too late to change and, anyway, it's sort of grown on me.

So writing this book was very much a voyage of discovery for me. I've learned so much about myself and my family, some of which I will share with you over the following pages.

Of course, I'm not too shy to tell you that I've made a huge success of my life – and I'll let you into some of the secrets that helped me to the top. It's not the conventional business advice that gets dished out so often – there are lots of surprises along the way. My hope is that you will be encouraged, maybe even inspired, by some of the ideas that have enabled me to achieve my dreams and ambitions, despite having few formal qualifications to speak of. I hope that you can attain some of your goals and that you will get as much enjoyment from reading this book as I did from writing it.

Chapter One

It's a struggle in Cyprus

I think now is an opportune moment to go back to the beginning – where it all started for me in Cyprus. The most important point in anyone's life is the day they were born. Everyone knows the exact date they came into this world and celebrates the occasion – apart from me.

I was born on 24 September 1959. Although, until I was ten, I thought it was 25 September. I only discovered it was a day earlier when I was planning to make my first trip back to Cyprus from our new home in England. My parents had a British passport, but I was born in Cyprus so I was a Cypriot citizen. I needed to be naturalised and while going through the process of getting my own passport I discovered I was born on 24 September.

Why didn't I know? Well, we never really celebrated birthdays. Why? I don't really know. A birthday wasn't a special occasion as far as our family was concerned. I can't ever remember receiving many birthday presents. Maybe it was because we had emigrated when I was six and all our immediate family was still in Cyprus, combined with the fact that money was scarce. But it didn't bother me because I knew no different. It was only much later on when I reached my teenage years that

I would persuade my parents to find the money to buy me the odd item of peer-pressure clothing. And by this time I had various part-time jobs, so I was able to treat myself.

My earliest memories as a child are going to nursery school in Cyprus with my brother Marinos. Our mother, Yianoulla, worked in the local sugar factory, while our father worked as an electrician at the British Army base in Limassol. We spent all day at nursery, from 8 a.m. until 4 p.m., five days a week, and I hated it. We had lunch there – usually a piece of Cypriot bread smothered in jam – then had to sleep on the floor for ninety minutes with just a cushion for comfort.

Even at three years old I always seemed to be in trouble. I could never sleep, a trait that I retain to this day. At nursery I would get up and talk, rather than sleep, and was always being told off for disturbing everyone else. I was the boisterous one, while my brother Marinos was much quieter and found it easier to accept authority. He just got on with life. If there was any trouble to be found, I was in the thick of it.

One of my pet hates at that early age was an appointment at the dentist. The only way my parents could persuade me to go was by bribing me with a visit to the local toy shop, where I would be allowed to buy a cheap plastic toy. I used to take these toys up on the flat roof of our rented house, which was my play area.

One day, having been told off by my mother, I went up there in a fit of pique with a hammer and nails, and nailed all the toys on to a piece of wood which was used as a barrier to stop people falling off. Once I had finished this work of art, I realised I was going to get into more trouble and took a pair of pliers and attempted to remove the nails from the barrier. In my efforts to pull out the nails I managed to catapult myself off the roof and landed head first in the shrubs below, which were in the grounds of the local convent. I knocked myself unconscious in the process. Eventually, I was missed and search parties were sent out to look for me. I was delivered back home, by now in a state of semi-consciousness, by two nuns who had chanced upon me.

If there was any danger to be found, rest assured, I would find it. On the morning of my uncle Sissos's wedding, around the age of five and dressed all in white as a pageboy, I decided to go and play out in the road. I dropped one of my favourite toys in a storm grate and tried to retrieve it by using a piece of metal to take up the grate. Unfortunately, as I placed my hand inside to get my toy, the grate came down and crushed my hand!

I was left screaming, trapped by the side of the road, dressed in my finery with my hand stuck in the drain. People rushed to help me and I was whisked to the local doctor. My hand was quickly bandaged up and I made the wedding. As a pageboy, my duty was to hold a candle that was almost as big as I was. With my damaged hand, there was no way I could do this. (Fortunately, there was soon another wedding and I got my chance to hold the candle.) For the wedding photographs I had to hide the bandage behind my back.

After the formal wedding ceremony was over and the party began, I was left to my own devices. As was the custom, everyone living in the street where my aunt and uncle were about to set up home was invited to the party. It was during these festivities that I decided it would be fun to take a glass and fill it with what remained of other people's drinks – mainly spirits, including good, old-fashioned Cypriot brandy. I then found a nice hiding place under a table and drank the contents of my glass.

Unsurprisingly, I passed out and was found comatose several hours later, prompting another visit to the doctor, who was now getting to know me quite well. It was the first time I had been drunk and I spent the next twenty-four hours in a different world. I wasn't to know it at the time but it was to happen to me again many times in the future.

So, living with me as a child was not easy for my parents. Mum was hugely houseproud and tidy, and our home was always spotlessly clean. Although money was very tight, every year we moved to a different rented property, one of which was in downtown Limassol, now the old shopping part of the town. It was barely a hundred yards from the sea.

This was a huge attraction to me. There were big rocks to clamber over in search of crabs. Armed with a fork from my mum's cutlery tray, I became quite an expert at catching them. Unfortunately, I was not so good at hanging on to the forks. I lost so many that at many mealtimes we were short of forks – something that I blamed on a mysterious kitchen pixie.

I didn't realise the dangers of crab hunting on my own and was eventually forbidden to go anywhere near the rocks. The ban came into force after one Sunday afternoon when I set off on a crabbing session in my Sunday best and new sandals. A wave took me by surprise and sent me head over heels into the sea. I managed to drag myself back on to the rocks and then had to soggily make my way home to face the music.

I would love to say that my parents, especially my mum, were sensitive souls. But the truth is that my mother is of solid Mediterranean stock with a temperament to match. A good clip round the ear was never far away. This punishment didn't seem to bother me too much or act as a deterrent as I went on numerous further escapades throughout my childhood years. And then came the biggest of escapades!

Once the British Army's occupation of Cyprus ended, there wasn't much work for my father, so eventually in 1966 my parents decided to make a fresh start in England. Some time later I learned that a friend had told my father that there was a big demand for bouzouki players in England! The bouzouki is a

Greek instrument similar to a mandolin. I couldn't quite picture hundreds of people waving wads of cash, waiting to snap up the first bouzouki player to step off the banana boat from Limassol.

However, surprising though it seems to me now, once we arrived in England my father got fixed up very quickly in a Greek restaurant-cum-nightclub, playing his bouzouki, and was soon earning decent money.

For me, going to England was not a concern – it was an adventure. We started selling all our possessions, so I knew the trip was imminent. When our final week in Cyprus arrived, we spent a lot of time visiting relatives and saying our farewells. There were plenty of tears and much advice given. I had just finished nursery at the time and I can remember my mother's father, George, who was a verger at the local church, sitting me down on his lap to teach me English. It didn't take very long. He taught me the word 'water'. I am sure he felt that would hold me in good stead and that if I came to any harm in this foreign land I could at least ask for a drink. In a strange way I could see the logic in his thinking. You can survive a long period without food but not without water.

But that wasn't all he gave me. My grandfather lived with my grandmother, Elathe, in a shack at the end of my aunt's garden. It was traditional for Cypriot parents to give their youngest child their home and then build themselves a breezeblock shack with a tin roof in the garden. Their home was a room with bed, table, chairs and a radio. The main advantage of this sort of arrangement is that grandparents are close at hand to look after their grandchildren – it certainly saves on baby-sitting costs.

From his humble home, my grandfather fetched a little hessian purse. He took great pleasure in opening it and showing me the contents. I expected pieces of gold to be contained within this secretive pouch. With great drama, Granddad pulled out several big, black English pennies, which he had been collecting over many years as he came into contact with English people who were either on holiday or working in Cyprus. He was saving them as some form of inheritance and obviously felt it was time for me to receive my share. It was an absolutely fantastic gesture and, to me, this was real treasure. I was even convinced that when I arrived in the mystical country that was England I would be king!

These pennies were my stash, and I suppose they were the origin of my penchant for having some 'walking the street' money – always hidden away in case of an emergency. Even then, it seems, I understood that cash is king. Ever since, I've always kept a little to one side so that I can move quickly in the event that I need something. Later on, 'walking the street' money would mean I could move swiftly to buy a company, rather than having to explain my plans to a bank in order to borrow some money.

With our worldly possessions packed in about half a dozen suitcases, we were picked up on our day of departure by the whole family. A cavalcade of cars arrived at the port full of people wanting to say their farewells. We were all excited, but I was more excited about the journey than where we were going and what we would be doing when we got there. It took us between ten and twelve days to reach Liverpool. We were all in our best clothes, all the males wearing ties, of course. I don't think mother would allow my father out of the house if he wasn't wearing a tie.

It wasn't exactly *The QE2* – more an old rust bucket than a five-star cruise liner. The boat was Italian with a mainly Italian crew, although quite a lot of them spoke English. We were all packed into one tiny cabin, but I wasn't too concerned about the cramped accommodation when there was a whole boat to explore.

On the first day, possibly before we'd even left Cypriot

waters, there was an announcement on the Tannoy asking if anyone had seen a small boy wandering around – that was me! Well, all the corridors looked the same, I didn't know the number of our cabin and I couldn't read any of the signs. I was quickly reunited with my family – it wasn't hard to spot me, I was the one crying and hyperventilating – and as soon as I received the obligatory clip round the ear from my mother, I knew things were back to normal and the crying stopped.

That scare didn't discourage me and I was soon off on my travels again, talking in Cypriot to anyone who would listen. Of course, nobody understood a word I was saying, although I was sure they did. They were just humouring me. I was also looking to spend some of my inheritance – my 'walking the boat' money – and had located the ship shop. It was a few days into the trip when I plucked up the courage to go inside and I soon found a plastic toy, a fire truck, that took my fancy. I placed it on the counter and emptied my pennies out, wondering how many of these coins would be needed.

But the woman behind the counter just shook her head because I didn't have enough. I was hugely disappointed. And after she had counted my ten pennies over and over again I finally got the message that I was well short of the proper purchase price.

Then one of the crew members I had chatted to a few times during my walks around the deck came into the shop and spoke to the lady. Before I knew it, I was walking out with the toy in my hand – and my money unspent. It doesn't get much better than that! Though it certainly got a lot more interesting once we reached our destination.

Chapter Two

Moving to Manchester

We eventually landed in Liverpool after stopping off in Venice and it was on Merseyside that I stepped on to British soil for the first time. My parents had friends there and we spent a week with them until we set off by train to Manchester.

To this day, I always think of Liverpool as the land of Old Spice, because the room we stayed in there was permeated with the smell of the aftershave of that name. Actually, it's a smell I quite like and has stayed with me ever since, even though it wasn't until many years later that I found out what it was.

In Manchester we stayed with friends for a week or two before my parents managed to rent a little two-bedroom terraced house in a place called Old Trafford. Living there meant absolutely nothing to me. It seemed an ordinary sort of area, pretty quiet to be honest, with not much happening – until our first Saturday that is!

That's when the world and his wife – and kids – descended upon us. We were so close to what I soon enough learned was the Manchester United football ground that it was hardly believable that I hadn't noticed it before. I hadn't even heard of Manchester United. The only football I had seen was in the playground or in the street – and now here I was right in the thick of it. It didn't take me long to take an interest in what was going on right on my doorstep. I could hardly ignore it, could I?

When I started my new school in England aged seven, the only words I knew were 'yes' and 'no' and, of course, 'water'! Despite my limited vocabulary – or perhaps because of it – it wasn't long before I started getting into trouble. I think it was my first or second day, actually – I wasted no time at all in getting myself known. It was break time and a box came round full of chocolate bars, so I dived in and took out a bar, only to find myself grabbed by the teacher and told off, while this young lad standing next to me burst into tears. Apparently, you brought your snack in and put it into the box in the morning and got it back at break time. Well, how was I to know that? I just took out the biggest chocolate bar I could find and started to devour it.

What I did know was that I was desperate to get into a match at Old Trafford. But I knew you had to pay and couldn't see how I'd ever have enough money to afford it. What's more, my parents wouldn't let me. So even if I did manage to scrape together the cost of admission, I'd have to go without telling them.

And then one of the kids who lived nearby and went to the same school explained that there were reserve games during the week. I wasn't even sure what reserve games were, but I did know it wasn't the main game. I worked out it was some sort of practice match, but you could get in for nothing. So, of course, we skipped school to watch the reserves.

I was about seven at the time and no one even asked why we weren't at school. We watched a game and I didn't have a clue who was playing, but it sparked my interest in football – an interest that was to take me from a reserve-team match at Old Trafford to a famous day at the FA Cup final nearly forty years later.

Dad was still working as a musician. His hobby, and his life, was music, even though he was an electrician by trade. He played the bouzouki incredibly well and had a great voice too. He had used his musical skills to make extra money when we were saving up for the trip to England. When we first arrived, my mother didn't work. She was busy trying to understand what the hell was going on in this foreign land. Without a car, the first thing she learned were the bus timetables.

Dad worked seven nights a week and earned enough for us to be able to buy a two-bedroom house in Gorton, a suburb of Manchester, for £880. You went straight in off the street – think *Coronation Street* and you've got it! There were two rooms downstairs and a kitchen, and up the stairs you had two bedrooms and a bathroom. The toilet was out the back, which was not handy – or comfortable – especially when it was cold, but it was all we could afford at the time.

We settled in and the change of address, even though it wasn't a million miles from our old home, meant a change of schools. By now I was eight and, perhaps not surprisingly, bouzouki-mania seemed to have died down a little, with the result that things were drying up for my dad in the musical world. He had to get a job in a factory. I never asked him what he did; I think it was something to do with palettes.

But what I did know was that his income alone wasn't anywhere near enough for the family, so Mum had to get a job too, finding work as a seamstress in a factory making leather coats. I can remember it quite clearly because, like that Johnny Cash song about the man who makes a car out of all the bits he gets from the car factory, she managed to make herself and everybody in the family a leather coat, using whatever bits of scrap leather she could get her hands on. The pieces didn't always match, but everybody got a coat.

By this time Mum had fallen pregnant with my youngest brother, George, so working was becoming difficult for her.

After George was born, the only way my mother could go back to work was if my nans came over from Cyprus to look after the baby. So the two little old ladies – Xanthi and Elathe – who had never set foot outside Cyprus, each came over on holiday for a few months at a time and were confronted by Manchester. It was quite a culture shock for them.

Marinos and I had become quite self-sufficient and were often given sixpence to buy saveloy and chips for dinner after school. We would eat it outside, and then play together until it got dark. It was a great time for the two of us because Mum was always busy and we could run rings round both our nans, as whichever one was staying with us had her hands full looking after George. Now and again we would take George out for a walk in his pram and the poor little mite would regularly fly through the air and hit the deck after we failed to negotiate a kerb properly.

At about this time we discovered the wonders of a place called Belle Vue, which wasn't far from where we lived. Belle Vue was a big entertainment complex, which regularly featured speedway and greyhound racing. But more importantly, as far as we were concerned, it was the biggest fun fair we had ever seen, a forerunner of places like Chessington World of Adventure and Thorpe Park.

It was sixpence to get in, but we had already spent most of that on our dinner so we had to find an alternative 'entrance'. It wasn't too difficult – the perimeter fence presented us with few problems! The atmosphere was great – to boys of eight and ten it was like being in heaven. We spent what little money we had on the slot machines that would take sixpences or shillings. It was an early lesson to me and my brother that gambling doesn't pay!

Gorton was, as we soon discovered, famous for its railway sidings, which provided us with a magnificent, free playground.

All around the sidings were air-raid shelters – great, big concrete constructions that had been built during the war. And as if this wasn't enough, the whole area was thick with raspberry and blackberry bushes. There was an even bigger bonus to be found on the ground – huge amounts of coke, which had literally fallen off the back of a cargo truck as the trains rattled through and which could be used to make a fire to keep us warm while we ate our raspberries and blackberries.

It didn't matter if it was raining outside – and it always seemed to be raining in Manchester – it was a fantastic place to hang out with your mates. We didn't get up to much mischief; we usually just sat there singing our silly songs, but the occasional dare did send one of the gang to try to 'liberate' some cargo from one of the railway trucks parked above the sidings. Lots of the cargo was absolutely useless, it wasn't worth nicking, but one particular dare did get most of the kids at school in trouble.

Several large boxes of blakeys were freed from one of the trucks. Blakeys were bits of metal with spikes that were put on the heel and toe of the shoe sole to stop them wearing out. Everybody stuck them on to their shoes because they made such a great racket. For weeks, the whole school went clonk, clonk, clonk, and the caretaker was none too pleased at the damage being done to the school floor.

We had great fun finding uses for the things that fell off the goods carriages. We played marbles with the ball bearings and then some bright spark, who shall remain nameless for fear of the law catching up with him even at this late stage, discovered that the metal washers we found were virtually the same size as shilling pieces. The arcade machines at Belle Vue weren't very sophisticated and couldn't tell the difference.

Armed with pockets full of washers, we would get on the bus to Belle Vue, jumping off again before the conductor reached us to ask us for the fare. This continued – on, off, on, off – until we reached our destination. It took much longer that way, but it didn't cost us a penny. Then we would climb the fence and make a beeline for the arcades. I suppose we must have looked pretty suspicious, and now and again the security people would chase us away. They even caught us once or twice, but we didn't care; it was all a game and this was our playground.

Of course, during all this time we were supposed to be in the classroom and not the playground. But the excitement of the sidings and the air-raid shelters, plus the lure of Belle Vue, was beyond anything that school could offer. It really was no contest as far as I was concerned.

Then one day a group of four or five of us decided we were going to go to another reserve game at Old Trafford. I can't remember who United were playing, but it was a great game and there were lots of goals. It was awesome. We had such a great time we decided not to go home but to go to Belle Vue instead. I knew my mum wasn't coming back from work until late, my dad was away working, and we didn't have a grand-mother staying with us at the time, as George was being looked after by a neighbour.

So off we went to Belle Vue. We got rumbled by security so we split up. We gave them the slip but then we couldn't find each other and, as it was getting dark, we each made our way home separately. Unfortunately, it was one of the few days when my mother had come home early. She didn't know where we were, so she went to the school to find out. Of course, that was probably the last place she was going to find us! Eventually, when we did get home, we got the biggest hiding of our lives.

That curtailed our activities for a while, but not for long. We were learning the language, mainly from hanging out with our mates and being immersed in the culture. It perhaps seems strange, but I faced no problems fitting in, despite my relatively poor English and my accent. There were lots of other immigrants in the area, so I didn't feel in any sense the odd one out. I know it sounds like a cliché but it was a real voyage of discovery for kids of our age.

Chapter Three

Our new life in London

I was nine when we got the exciting news that we were going to London for the weekend. My dad, whose musical work hadn't completely dried up, had been offered a gig near Finsbury Park, which was a popular area for the local expatriate Cypriot community. We were going to stay with a distant cousin of one of my parents while Dad played at this club on Saturday night.

For a lad of my age, it was all terribly exciting. We took the train, Dad carrying his beloved bouzouki, and ended up at our cousin's house, a semi-detached in Turnpike Lane in north London – I thought it was lovely. It was my first experience of London and I will never forget it – for all the wrong reasons.

On the night when Dad went to work in the club, we stayed back at our cousin's and went to bed fairly early, only to wake up in the morning to find that Mum wasn't there. There were some extremely glum faces around the place and it wasn't long before I realised that something had gone very, very wrong.

The nightclub in which my father was working was on the fourth floor of a building in Seven Sisters Road, near to what was then called the Astoria, where the Beatles once famously performed. The club was also a bit of a gambling den and somebody had taken umbrage over something that had happened there that night and decided to chuck a petrol bomb in through the window. Definitely not what you want to happen when you're on the fourth floor of the building strumming away at your bouzouki.

It was in the days before those troublesome twins Health and Safety had been born, though in this case they would have been a huge help as there were no proper fire exits – the only escape route was the window. It was a case of burning to death or jumping from the fourth floor. The ones who didn't jump died, and some of those who jumped died too. My father decided that jumping was the lesser of two evils – he didn't fancy choking to death in the thick, acrid smoke that was beginning to engulf the building. He spotted a white van parked in the street below and decided it would break his fall. It didn't just break his fall; it broke almost every bone in his body.

He bounced off the van into the middle of the road and was unconscious when he was taken to the Whittington Hospital in Archway. He was in intensive care for a week, and when he did finally come round, it was touch and go whether he would survive. Even at the age I was, I knew it was a serious situation, but I couldn't help feeling he looked like the bloke you saw in cartoons in plaster from head to toe. His arms and legs were in traction, he had weights attached to various parts of his body and there were screws through his legs. He was also allowed two little holes in the plaster through which his bodily fluids could pass.

He spent a total of six painful months in hospital and for most of the time he was in such a critical condition that he couldn't be moved, so there was no way we could go back home to Manchester. Our weekend stay in London stretched to a lifetime. My brother and I hadn't even said goodbye to our friends.

Eventually, Mum found a one-bedroom basement flat with

a shared bathroom in Queen's Drive near Finsbury Park, not far from the nightclub where Dad had been playing that fateful night. I'll never forget that flat – again for all the wrong reasons. It was damp; it had only the one bedroom, a small sitting room and a sofa that had seen better days and was practically alive. There were two armchairs that were of similar ilk. Mum had the bedroom, which she shared with my younger brother. I slept on the two armchairs put together to make a bed and my brother had the sofa.

We spent a good few months at the flat, during which time my brother and I didn't go to school. It was about this time that man landed on the moon on one of the *Apollo* missions, but our lives certainly weren't taking off. After a couple of months living in this hell hole, we managed to find, through friends and relatives, another flat in St Thomas's Road, in another part of Finsbury Park. St Thomas's Road runs between Finsbury Park Tube Station and Highbury. Yet again, we had landed near another famous football ground. We were only a decent free kick away from Arsenal's headquarters.

Mum got a job as a seamstress in order to pay the rent on our new home and we were sent to the local junior school called Ambler, which was in Blackstock Road. To my horror, having just finished the second year of junior school, I found I had to do it all over again at Ambler. There were two main reasons, one being that my birthday towards the end of September meant I was on the cusp of two school years. The second reason was that I had bunked off so often that I was way behind in my studies.

We returned to Manchester for one day, with a man and a van, which we loaded with as many of our belongings and furniture as we could cram in, and brought it back down to London. With Dad still in hospital, the house in Gorton had to be sold.

My father was finally discharged after six months and joined us in the flat, but things were never the same. I think the time Mum and Dad had been apart was instrumental in ending their relationship. Also, my father hadn't just broken bones, but had sustained some severe head injuries, although in time he made a complete recovery. But the relationship never really worked again. They just seemed to drift apart and finally separated eighteen months later. But they didn't go quietly. There were plenty of rows. My mum's a strong and dominant person, while my father is measured and calm. It was a classic case of chalk and cheese.

I tended to side with my father because I felt he suffered more than anyone else from my mother's hot temper. We were always terribly close and I was convinced he had a rotten deal. Mum was a livewire around the house and you had to do exactly what she wanted. She didn't take prisoners and getting a clip round the ear was a very common occurrence. It was definitely not an option for her to come back home from work and find the house in a mess.

We were not treated in the same way as our friends, who were looked upon as children by their parents. We were always expected to act like mini-adults, tidying the house, running errands, doing our chores, generally pulling our weight – what little there was of it – and God help us if we didn't! But we were incredibly self-reliant, typical latch-key kids. After all, we had been uprooted from Cyprus to Manchester and then to London.

So my brother and I felt different from those we grew up with. For example, my parents wouldn't go to the school open days – Mum had not been to school and didn't really see the point, while Dad was still trying to put his life back together again. It was embarrassing that they never came. Because we were incredibly strictly disciplined at home, we took some of that with us into the outside world. So although we could have got up to all sorts, we were never in trouble with the police.

Perhaps this regime helped set me on my way in my career, but my brother, who was always the sensible one, took a different route and has been a career civil servant all his life.

In short, I did not enjoy a normal childhood like the one I've given my own children. We were expected to act a lot older than our years from a very early age. And we managed to do that. It proves that children are incredibly resilient. But there's no question that it left me with some emotional scars. I was always very envious of friends who had a stable family life with a mother and father who did all the normal things that parents did, who were there for them whenever they needed them and who treated them as children.

My brother and I certainly weren't molly-coddled. We were left to our own devices and learned very quickly to make our own decisions and our own way in life. So while I missed not having that stable family background, it was also an advantage in later years because it gave us confidence in our abilities and we were never afraid to make decisions. We grew up – but a lot quicker than most other kids.

When my parents split up, Dad moved out and rented a room above a restaurant where my brother and I would visit him at weekends. He worked in the restaurant by day and as a musician at night. Meanwhile, we eventually moved from our rented flat to a council flat in a three-floor tenement block in Tufnell Park called Blake House.

We were on the top floor, and with the tenement being built 'in the round', there was a play area in the middle with climbing equipment and a five-a-side football pitch, which we made full use of. It wasn't exactly the lap of luxury and I remember there was a chute outside the door to put your rubbish down. There was no lift, only concrete stairs, which always seemed to smell of stale urine.

The flat had steel windows, which had warped over the

years. It was drafty and cold in winter, so we used to tape up the windows with masking tape or brown tape in an attempt to keep out the wind and rain. Of course, the tape meant you couldn't open the window on the days when the temperature soared – a minor inconvenience!

There was no central heating and the only warmth came from a small gas fire my mother had bought 'on the knock' – in weekly payments – from a guy we used to call 'The German' because, surprisingly enough, he was German. Basically, every bit of equipment in that house came from The German, including all the furniture. And every Saturday morning, he would come round and collect his money. I think Mum was paying him a fiver a week in those days. Sometimes Mum would have five pounds and sometimes she wouldn't and she'd have to tell him to come back. And if you didn't pay for several weeks, he'd add on another lot of interest. He wasn't as cheap as the shops, but they didn't take irregular weekly payments, did they?

Despite the gas fire we were still freezing most of the time. There was more ice on the inside of the windows than on the outside, and when we went to bed at night we would breathe out great plumes of condensation from our mouths. It was freezing everywhere, even in the toilet, although we were much posher now – the toilet was inside the house. And we did have three bedrooms. I shared with George, and Marinos and my mother both had their own rooms. I was eleven and about to start senior school, a comprehensive called Woodberry Down, where my elder brother already went.

The school's main claim to fame in later years was that it was where the two sisters in *Birds of a Feather* (played by actresses Linda Robson and Pauline Quirke) were educated. A few years ago I met Pauline in one of my Contessa stores in Beaconsfield. The staff got all excited, but I avoided eye contact with her because I didn't want to invade her privacy. She came up to me, however, and said, 'It's on tonight. I've got to rush home, my hubby never misses it. *Dragons' Den*, we love it!'

We had a long conversation and I asked her why Woodberry Down kept getting a mention on *Birds of a Feather*. She told me that one of the scriptwriters had an association with the school. I was actually quite star-struck because it was one of my favourite shows and I think she's a fantastic actress. I then slightly ruined it when I told her I thought she was amazing in *Telstar*, which I'd seen in the West End. 'I wasn't in it, love,' she replied. 'It was the skinny bird, Linda Robson. She was in it.'

Woodberry Down didn't need any 'product placement' on *Birds of a Feather* as it was a very good school with a tremendous reputation. It took me about an hour to get there but it was well worth the effort. And one of the few benefits of coming from a one-parent family was that Marinos and I got free bus passes and free school meals.

Back home things continued as before. When Mum was working we had our various duties. Every Wednesday, for example, we had to take the washing about a mile to the launderette, put it in the dryer, fold it up and bring it back to iron it – all before Mum got home. And if it wasn't done to her satisfaction when she did get back, she would explode. Not only that, but she'd expect us to have Hoovered and tidied up the whole house and cooked a meal as well. It might seem harsh, but we didn't think it was that bad. It was what we were used to and we didn't know any other way.

But Mum's moods were a key factor. One day we'd done all the washing, all the ironing and cooked a meal but I had made the mistake of leaving the previous day's newspaper on the floor in our bedroom. Well, World War Three broke out!

Unlike my brother, I always argued my case with Mum, but that only led to blazing rows, and then I couldn't wait to get out of the house. I would walk to King's Cross, a couple of miles away. I loved all the hustle and bustle – literally an innocent abroad in those days, its seediness didn't really hit me. I would hang around in the arcades for a few hours, waiting for Mum to calm down.

Money was incredibly tight and we all had to fend for ourselves. There was certainly no pocket money, and if I needed any cash, I had to earn it. I had a variety of jobs, one of them delivering cards for a mini-cab company. I was twelve and it was my first taste of direct marketing. I loved walking so I enjoyed the work. There was a map of the local area on the cab-office wall. 'Go and do these streets,' they would say, handing over 5,000 cards. I had to put two or three cards in each letterbox and was paid a couple of pounds – good money for me in those days.

Although I didn't know it, the first time I did the job it was a test. The owner of the cab firm wanted to see whether he got any calls from my 'drops' or whether I had dumped the cards in the bin, as many did. Thankfully for my career prospects, such as they were, he got calls and I did the job for several years, sometimes earning as much as £3 or £4 a time. It meant I didn't need to ask Mum for money and was able to save as well as buy some clothes.

Strange as it may seem, I was beginning to enjoy school, even though I was dyslexic. Of course, dyslexia hadn't been invented then, so I was just considered thick! I was in the lowest form, except for maths, but I enjoyed sport, especially rugby and football, and it was partly through playing sport that I was able to start communicating with my fellow pupils and teachers.

I was terribly argumentative and most of the teachers hated dealing with me. I suppose I disrupted their routine. Some of them, however, were willing to enter into a debate with me, and I had an excellent relationship with them.

My routine was pretty hectic. I played rugby for the school

every Saturday morning, did the card drops for the taxi firm in the afternoon and then worked in the Wimpy Bar at Chapel Market on Sundays. In the summer, when there was no rugby, I did the card drops after school and the Wimpy job on a Saturday and Sunday.

I earned £5 a day in the Wimpy Bar plus any tips, which usually doubled my take-home pay. I was always ecstatic when someone didn't turn up for work because it meant I had a second section to look after. The manager, a Turkish Cypriot who seemed to be nipping out to the bookies every five minutes, made it clear we weren't going to get any payment for the extra work involved. I kick myself now, but in those days of youthful naivety it never occurred to me to insist on any additional payment. Just the prospect of all those extra tips from satisfied customers made me happy. A big tip in those days was 50p.

By fourteen, I'd joined the students' union and entered my 'socialist' phase: I'd read *Animal Farm* and believed that everything had to be fair. When I began to work, however, I realised that it didn't work that way.

At school, I started a tuck shop that made money for the school fund. This was good fun and made me one of the most popular pupils in the school. I would sometimes weigh the crisps on the chemical scale in the school lab, and if the packets weren't the weight they should be, I would send them back to Smith's complaining that we had been undersold. It worked a treat and I would receive a free box of crisps in the next delivery, adding to the profits.

Alongside my first retail enterprise, I also came up with my first incentive scheme. The school didn't want any litter scattered around by tuck-shop customers, so I offered a free bag of crisps to anyone who picked up twelve empty crisp packets. It worked a treat and I've used incentive schemes in all my businesses ever since, though I suppose a free trip to the

Caribbean, which is sometimes on offer for my employees now, is a lot better than a gratis bag of salt and vinegar.

I was always busy trying to make money even in my early teens. I needed my 'walking the street' money, unlike my brother, who could go out with no money in his pocket. I needed to have money in case an opportunity came my way, although what sort of opportunity I thought might fall into my lap at that age God only knows!

I couldn't find work for the whole summer holidays, so spent most of the time fishing down at Hampstead Heath ponds, about two miles from where we lived. Off I went with my fishing rod, a couple of cans of Coca-Cola, a sandwich I had made for myself and a transistor radio. I had several radios from which to choose, as I would buy broken ones from the other kids at school for about 50p and fix them for resale.

I would spend the whole day fishing – the sun shining, a drink, a sandwich and the cricket on the radio. There always seemed to be a Test match on when we were out fishing and that led to my love of cricket. It was a cheap day's entertainment – the only outlay was the cans of drink and a pint of maggots from the local fishing shop. In between listening to *Test Match Special* and waiting for the fish to bite, I would dream about becoming sixteen – at that age I'd be able to do whatever I wanted.

On the bottom rung of the school ladder, I was in a class of difficult kids who either weren't very bright or simply didn't want to learn – most of them destined for life's scrap heap. One English lesson, the teacher didn't turn up because she was ill, and the head of year took the class instead. This chap had served in the Royal Navy, and had the beard and dress sense to match. He was every inch the stereotypical sailor pictured on the fag packet.

As he talked to us about his time in the navy, not many of the boys were paying much attention, but I was fascinated by boats and water. 'How do ships stop?' he asked. 'Do they use their brakes like cars?'

'No, they chuck their anchor overboard,' someone piped up.

'No, that's how they stay put.'

I put my hand up and explained that if a propeller goes one way to take you forward, the other way would take you backwards, and you'd come to a stop. He looked at me and asked me whether I had just worked that out. I told him that I had. At the end of the lesson he summoned me to his room and we chatted for about an hour. We talked about all sorts of things, and he worked out that I wasn't that thick and shouldn't be in that class. He had my academic records in front of him, none of which showed much promise except for maths, where I was always at the top of the class, getting 90 to 95 per cent in tests. He put me up to the top stream and told me that this was the right place for me. I was also to be given extra English lessons. At last, I thought, someone believes in me. Maybe it would put an end to other pupils labelling me a dunce or stupid – along with everybody in the lower class. There was no political correctness in those days. Nowadays it would be called bullying, plain and simple.

So my last couple of years at school weren't too bad. That teacher helped me to see that there might be greater opportunities for me, even if I was never going to be a great academic. Despite being in various tutor groups, I failed my O-levels miserably. I got a Scottish certificate in colouring in maps, and the only reason I got that was because I loved the geography teacher. She was Scottish and a fantastic teacher. I think I might have even ended up with a CSE in English and maths at some stage. And that was it. I got lots of Unclassifieds.

My dad, now in his forties, had remarried and had two more children, Xanthos and Christos. Xanthos was named after my dad's mother, Xanthi, who was quite a character. She used to sit on the veranda of her little bungalow on the main road in Limassol and drink half a bottle of brandy every evening. When she came to England to look after us, she couldn't afford to drink brandy, so every evening she sent me over to the boozer on the corner of our street with a jug and a shilling so that the landlord would fill it up with beer for her.

Dad's new wife, Kyriacou, came from a town in Northern Cyprus called Kyrenia, though she and my dad had met in England. Like my mum, she was a seamstress, but the similarities end there. My mother is a tall lady, whereas Kyriacou is short, like my dad who is only about five foot six inches. She is a church-goer and undemanding, the exact opposite of my mother. My brother and I would visit each weekend, just for a few hours, and it was always a relaxing time in our lives. The new woman in Dad's life accepted us and we accepted her – there was no stress, no hang-ups.

It was a shame that Mum and Dad couldn't get on. They say opposites attract, but not in their case.

Chapter Four

Learning what business is all about

As the countdown to my leaving school began, I started to look for a 'proper' job. I was already working weekends at the Wimpy Bar, and although it may not have been the most glamorous of positions, it was a fascinating glimpse into the world outside the tenement block where we lived: I had a boss, I had to turn up to work, I was given responsibility and I got to deal with the public. I was excited by the prospect of a proper job and realised that work was going to teach me far more than school had ever done – and give me a reward as well.

As I'd always had a job of one sort or another and had found various ways of making money, I thought it wouldn't be that difficult to find gainful employment. After all, I was confident and reasonably articulate. But I was in for a shock. In the past, I'd just turned up, got taken on, washed plates, worked as a waiter or worked behind the grill. But dyslexia made even the simple act of filling in an application form a major problem.

What's more, I wasn't sure what I wanted to do. I'd always fancied doing 'something in the City' as I thought that would guarantee loads of money. I dreamed about going on holiday to Butlins in Minehead – that really was the summit of my ambitions. I used to look with envy at the big, mock-Tudor houses on the main road, which I thought were all owned by people who worked in the City. Looking back, I was almost certainly wrong about this – and the houses weren't even mock-Tudor. They were just big houses with a bit of timber cladding and they weren't even detached! I dreamed of owning one of those houses on an A-road, even with all that traffic roaring past the front door.

So I started applying to all the City institutions – for anything. It could have been anything. Whatever was advertised, whatever the agencies had, I'd apply for. I turned up for one interview as a Telex operator. I didn't even know what a Telex operator was. I couldn't type and I couldn't spell – that particular interview didn't go very well. The guy interviewing me went through my application form and took great pleasure in pointing out all the spelling errors. There was a mistake on almost every line.

I must have made a hundred applications for jobs from junior stockbroker to office boy to Telex operator, all of them without success. But I kept on going. I scoured the *Evening Standard* every day and visited every high-street employment agency I could find. What I didn't work out was that the person sitting behind the desk at the recruitment agency – for whom I usually had the greatest respect – was entirely commission-orientated. That's how they earned their money. They didn't really care where they sent you. There was no analysis of your strengths and weaknesses. They didn't even ask you what you wanted to do. You want a job? There's a job going at such and such a place. I've got a card here. I'll ring up, make an appointment and see if they'll see you. I'd be sitting there, wearing my only suit, a hand-me-down from my brother, and the guy at the agency would ring up and say to some prospective employer, 'I've got a young man here, a very smart young man, and I think he's just what you're looking for.'

I turned up at these interviews more in hope than expectation. I got to know Bank Tube Station very well. I must have gone up and down that escalator forty times for job interviews. Slowly but surely, my confidence was beginning to seep away but I was still determined to find myself a career. I didn't want to work on a building site or as a gas fitter or plumber. A lot of my mates went on to become gas fitters, plumbers, BT employees, but although I was pretty good with my hands, I knew I could do work that relied on my brains instead.

At one stage, I did swallow my pride and go for an interview with BT. But they turned me down. I reckon it had something to do with the damned application form! That was a low point for me – being declined by BT.

I wasn't getting much help – I had received no careers advice at school or parental guidance at home. My mum was busy working and running the house – all she wanted to know was whether or not I'd got a job, any job. What's so wonderful about some of the programmes around at the moment like *Dragons' Den* and *The Apprentice* is that they show kids they can achieve something in life. Back then, where did a sixteen-year-old go to start his own business? It would have been an easy option for me to become a labourer, plumber or gas fitter – to get an apprenticeship (without the help of Sir Alan Sugar!), but I continued to search for a career.

Then I saw an advert in the paper for a job as a cadet in the police force based at Hendon. I thought it might be for me, so I decided to sit the exam. Before the interview, one of my teachers gave me some advice. He told me that the police who'd be doing the interview would all be *Guardian* readers, so I walked in with a copy of the *Guardian* under my arm. I'd never read the *Guardian* before – my paper was a new one that had good coverage of sport: the *Sun*.

There must have been thirty of us there for the interview at

New Scotland Yard. About seven got kicked out after the medical. Playing football and rugby kept me reasonably fit so that bit wasn't a problem. Then we had to do an exam. Luckily for me, it was a general knowledge multiple-choice exam which I was good at from reading the *Sun*, so I got through that quite easily too – something of a shock to me with my poor previous exam record.

Now down to about twenty, it was time to go before the interview board, which consisted of three very stern-looking people, all of whom appeared to have a very high regard for themselves. There was more gold braid in that room than on the average ocean cruise liner. As they asked me questions, I began to realise how careful one has to be when choosing one's words; it did not go well for me.

I was disappointed not to get in but my heart wasn't really in it anyway. One of the questions I was asked was, 'How would you feel if you were put out on Dartmoor in a tent and asked to stay with a team for two or three days in the middle of winter?' I told them I thought it would be quite a challenge and it would be fun. I don't think 'fun' was the right answer. I don't think you were meant to have fun. I think you were meant to find it character-building or some such.

I shan't use the word 'racism', but I don't think I was the type they were looking for. I don't know how many people from an ethnic minority were in the police back in those days, but not a lot would be my uneducated guess. One of the boys came out of his interview looking as pleased as punch because he'd got in – they told you there and then whether you'd been selected. I got talking to him and, frankly, he was as thick as two short planks. I often wonder whether he ever became commissioner.

It was a tough time and I was beginning to realise that there is prejudice out there and that life isn't always fair. But then, out of the blue, I got an interview for a job as an office boy/clerical assistant for a company called Wright Dean in their offices in Borough High Street.

I arrived a bit early for the interview and sat in reception, feeling extremely nervous. There was this rather attractive girl called Doris there and I started chatting to her, asking what the firm did. I discovered that they were Lloyds' brokers. As I talked to her I started to relax and got a bit bolder. I started to chat her up and thought that if I didn't get the job at least I might get a date.

Borough High Street plays a big part in my life and I've got a shop there now, but when I went for that interview I owned absolutely nothing except the clothes I stood up in. I was interviewed by a man called Bernard Campion. He was six foot two inches with greased-back jet-black hair and a big black moustache, and he was wearing brogues and a smart City suit. He looked every bit the City gent – or at least what I thought a City gent should look like. But though he was dressed in all the right gear, he was only the office manager, he wasn't a broker. Later I found out that he came from an underprivileged background – just like myself – and had made his way at the firm, starting from the bottom of the pile about forty years earlier. He was a lovely man and very polite.

Three or four days later, to my shock, horror and amazement, I was offered the job. The wages were £20 a week. It was the only offer I'd had, so I accepted it and started straight after school had broken up. Not only was there the money to look forward to, but also the chance to get to know Doris, whose name was actually Debbie.

It wasn't a whirlwind romance. I spoke to Debbie regularly at the office – it was part of my job anyway, but it was only at the firm's Christmas party in December 1976 that I managed to consume enough alcohol in order to feel brave enough to ask her out. In fact, I offered to walk her home after the 'do'. It turned out that she lived at the Oval and I said I knew exactly where it was, though actually I didn't have a clue. To me it was just somewhere in south London where they played cricket.

Obviously I didn't have a car – not on £20 a week – so we got the tube to the Oval and then walked to her place. As we got close to her front door she said, 'Do you want to see my Christmas tree?' I thought it was the best offer I'd had all night. She then gave me a peck on the cheek, said, 'If you cross over the road there, you'll be able to see it in the top window,' and went indoors!

It was about one o'clock in the morning and I had to get home to north London. I got back to the tube station pretty damn quick, but the last train had long gone. There was no question of taking a taxi, so it was shanks's pony. My long trek north took almost four hours, giving me plenty of time to think things over.

Our next date wasn't much better. Mum had gone to Cyprus over the Christmas break, leaving me and my brother to look after the house. We took the opportunity to have a New Year's Eve party, and wrecked the place. Next morning, Debbie rang. I tried to persuade her to come up by tube so that I could meet her at Tufnell Park Station, but instead she took a taxi. When she got to my street, she spent ages looking for the smart house she'd got the impression I lived in, but all she could see was a big tenement block. She rang from a call box, and as I looked down at her in the street below, I had to admit that I lived in a flat and one that was in dire need of a clean.

There were things that I didn't tell my work colleagues too. In order to pay for the tube journey to and from work, I continued to work at the Wimpy Bar on Sundays. But it didn't seem right. Here I was all suited and booted during the week, thinking I'm going to be a City gent and make my millions and then getting into my jeans and working in a Wimpy Bar at the weekend.

At the office, I had to be in by seven thirty every morning to take all the Telexes off the Telex machine, read them, cut them, paste them on to A4 pieces of paper, and work out who they were meant to go to. These were 'risks' coming in from other countries. So if it was a North American 'risk', I'd give it to the North American broker.

I would pile these on to the broker's desk so that when he came in he would have his day's work ready for him. He would take the company minibus over London Bridge to Lloyds of London, place the 'risk' and then return to Borough High Street where the back office would process it. When everybody came in, I'd go and get coffee or tea for all the brokers. Once I'd done the drinks, I'd have a list of files that I would have to dig out for the brokers to work on. And then, later in the day, I'd have to put all those files back where they came from. As you can see, it was an exciting job.

Working in the office meant that I had to write a lot. There were no computers in those days and I had to write line slips, 'risks' and policy amendments for the brokers to take to the underwriters to get signed or initialled. All of this helped me to deal with two of my weaknesses – spelling and handwriting. You weren't going to get your document signed by an underwriter if it wasn't written up properly and the spelling wasn't up to scratch.

So Debbie bought me a pocket dictionary from the stationer's nearby, a place called Ryman. I kept it in my pocket at all times. I also popped into Ryman to buy myself a calligraphy pen and must have spent a couple of weeks every night learning calligraphy and within a month I'd taught myself to write all over again.

It was about recognising my limitations and knowing how to deal with them – an important lesson that would stand me in good stead for the rest of my life. If I hadn't accepted that my writing and spelling were rubbish, I'd have been out of a job.

And, in fact, because I'd learned to write in a formal style, everybody thought I was brilliant.

Not only was I learning things, I was working with nice people, including a couple of guys and a girl who had started at the same time as me. Within a year they'd all got promoted to junior brokers but I was still coming in at seven thirty every morning, cutting up bits of paper and making the tea. I made lots of friends and was invited to everything, but perhaps I was invited as a token ethnic or because I was good for a laugh. I knew I would always be an outsider, and sometimes I was made to feel like one.

Once again, as with the police, I was learning that it isn't an even playing field out there. They don't teach you that at school. Because I went to a comprehensive in north London where most of the kids were from ethnic minorities, we were all in the same boat. We lived in similar housing and all had similar problems, and it was only when I went out into the wide world that I discovered that actually everyone isn't the same. We're not all in it together – far from it. Like anyone faced with this situation, I had the option of being bitter or accepting it. Whether I liked it or not, these were the rules of the game.

I built up quite a rapport with an old guy called Bill, from south London, who had taken early retirement from the docks and had been employed as a part-time filing clerk. A 'spit and sawdust' man and a big Millwall fan, he gave me a lot of stick, but was highly amusing with it and I think I took it well. He also began to explain to me how the world really worked, that some brokers had their jobs not because they were better than me but because they had family contacts and, in most cases, a better education. Once the penny dropped, I started to become resentful.

'You ain't going to change it, son,' Bill would say.

Bill never treated the firm, or its employees, seriously. He lumped all the staff together under 'privileged posh', but he had a great sense of humour so he mocked them all, which was better than being annoyed or jealous. None of this is to say that the 'privileged posh' were bad people. Some of them were absolutely marvellous and the fact that they came from a totally different socio-economic background just meant that they had their own rules, as I'd had in my north London comprehensive. It didn't make them better than me, and it didn't make them worse than me.

It was a fantastic apprenticeship. There might not have been a great deal to learn in the job itself, but I learned a lot about the ways of the world, life and the way the City worked. I would never have planned to hang around for a couple of years to learn these things because I thought I knew everything anyway.

By the time I left, I had an old head on very young shoulders. I didn't have to be told things twice. I realised how British society worked, how the institutions worked. I saw their short-comings, didn't like some of them, but understood them. I could have got a chip on my shoulder but Bill helped me to avoid this.

The job meant that I could mix with my peers who had come from humble backgrounds, and with those who had been to public school and university. I wouldn't change my accent; I didn't think I needed to. I remained true to myself, and if somebody tried to put me down, then I was able to fight my corner. It didn't happen very often but occasionally I did have to stand up for myself and what I believed in.

Bill had an opinion on almost everything – whether you wanted to hear it or not. To most people, he seemed closer to Alf Garnett than Jim Callaghan, who was prime minister at the time, but I valued his perspective. He was a parental figure for me. I'd tell him what was going on and what was bothering me and he had the knack of making everything seem clear to me. I think everyone needs a Bill. He became my best friend and he looked after me. I remember as if it were yesterday him saying, 'One day you'll be a millionaire.' The words could have come straight from the mouth of Del Boy. Bill not only taught me the rules of the game but also told me that as long as you know the rules, you've got a chance of winning.

The lessons that I learned at Wright Dean – to respect everyone, whatever their background – have stayed with me for the whole of my working life. I still try to connect with the most junior members of my staff, the people working in the stores. In all the businesses I now run I show as much respect to those working at the sharp end as I do to any director or senior manager.

At the end of my first year, I got a rise, which meant I was earning £1,500 a year – about £30 a week. I felt I could be there for ten years doing the same job and not earning very much, so I began to look around for another job. After about six months into my second year, a broker on the other side of Borough High Street advertised for an admin clerk, paying £2,500 a year. I applied for it – and got it. I was quite sad to leave, but it was £50 a week and I needed the money.

I lasted two months. I hated it, absolutely hated it. It was a much bigger office and nowhere near as friendly. I'd look at the thirty-year-olds there and think, I don't want to be like that when I'm thirty. I began to realise that this wasn't what I wanted to do for the rest of my working life. This industry wasn't for me. My mind works 24/7, I had so much more to offer, but all I was doing was shuffling paper around. It was time to move on and find a new way to make money.

Chapter Five

Just watch me go!

One day I spotted a little advert in the *Evening Standard*. I've still got the cutting, which read, 'Tyme Limited sales assistants required, 1 Old Bond Street.' The salary was £5,000 – double my own. Debbie urged me to give it a go.

Tyme, which sold watches on the corner of Old Bond Street and Piccadilly, was part of Watches of Switzerland, which in turn was part of H. Samuel, the high-street jewellers. I now owned a couple of suits, so on the following Saturday, I put on my best one with my favourite tie and jumped on the number 12 bus, which took me right into Piccadilly. I was interviewed by a guy called Derek Jeeves, who offered me the job there and then. I couldn't believe it. I went and told Debbie, 'I got the job – £5,000.'

I would love to say that this was all part of some structured plan of progression, but it wasn't. I just wanted more money and to get out of the rut I was in. I gave in my notice. When I told them I was going to work in a shop, they looked down their noses at me, but I didn't care. I was going to be earning more money and that was all that counted for me.

Tyme's still there, by the way, and a few years back I nearly bought Watches of Switzerland, but, after discussing it with Mrs

P, I decided it was more of an emotional move than a business one and I called time on the idea. I have rarely consulted Mrs P on business matters, but in this instance I was worried that my heart was ruling my head.

On my first day at Tyme, I knew it was what I wanted to do – and by the afternoon I was even more convinced I'd made the right move. I sold a Rolex!

I'll never forget it. It was late in the afternoon when an older man, a very serious City type, aristocratic-looking and in his sixties, came into the shop with his nephew, a young guy with a moustache, who was wearing a leather jacket. The old boy told me he wanted to buy a watch as a present for his nephew. I brought the Rolexes out, shared what little knowledge I had of the product with them, gilding the lily on the way.

And to my utter incredulity, he said, 'Yes, we'll take it.' I was ecstatic. I had sold a watch for about £1,600. I was flying. I'd made my first sale. It was down to me and no one else. I'd persuaded someone to part with £1,600, a huge amount of money for a watch in a shop where we also had timepieces costing much, much less.

I sat down behind the desk feeling very smug and began to recount my success to one of the other salesmen, who shattered my illusion somewhat by saying that the man would be back next month with 'another nephew, who will also be wearing leathers, and have a moustache and God knows how many tattoos. It'll be one of his little boys.'

Naively, I asked, 'Is he a poof, a queer?'

'"Gay" is the word you're looking for, Theo. There are a lot of gays around here.'

Whatever the reason for the sale, it didn't stop me being congratulated by the manager, Derek. I asked him why he hadn't told me the old boy was queer. Derek looked up and said, in a very camp voice, 'I thought you knew, love.'

Then the penny dropped. My manager was gay too and I was sure I was going to get the sack for insulting him. But it all blew over. Derek later admitted that he thought the whole incident was hilarious, and the more I worked with him, the more I realised what a good guy he was. Looking back, I am astonished I didn't suss out that he was gay.

It was a tiny shop – no more than 800 square feet – and people used to have to press the buzzer to be let in. It looked good upstairs, but it was crap downstairs and infested with mice. But that didn't bother me one iota. I loved people coming in; I loved serving them; I loved talking to them. All of a sudden, at the age of eighteen, I had become a salesman and was having a ball. And the reason I enjoyed being a salesman so much was simple. I was bloody good at it – and there was very little paperwork. All we sold was watches so I learned almost everything there was to know about them.

Some of the watches had yellow price stickers on the back. You got 5 per cent commission on every yellow-sticker watch. After about two weeks I was selling more yellow-sticker watches than anyone else. Head office was ecstatic because we were getting rid of old stock, stuff they were keen to shift. Customers would come in wanting a particular watch at a particular price – and I'd sell them something completely different, usually with a yellow sticker on.

I made a point of selling customers exactly what I wanted to sell them. They'd leave feeling happy that they had received personal service and with a watch they really wanted, although it wasn't exactly what they had come in for. For the first time in my short working life, I felt I had enough money. I was even earning enough to marry Debbie. We waited until shortly after my eighteenth birthday and got married on 28 January 1978.

At the time, Southwark Council was offering 100 per cent mortgages for first-time buyers. Together we were earning

£9,000 a year and Deb's nan gave us £750 – money she had set aside for her funeral. With that extra funding we became the proud owners of a £9,000, one-bedroom converted flat in Peckham.

At work I was still finding out what I was all about, what I enjoyed doing, what I was good at. I thought I could do most things but I knew I could do a sales job exceptionally well. I was young and in a hurry and enjoyed making money, especially commission. Being rewarded for the work I put in spurred me on.

It was the beginning of my love affair with retailing and watches, both of which continue to this day. As I write this, I'm wearing a watch that cost £15,000, three times my annual salary all those years ago. If anyone had told me then that I'd have a watch worth £15,000 and be the owner of God knows how many shops, I would have told them they were mad. Incidentally, David Butcher, one of the guys who started at Tyme a couple of weeks before I did, is still with the company, managing the Watches of Switzerland branch at 16 New Bond Street. I still buy my watches from him.

I was riding that great wave called the learning curve. I'd learned about the City and I thought I'd learned about prejudices. I certainly didn't think I had any and considered myself pretty streetwise. Here I was working with a camp bloke in the middle of the West End, meeting people from different walks of life every day, from Nigerian chiefs to Arab sheiks, from City types to American oil barons. I carried on selling watches for some while, working with Derek and David, and loved every minute of it.

Obviously, I felt I was going to get my own branch, but I only wanted a big branch. I knew they weren't going to let a nineteen-year-old take charge of stock worth millions of pounds. It was going to take a while, but I had already gained some recognition. If something needed selling, it got sent to us and it was my job to get rid of it. There were, for example, some *objets d'art* made by a well-known silversmith that the other branches just couldn't sell. I sold the lot in about two months. Oh, and of course they all had yellow stickers on. The commission came in really handy as Debbie, now Mrs P, was pregnant with our first son, Dominic.

My ambition to become a millionaire had been dampened down by the sheer reality of life and the responsibilities of marriage and a child on the way. Maybe my dreams were just dreams. I would do well, but owning that mock-Tudor house would probably never come to pass. I resigned myself to the fact that I'd probably be working for Watches of Switzerland for the rest of my life.

Debbie and I were thoroughly enjoying our time together and not even a tube and bus strike that year seemed a problem. I was quite happy to get up early and walk from Peckham to Bond Street. It took me about two hours but I never considered it a chore. I was in love with my job and my new wife . . . and then something happened that would change both our lives for ever.

It was a chance meeting that allowed me to leave Watches of Switzerland and move on, something I thought I would never do.

Chapter Six

Living an Imperial life

I got a phone call from a guy who said he'd met my mother at her place of work. She had told him how proud she was of me. I quickly explained to him that mothers usually are proud of their children, but, undeterred by my rather feeble response, he said he would like to meet me and, although he didn't explain what he wanted, I agreed to see him for a drink.

He was an insurance salesman, called Adam Phokou, who had met my mother when he had arranged some insurance for her boss. She had told him that he had to meet her son, who had also worked in insurance for a while. He was smart, well spoken and well mannered, and over our drink told me all about his exotic sports car. It sounded quite exciting and I was more than a little intrigued, although I had no idea what he wanted from me. He suggested I meet him the following Monday night at his offices in Tottenham Court Road.

'You're in the office Monday night?'

'Yeah, we're in the office every Monday night. I'd just like you to see everybody, see what we do.'

By this time I had worked out that he was going to try to sell me some life assurance – it wasn't rocket science on my part; after all, he was an insurance salesman! But I had got on really well with him at our first meeting and nothing altered that view when I met him at his offices.

Adam worked for Imperial Life, which was a Canadian-owned outfit, and as I stepped into his office the first thing that struck me was the sheer volume of noise. My previous experience in insurance had been quiet. There might have been a bit of hullabaloo after we had had a few drinks, but during office hours it was always pretty calm.

I told Adam I'd worked in the insurance industry before, and while it was a possibility I might return, I really loved selling watches and got paid a huge amount of money. I didn't want to go back into insurance anyway. It was full of boring blokes in grey suits. It just wasn't me.

I was still trying to take it all in when a young man came charging in carrying two of the biggest bags of McDonald's I had ever seen. (McDonald's was quite new in the late seventies.) He barged into me and I very nearly ended up wearing a couple of Big Macs. He quickly apologised and walked on into the main office where everybody descended on these bags, grabbing their Big Mac and chips as fast as they could.

Adam then explained what all these people were doing in the office – apart from consuming their Big Macs. They were making appointments for the rest of the week, to sell life insurance, household insurance, mortgages, finance and so on. During the week they would 'prospect' – meet people and ask for introductions – and then on a Monday night they got together in the office and hit the phones to make appointments with the people whose names they had accumulated during the week.

The aim was to fill their diaries for the week. All the junior staff had to show these diaries to their team managers, one of whom was Adam. Once you had filled your diary, you could go home. However, it was very rare to fill the diary before 9.30 p.m. or 10 p.m. and you had to stop making calls then anyway as people got fed up if you called much later. So everyone spent Monday night working. Well, that was certainly a new one on me.

Adam then pointed to a board on his wall, which listed all the people in his team and beside each name a red line, which showed how much commission they had made. We were only halfway through the month and there were figures like £1,000, £2,000 and £3,000. My eyes started to water.

Astonishing though it seemed to me at the time, one of the guys in Adam's team had made my whole annual salary by halfway through a single month. He told me that this particular guy was exceptionally good, but pointed out another who was new and had earned only £1,000 so far that month. But £1,000 was still a huge amount of money to me and it opened my eyes to the rest of the insurance industry, the non-Lloyds' brokers side, and how much money could be made.

A few days later, Adam called and asked if I wanted to see the operation in action again. The opportunity to earn so much more money had me intrigued so I went along for several more Mondays. I realised I was being checked out as I sat there listening to other people's phone calls. One time I even went to get the order from McDonald's. What I didn't realise was that I was being groomed to take over from the lad who was doing the McDonald's run.

I wasn't about to be handed the keys to a company Ferrari – even if I had been able to drive it. And I wasn't going to be earning a multi-million-pound salary. My sole job would be to fetch the McDonald's while I learned the business.

At home, I discussed the job with the now heavily pregnant Mrs P and the first thing she pointed out was that it was commission-based. Fortunately, for the first six months they would guarantee a minimum salary of about £800 a month, so even if I was no good, I'd still be earning twice what I was earning at the shop. If it all went wrong, I'd be able to return to retail. It was with a very heavy heart that I handed in my notice at Watches of Switzerland. The following Monday I started at Imperial Life.

I spent my early weeks shadowing Adam. He also came out with me to see the prospects I came up with, mostly people I knew as it was usual to start off with friends and family. The theory was that family members normally indulge you and let you take over their insurance. You just have to hope that you don't do a worse job than their existing broker.

What this job taught me – and I hope my children will have the same chance to learn it – was a pure and simple work ethic. It was instilled in me from the moment I joined Imperial Life and it has guided me every single day since.

The central London branch was predominantly Jewish; 70 per cent were Jewish and most of the remaining 30 per cent were Cypriot, but the managers were Jewish. The work ethic was all-consuming, almost compulsive, whether you were Jewish or Cypriot. I had never experienced anything like it. They simply didn't let you go home on a Monday night until you'd filled in your diary. It was like being back at bloody school. And I didn't want to hang around until ten or eleven o'clock at night trying to fill my diary. You had to make sure you had enough prospects and started filling in appointments the week before, so you didn't turn up on a Monday with an empty diary.

We had to have a minimum of four or five appointments a day, every day. The pressure was unbelievable. Sometimes they would treat you like a child and you'd feel like crying. You had to go and show your diary and ask if you could go home, but they'd always spot a time where you could fit in another appointment. If they thought there was a chance you were putting in bogus appointments, they'd offer to come with you that day, so you had to keep on your toes.

I couldn't take it. I thought, I'm an adult, I'm a married man, my wife's expecting our first child and I can't go home. I have to stay at 'school' until I fill my appointments. And I have to do five appointments every day.

I didn't drive so I had to do my appointments by bus, tube and train. They usually lasted a minimum of an hour and it normally took me an hour to get to each appointment. That was ten hours before any problems or overruns, and a lot of the appointments stretched well into the evening so a working day was from ten in the morning until ten at night. I was virtually a stranger at home when I did manage to get there!

I thought there would be a chance to be home at weekends, but on Saturdays there were activities, run by the branch, that you had to take part in whether you liked it or not. In fairness, they all included your family. It was a clever tool but at the time it went right over my head. Some of the weekend trips were fantastic and I enjoyed them immensely. I got to do things that I wouldn't have been able to afford to do on my own. There was always a dinner afterwards in a posh hotel, where you had to dress up in black tie.

They didn't just want to win your heart and mind; they wanted to win the hearts and minds of your family too. And the managers' wives were indoctrinated early on so that when they met other employees' wives they would indoctrinate them as well as the kids. It was as close to being a cult as anything I have ever been involved in.

There was no escape. There was only one day in the week when you could see the rest of your family and friends – and that was Sunday. They absolutely owned you the rest of the time and all you ever thought about was the company, the work and how your figures were stacking up. There might not have been a company song, but there was a company life and I was living it. And when you recruited other people to join the company you found yourself, almost unwittingly, repeating to them all the things you had been told.

Almost without realising it, you became part of the recruiting process, bringing other people you knew into the office on a Monday to meet your managers. You were completely brainwashed. I was young and I went along with it. Despite feeling that in some ways I was being manipulated and as though I had gone back to school, I was enjoying it. After all, I was wearing a decent suit and making decent money. I wasn't at the top, but for someone of my age I was close. I was appearing in the monthly newsletter every month as the rising star. Every month I'd win something with the company's logo on it: a penknife, which I've still got somewhere, a pen or a watch. I even had a company tie and a company lapel badge. And every time anyone appeared in the staff magazine there would be a mention of their wife and their children or their girlfriend or mum and dad.

I didn't recognise the psychology behind it. My main concern was making money, especially as Mrs P had stopped work. We were doing well, and I was thinking of selling the flat and buying a house. I had even started taking driving lessons.

Earning as much as I did made me a bit complacent and I didn't always try as hard as I could have done. One Monday I had had a particularly bad day and at the end of it my manager wanted to take me out. I just wanted to go home but they wouldn't let me and I got the hump. Eventually, I was allowed to leave, but I took the hump back home with me.

The following day, Adam called and I was expecting the worst. I thought he was going to have a go at me, but he didn't even mention the previous evening's shenanigans and said we ought to go out for a bite to eat. As I got into his car, he said he had to stop off on the way at a garage in Camden Town. He had a beautiful Alfa Romeo sports car – he was an Alfa man; he was half Italian and half Cypriot, and he spoke a bit of both languages.

When we reached the garage I followed him in, and about an hour and a half later I left with a piece of paper in my hand – a sales invoice for a car I'd just bought. I had no driving licence and had only just started taking driving lessons, but I was the proud owner of a blue Alfa Romeo Sud 1.4. To say I was chuffed to bits was an understatement.

Mrs P was a bit dubious, so I explained it was second-hand and had cost only a thousand quid or so. When she quite rightly pointed out that I hadn't got a driving licence and that we now had £80 a month in hire-purchase payments to worry about, I began to see the problem. We would now struggle to pay for the flat – all for a car that neither of us could actually drive. She had a point!

I tried to explain that it would save me travelling to work by train every day, but Mrs P, as sensible and practical as ever, wanted to know what was wrong with using the tube or the bus. I had to admit that it was working fine getting about by pubic transport. I knew the tube lines inside out and could get anywhere within an hour.

All of a sudden, I was in debt up to my ears and I needed to work much, much harder. I was part of an unbelievable organisation. In retrospect, I think it was fantastic for me. They'd taken a young man with ambition but no direction and little education, who was dyslexic and had the concentration span of a particularly dim-witted goldfish, and moulded him into a focused, incredibly hard-working selling machine. I had become a company man and they had done it without me even having a clue what was really going on.

Although the firm was smart, it wasn't perfect. Every now and again they dropped a clanger, for example when they brought in new employees in their thirties and forties from the schmutter business – the rag trade. These people wanted to move into a new profession, but most of them didn't make it.

Now and again they'd bring in a cynic who could see through all the psychobabble. One of these was a guy called Matheos Matheou, Matthew Matthews to you and me. He was a Cypriot, a good ten years older than me, and we would go on to be great friends. Matthew had come over to the UK to study as a TV engineer, but was never the sort of person who was going to spend his time studying, and started up his own business as a driving-school instructor.

Adam recruited Matthew and suddenly I found there was this bright guy working in the office, speaking the mother tongue. In the mistaken belief that I originated from Limassol, a major city in Cyprus, and he from a small village in Paphos called Neokhorio (new village), I affectionately referred to him as 'the peasant'. Only now, in writing this book a lifetime later, have I discovered that my grandfather originated from a village called Lisos, which is a stone's throw away from Matthew's village. So I suppose there is a little of the peasant in me as well. I can already taste some humble pie.

He should never have been recruited; he just slipped through the net. Matthew wasn't cut out for the job and some Monday evenings when we had to fill in our appointments, he'd be encouraging me to write down any old names and times. He couldn't wait to get out of the place and we would invariably end up at the Sportsman Casino further down Tottenham Court Road to have a drink and play cards. I often told him it was ridiculous. I couldn't go because my missus was expecting a baby, I had a mortgage and a car loan to pay, and I didn't have any money to spare – certainly none to take to a casino.

But Matthew promised to teach me to drive and the ways of the world if I would keep him company at the casino and I found myself making up appointments so that I could go for a drink with him. I would end up playing cards with him and his friends, and gambling away £50, which was a significant amount of money for me in those days. However, when you compare it to the education I was receiving, it was cheap.

Matthew was wrong as far as the management was concerned and it was inevitable, I suppose, that he and the company would go their separate ways. It was a shame he had to go as I had grown very fond of him – he was a younger version of Bill. But despite leaving, Matthew kept his promise and taught me to drive, in a yellow Escort with dual controls.

He went off and bought into a small insurance brokerage firm that had an office in Clapham. He was always savvy enough to work for himself. Matthew became a close friend and adviser to me, and likewise, I became an adviser to him. Only last year – thirty years on – I repaid him for those driving lessons by teaching him to skipper my yacht.

Poor Adam got an absolute kicking for recruiting Matthew, who was clearly a non-believer as far as Imperial Life was concerned. That's when it dawned on me that Imperial Life wasn't the place for me because, not being of the Jewish faith, I was always going to be looked on as an outsider. I could also see that because Adam was mild-mannered and polite, he was pushed around by his managers. Sometimes I would ask him why he put up with it.

Everybody was trying to climb up the ladder to be top dog. Everybody fed off other people's earnings. My manager, Adam, earned on my earnings; his branch manager earned on his earnings; the area manager earned on the managers' earnings. I was never going to be one of them, I was always going to be Adam's boy, and the hierarchy considered Adam to be thick (I'd been here before). It seemed they mistook Adam's politeness and mild manners for stupidity. Although he was one of the brighter ones, he didn't play the political game – and that made him stupid in the eyes of certain grease-pole climbers. I began to grow disillusioned with the whole set-up.

It all came to a head one training session. As I was nodding off, the guy running the session, a smartly dressed, middle-aged grease-pole climber who was deeply in love with himself, woke me out of my reverie by slamming his fist down on the table in front of me. Startled, I looked up to hear him shouting at me. He was reminding me of his lofty status within the company and how he'd given up his time to teach me.

I waited until he had stopped his tirade, then asked him whether he had finished. I was a young kid in the firm and wasn't supposed to answer back, but I did, and told him in no uncertain terms that the reason I was falling asleep was because he was so boring. I added, for good measure, that there was absolutely nothing he could teach me as he was telling me things I had learned years ago on my grandmother's knee. I told him he was a half-wit but that he shouldn't treat me like one. Once I had got all that off my chest, I upped and walked out. I was hardly going to get a promotion after that.

I was twenty-one and pretty disillusioned. We'd moved house and were living in Carshalton in Surrey. We had a child as well as a mortgage and car loan. It had been five years since I'd left school. What was I going to do with the rest of my life? Of course, I'd learned to drive by then and had even changed to a better car. I saw a job advertised selling mortgages at Legal & General, a company I had come across several times. They were offering a car, a good basic salary and a generous bonus scheme, and it was in Kingswood, Surrey, which was ten minutes' drive from where I lived.

It sounded perfect, so I went for an interview, taking with me all my payslips from Imperial Life from the last two years. Hey presto, I got the job, along with a company car, expenses, a good salary and a staff mortgage. It seemed all my dreams had come true at once. I could substantially reduce my mortgage payments and sell the car, which I was still paying for. I got my own little rust-coloured Vauxhall Chevette and I worked for a company that people recognised.

I thought I was set for life. I thought if all went well, we'd eventually be able to move house again and I might even get a Cortina as my next company car. There was no pressure, no hot housing. I was given leads from other brokers as well as company leads that they had because they had been around for five million years or so. Legal & General had beautiful offices in a big, old, converted mansion in Kingswood with cricket pitches and football fields, so I could play cricket or football, and in ten minutes I'd be back in the house. It doesn't get much better than that.

But I hated it. It was great for about three months and then I got bored. There was no excitement. There were a lot of lovely, lovely people, but there was no buzz, no excitement and I thought I could still be there in twenty or thirty years and end up like all my colleagues, just being nice to everybody.

Yes, of course, I could make progress, perhaps become a manager, get a bigger house and have a new company car in the drive. But I wanted so much more. I was earning well, although not as much as I would have done had I stayed at Imperial Life, things were comfortable and I had much more leisure time on my hands. But I still wasn't satisfied.

Chapter Seven

Starting out on my own

I had become friendly with a guy called Michael McCroddan, who had joined the company about the same time as me. He was an ex-policeman, who had been in Special Branch, and who had left the force after twenty-five years, looking for a career change. Like Adam, he was mild-mannered, honest and non-political, which I thought was rather strange for an ex-copper! He could see that I had fallen out of love with the job and was just going through the motions.

I told Mike I had found a niche in the market at Legal & General involving commercial finance as opposed to mortgages. Selling mortgages never really appealed to me, whereas commercial finance, providing loans for businesses to buy equipment, factories and offices and for property investment, did. Legal & General had a fledgling commercial finance department, involving commercial properties, shops, offices and businesses, and I found it exhilarating.

On some occasions L&G didn't want to get involved, so I'd done a few deals on the commercial side via other banks and found myself contacts who were much more commercially minded than L&G. I discussed the idea of striking out on my own with Mike. In this way, I could work with L&G or any other insurance company to get the best deal for my clients. I knew that selling insurance was a highly competitive market, and that there were too many players out there, but I thought I could find a gap in commercial finance. After all, many of Mike's mortgage clients needed finance for other things, if they ran a restaurant or a shop or some other business, and I asked him to pass on their names.

The reason there was a gap was because someone had to put together people who wanted to borrow money with those who wanted to lend it. Of course, many people would go to their local branch of one of the big banks and ask for a loan. However, if the business was complicated, or the level of the loan was above what the local branch could authorise, all too often the request would be turned down. Many people with good business ideas were desperate to find someone to support them.

Meanwhile, there were smaller banks, Licensed Deposit Takers, who paid out higher rates of interest to their depositers, which meant they needed to charge higher rates when they loaned money. If one of the big banks loaned money at base rate plus 4 per cent, these outfits would do so at base rate plus 7 per cent.

I networked like mad to get to know local accountants and lawyers, who often had clients desperate for finance. My experience at Imperial Life had taught me all about prospecting for clients. I'd also built up an excellent knowledge of the banks, and what sort of investments they were looking to make, so I knew where to match up an entrepreneur. Once I'd put the two sides together, I would take my commission. In the days before the internet, when information was relatively hard to come by, it was much easier for me to set myself up to do this than it would be now.

At first, I planned to work from home, which meant getting a bigger house. Fortunately, I could hold on to my L&G cheap mortgage for a year after I left the company, which would help cover my early costs, after which I was sure I'd be doing well enough to pay for the higher cost of the mortgage.

By the time I'd moved house, Mike had decided he would leave too and would share an office with me. We would each play to our strengths, with him focusing on mortgages and me looking after the commercial side.

We rented an office in Croydon from one of our former L&G clients who was allegedly importing wood pulp from Russia, although we never really knew what business he was in. It was at the height of the Cold War so it might have been interesting to find out since he spent a lot of time in the Eastern Bloc countries, but Mike and I didn't ask too many questions, especially as he was only charging us £50 a month for the accommodation. It was a rickety old building with a shower in the office! We put a nameplate outside the door. I lived in Surrey, Mike lived in Kent, and so we called it Surrey & Kent Associates. We got a credit licence (just by sending off the application with the requisite fee) and off we jolly well went, even though we were still working our notice at L&G.

One morning, we were beavering away when I heard a rat-a-tat-tat at the window. I looked up and, to my horror, recognised our caller – Tim, the area manager of L&G. The colour drained from my face as he looked around our cramped offices. I was terrified he'd recognise the desks; they were from an L&G storeroom, where the firm kept a load of furniture for disposal. I'd given the storeroom guy £20 and he had delivered two desks, two chairs and two filing cabinets to the offices of Surrey & Kent Associates. But I needn't have worried, our unannounced – and unwanted – guest had no idea.

He told us he thought we were both making a terrible mistake and that we had bright futures with L&G. He said we both had expertise in our own areas and were earning good money – and that one day we could be doing his job. But that's exactly why I had left – I never wanted to end up doing his job. Tim was with us for almost an hour, reminding us of the careers, stability and security that we were leaving behind. He knew I had just taken on a bigger mortgage and I had to stop myself from telling him that my reason for doing so was that I knew I was leaving. He said there was no way we could make it without the support of the company.

'You'll have to buy your own cars, pay your own rent, and if things go wrong, you could end up selling matchsticks at Victoria Station.'

That was it. I don't think anyone had ever said anything that had motivated me more. Here was this boring half-wit who thought he was a sophisticated man about town but who was in fact a grey-suited, old whatsit, lecturing me about my future. Now I knew I couldn't fail however difficult it was going to be. I wrote down his comment about the matchsticks on a big piece of paper and stuck it on the office wall – and it stayed there all the time I had those offices. It was all the motivation I needed. It was my driving force – I simply wasn't going to be selling matchsticks at Victoria Station and this guy had got it all wrong.

We worked our notice and left. At the age of twenty-three, I was running my first business; I was my own boss. I didn't have the boys at Imperial Life standing over me telling me how many appointments I had to have. I didn't have L&G as my comfort zone. I had my own business cards and I could do whatever I wanted to do – go to work when I wanted, not go to work when I didn't want to. I had to give back the company car and bought myself a Golf GTI, all white with spoilers, the whole lot on HP.

I was excited again. I was driven. I was doing what I wanted to do. There's a big wide world out there. For me, it was the best decision I ever made and Tim's words were the best words of encouragement anyone's ever given me. He might not have realised it at the time but I owe him plenty. And what's more, the work ethic that I'd picked up at Imperial Life several years before had returned and would never leave me. As well as being excited, I was frightened. The two emotions go together in my life experience, but the buzz outweighs the fear. I kept telling myself I wasn't going to fail. I just needed to fill my diary, like I had at Imperial Life.

I saw Matthew regularly and he continued my education in the ways of the world. Now and again we went to the Sportsman, but I'm the world's worst loser so I stopped going – it wasn't losing the money that mattered; I just couldn't handle the idea of losing. And a good man must know his limitations as that great philosopher Clintos Eastwoodos once said as he put a Magnum to someone's head. To be fair to Matthew, he didn't get too involved financially. For him, it was just somewhere to go. But often when he rang I'd tell him I was too busy. 'Bloody hell, you might as well go back and work for Imperial Life. They worked you less hard than you're working now,' he'd say. And he was right. I got in early in the morning and worked every single night, and we did a lot of socialising too, attending business lunches and dinners. There was a huge amount of networking. We both worked very, very hard. But we loved every minute of it.

I had never made so much money. One of the reasons was that during our notice period at L&G, we had set up lots of prospects that came to fruition. Mike bought a new car and we soon moved into a bigger room in the building for £80 a month, although there was no shower. Within two months we needed a secretary.

We chose to go to the Job Centre rather than to an employment agency because there was no fee, and they sent us a girl of eighteen. It was the height of summer and she turned up wearing a mini-skirt that barely covered her buttocks. She couldn't type and had no idea about office procedures, but she had a great personality and a great presence – and, more to the point, she was cheap. When my mother visited the office and saw her, she ran off and told Mrs P that we had employed a girl who wore no clothes. Our new secretary was Josephine Cocks and she would stay with me for many years.

Mike wasn't to stay anywhere near as long. He had been in a relationship that broke down and then he met the love of his life, Penny. She lived in Hertfordshire, which was a long way to travel from Croydon every day, so our business relationship came to an end. I still keep in touch with Mike and have been to his daughters' weddings and his fiftieth birthday. He's a super guy.

Soon after Mike and I parted company, our landlord dropped dead and I had to move out. Luckily, I found offices nearby in Wellesley Road, in Croydon. They were in the attic space of a converted house, had been recently decorated and overlooked the whole of Croydon. I had one office and Jo the other, and they cost me just £400 a month. This was a lot more than I had been paying, but by this time the business was established and I had a regular income from clients.

I replaced the second-hand furniture I had liberated from Legal & General, which was riddled with woodworm, with a nice mahogany desk and filing cabinet and a really pukka captain's chair. So there I was in a Victorian building with a proper desk and a well-polished brass plaque reading, 'Surrey & Kent Associates,' and I was all on my lonesome. All the accounts had been opened in this name so it made sense to keep it.

The commercial side now made up 95 per cent of the business and I had very little residential stuff. The commercial business brought in renewal income, but I also began to manage a few properties I had financed for clients' syndicates. Most of these were Asian and, on the surface, they appeared to be really close associates. They went drinking together, they dined in each other's houses, but, as far as I could see, there was a level of mistrust.

I had been introduced to them by their accountant and had financed a couple of parades of shops for them. They were multi-tenanted properties and I was asked whether I would look after property. At first I had been reluctant, as it wasn't something I'd done, but thinking that it couldn't be that difficult, I found out what other people were charging and took the work on.

The great thing about it was that it gave me a guaranteed income – and it more than covered the rent, electricity, gas and all the other incidentals. The experience gave me a better understanding of various aspects of the property market and business. Although I enjoyed the work and was delighted with my success, there was a problem: I was really lonely. I simply didn't know how not to work late. It wasn't that I didn't want to get home to my wife and now two children, I just knew no other way of operating.

It had been instilled in me that evening was a prime time for selling, networking and meeting people, and going home to the family wasn't going to achieve any of that. I would ring people – business people, accountants and solicitors – and we would have a drink or dinner after work. On the rare occasion when I did go home early I felt guilty. The word 'network' had never been explained to me but I knew that what I was doing was very important to the business.

It was a simple equation, a numbers game: you had to have appointments, you had to see people. If you had appointments and saw people, you did business and made money. What could be easier? Cheques came in, and those cheques then paid the rent and the secretary, and allowed me to pay for my car and everything else. I was earning twice what I had been getting at

L&G, but I wasn't accumulating fabulous riches, even though I had a few tens of thousands pounds' worth of property interests. It was a living – a good one – but only a living. It wasn't really a proper business at this stage; it was one man and his dog. Apologies to Jo, but you know what I mean! Somehow, I realised, I had to change things.

Chapter Eight

I become an employee again

I had kept in regular touch with Mike and we often spoke about my predicament. Then one day he called and said he had seen an advert for the position of managing director of a commercial finance business at a large estate agents. At the time commercial finance was in its infancy, and while banks did provide loans, there were very few individuals who were broking commercial finance. I wasn't looking for a job, but Mike thought there might be an opportunity for me.

Given how I'd been feeling, I decided to look into it and made some enquiries about their business. When I discovered that Hanover Druce was a publicly quoted company and had a big commercial estate agency business, I thought it was worth a look. I rang the managing director of the group, Steven Parnes, and had a chat. I said I hoped I wasn't wasting his time, told him I didn't know much about his business and explained that I was a one-man operation looking to broaden my horizons. I told him that he could ask for references from the West End banks I had been dealing with for years. The flexible approach I proposed appealed to him and he invited me to their Manchester Square offices near Bond Street.

It was just like walking into the office at Imperial Life.

Druce was a Jewish estate agency with the same ethos and the same work ethic. They had grown steadily, made acquisitions and progressed into a public company. Lots of the offices occupied by the company were owned privately by the partners and the company paid rent to them personally – the normal stuff. Steven and I got on well. I showed him a portfolio of the last thirty or so deals I'd done, and he was seriously impressed. He asked me how I got the business and whether I dealt with any other estate agents. It seemed to make sense, as they had so many clients looking for finance, that I should take over that area of the business.

It wasn't exactly what I'd had in mind, but I ended up working for them as the MD of a newly formed subsidiary called Druce Commercial Finance, and getting 20 per cent of the share-holding of the new company. I was excited by this opportunity, but rather disappointed when I arrived at work, expecting a new luxury West End office, to be confronted by a desk behind a door, while Jo had to go and sit in the secretarial pool.

I felt I was back to square one again – I was an employee. I even had to share my desk with one of the insurance clerks who wouldn't talk to me because he saw me as a threat. His name was Jon Schryer and, as it turned out, he was a smashing guy. He now runs his own brokerage firm and looks after all my personal insurance.

As I went round meeting the various department heads, they looked at me – a young upstart – like something attached to the bottom of their shoe. I was being touted as the blue-eyed boy who was going to do all this commercial business for the group and make them loads of money. That was the bigger picture – and they had that all worked out. What they hadn't got very clear were the finer details, like a fax machine and a typewriter for my secretary.

I was the managing director of a new company, but the

company didn't actually have any business, offices or employees – apart from me and Jo, of course. I had taken over something that Steven Parnes had done himself, now and again, for some of their clients. I'd given them 80 per cent of my business and in return I'd got 20 per cent of nothing. I had been seduced by the nice West End offices and the name. I couldn't believe how stupid I had been.

I didn't know what to do. I could walk out or try to make it work. I had already given them details of all the deals I had pending from my Surrey & Kent days, and they agreed I could keep the fees on those deals. But after that, any future deals were down to the new company, Druce Commercial Finance. It took me a week to get my head round these new arrangements and on top of that I was running into plenty of resentment.

The office, with a valuations department, a commercial department and a residential department, was riddled with politics and I was the poor little immigrant boy, only twenty-five, who had arrived as the MD of a new company. But I felt I had to make the best of a bad job and not give up. So I bought some very sharp suits. After all, I was managing director of a subsidiary of a publicly quoted company, so I felt I should at least look the part. Financially, I was doing quite well. I was guaranteed £30,000 a year plus bonuses, commission, a company car and expenses – and I think that's what tipped it for me. Back in 1985 and at my age, it was a pretty decent salary. I still wasn't sure how it was going to pan out, so I met up with a couple of mates who worked for banks and went through it with them. They told me to stick with it and try to make a good fist of it.

The MD of the financial services department also saw me as a threat. He thought I should have been part of his empire, and not be heading up a separate subsidiary. Here I was, trying to schmooze colleagues to give me their business when they already had their own pet people outside the business with whom they dealt. Did I really need all this hassle? As my own boss, I'd had my independence and I'd been earning a good living. But I was willing to give it a go: to build things up from scratch with the eyes of everybody in the organisation focused on me and my efforts.

After a fortnight or so working under this scrutiny, trying to put a business plan together, to do budgets, to set targets, I went to see Steven and told him it wasn't working out. I was meant to be the MD of this subsidiary, but I was sharing a desk behind a door with an insurance clerk. I wanted a proper office, staff and a car. Steven said, 'Get the business plan done and then come back to me with the car you want.'

I realised I had to make a go of it and stop being distracted by other things. In truth, I'd never put together a proper business plan before. So I fell back on my work ethic to drive me and very quickly I'd learned how to put a business plan together and to sort out a budget and targets. Eventually, I presented it all to Steven and he approved it on the basis that they would have lots of income coming in so he couldn't bitch about the extra expenditure I was planning. I had piled on the income so that the expenditure didn't look all that high – and Steven went for it.

To celebrate, I promptly went out and bought myself a Porsche 944, which was 25 per cent more expensive than the budget he had just agreed. But I told Steven not to worry, I would put the extra 25 per cent in myself – and, of course, I would own 25 per cent of the car myself. I thought that was fair and – more importantly – so did he. Buying that Porsche created absolute havoc in Manchester Square because no one else in the company had a Porsche, not even the other managing directors, all of whom were far more senior than me and were sitting on the management board. Worse than that, the car was German. It never occurred to me that it might upset what was essentially a Jewish company. I couldn't have acted more naively if I'd tried. It had been an emotive issue within the organisation for years and years, and the company had stuck with its 'no German purchases' policy for all that time. They all had English cars, with Jaguars being the top choice among senior managers. And here I was, in all innocence, showing off my German-produced Porsche. It went down like the Hindenburg. I was told I had to get rid of it, but that wasn't going to happen.

It became clear to me that it was bugger all to do with religion and the war and more about keeping expectations down. It was convenient to say, 'We're Jewish so we don't have German cars. No, you can't have a BMW.' And then, suddenly, they realised that we were in the 1980s and not only were the war years long behind us, but they were being a bit short-sighted in their approach to their employees. So they opened the floodgates with regard to German cars and I got to keep the Porsche.

Next I went out and found an office suite in a beautiful period building in Wigmore Street. It was far too big for me but I persuaded David Oatley, who was the MD of the insurance broking arm, to join me there. David wasn't enjoying working in the offices in Manchester Square because they were too small. There was so much space in Wigmore Street that we could both have big offices. Mine even had chandeliers and an Adam fireplace. I was getting serious delusions of grandeur, and when David saw the offices, he said that I would never get them approved.

By then I'd already done some decent-sized deals and had proved to the company that the business had a future. I had showed that the budget was fine and that the targets would be met. I felt sure that as long as David came in with me I'd be fine with the costs. So I went to see Steven. I explained that David and I would share the costs and that the whole lot was within budget. To my surprise, he didn't even flinch and approved it on the spot.

We took the offices and immediately kitted them out from top to bottom. When Steven made his first visit about three weeks after we had moved in, his jaw dropped. It looked quite substantial, almost palatial, and he wanted to know how much it had cost. I think by then Steven realised I was pushing the boundaries all the way. But I wasn't worried. I felt no fear. I always knew that what I was doing would be all right in the end. It seemed important to me to make a statement of intent, and all these things – the smart suits, the expensive car, the plush offices – were about ensuring that everyone understood I was taking things forward. It is crucial in business to create the right image.

Happily, we were delivering the numbers and the business was establishing itself. It was growing rapidly and we were making the most profit in the group every month. This was my first true business. I had been in business on my own before but this one was budgeted and structured; I had employees; and I was accountable. I was always willing to be flexible and bend the rules as much as I could without actually breaking them. I was also finding out whether I was entrepreneurial or just an employee. I was managing this business, but I had also set it up. It hadn't existed before I came along. There wasn't a Druce Commercial Finance when I joined the company.

My charm offensive was working and I was getting regular referrals. Good business was coming in from within, and good business was coming in from outside. When I had been running my own business, one of the things I got very good at was refinancing what I used to call 'hospital cases', businesses and deals that had gone badly wrong, and those that had huge arrears on their mortgages and other debts. These were people with overdrafts, whose banks were just about to send the administrator and receiver in.

What I did was quite simple. The businesses often had a range of loans here, there and everywhere. Because they were so much in debt, and behind on their payments, their credit rating was awful and no one would lend them any more money to keep going. On top of that, they were obliged to keep making repayments. We were able to spot the companies that had sufficient assets to sell should things go wrong and enough prospects to have a chance of being turned round.

For a fee, we would offer to take control of all their debts and help put them back on an even keel. If, for example, their total debt was £100,000, we would take out a year-long loan (or perhaps even one as short as six months) for the full amount, plus the interest they would have to pay to the bank, say a further £15,000.

The main problem initially was persuading the banks that they were safe taking on these bad debts. The banks were worried that the money they held on deposit to cover the interest would run out, but I explained that we would refinance these loans off their books before that happened. They were cautious about the whole concept, but I persuaded them that the proof would be in the pudding. It soon became clear that the system worked.

Meanwhile, we put the £15,000 interest on deposit for the bank to draw down on a monthly basis, and the company used the rest of the money to pay off their debt. With that done, they could approach other financial companies with a clean credit rating and so move the business forward again. Where previously no bank would have supported them, now they were happy to do so. During this period, we explained to them beforehand that they would have to pay a very high rate of interest, perhaps 5 or 6 per cent above base rate, which was covered by the £115,000 they had borrowed. It may have been a back-breaking loan, as we called it, but it was short-term, intensive-care treatment.

At the end of the year, the company paid back to the bank the £115,000; the business had a consolidated debt with a good payment history that it could finance much more easily at a lower interest rate; and we took a further commission on the way out. So we had made two sets of commission; the bank made profit on the interest, with minimal risk because it would have first claim on the assets if the company still could not recover. Meanwhile, the 'hospital-case' business had broken out of the vicious circle, because it had no interest payments to make and a clean credit history. The extra breathing space gave them the time to sort themselves out.

We established ourselves in this niche market and I took on two assistants to help me, Mike Watkins, who was known to me from my old Surrey & Kent days and who worked for Scottish Life, and Richard Lewczynski, who worked for a small bank with which I did business.

I transacted some big deals while I was at Druce, major West End property deals, which brought in equally major fees. Business was good and I established a rapport with quite a few small banks that were actively looking for business, trying to establish themselves. We were also able to pass on to other parts of Druce work that brought in further fees, in valuations, insurance and property management.

While I'd once worried that I'd given away 80 per cent of my Surrey & Kent business for nothing, I was now earning a decent salary and bonuses, and feeling very, very smug. I was there for two and a half years and was maturing and making fantastic contacts. At twenty-six I was no longer a boy and didn't have the same emotional hang-ups. If I was being told off, I could handle myself, but, truth to tell, no one told me off any more. I was the main director of the business, I had people who looked up to me, I was respected and banks would contact me to try to get business from me. It was all change. Whereas I used to take banks out to dinner, now it was the other way round because the banks knew I had a stream of deals that would interest them. They were the ones doing the networking and I was able to sit back and enjoy the ride.

The banks even began to ring me when they had problems. I was flattered to say the least. If they were about to put the receivers in, they would call me to see if I could do anything to help them out and avoid them having to take legal action, which would bring them extra costs. It was in everyone's interest to try to save the businesses. It was the beginning of the financial revolution in the 1980s, just after the Big Bang, and the banks were quite happy to let me play the system because they earned fees and got rid of problems at the same time.

A problem client for a bank takes up an inordinate amount of time. The idea is to convert that problem client to a good client on someone else's books. Each time I resolved a problem, I got more fees and so it went on. It was like being on a fairground carousel – and it was just as enjoyable! It was great, sending the clients round and round – they were on the same carousel as we were and it worked. We were earning fees all the way.

People within the organisation had come to realise I was the real deal and that I wasn't this flash little Herbert with a cockney accent who was ducking and diving all the time. I was running a successful business and respect was given to that business – and to me.

Working with my clients, whether they were manufacturing garden sheds, running a restaurant or a property business, I got to understand the workings of all sorts of companies. What they did was immaterial, it was what I did that counted in terms of getting them back on their feet. Many of the business people I helped became friends and I'd go to their houses, and they'd come to mine. I began to realise that our house was very modest compared to most of theirs, and that really bugged me, I can tell you.

By now I had this burning desire to do it for myself and not just work for an organisation that could be extremely generous but at other times, depending on the mood of the individuals involved, extremely frustrating and challenging.

I then chanced upon an idea that was to make a huge difference to my business prospects. It was simple really, like all good ideas. Insurance companies need to have some guaranteed income to service their clients' pensions, so, in addition to some fairly speculative investments, they had to buy government gilts, pieces of paper actually, that guaranteed they would get all their money back after twenty or thirty years and in the meantime would be paid an interest yield twice a year.

On the basis that they were accustomed to buying guaranteed paper and bonds from blue-chip companies to satisfy their requirements, I thought, wouldn't it be sensible to obtain a higher yield from those self-same blue-chip institutions. Your covenant was the same, your risk was the same, except instead of receiving, say, 6 per cent, you would receive 7.5 or even 8 per cent.

That was an attractive proposition and a lot of these blue-chip institutions occupied premises, in other words, they had property like warehouses, offices and shops.

Here is an example of how it works:

Acme Inc. is an insurance company who need a guaranteed 5 per cent per annum long-term return over twenty-five years in order to guarantee the pension payments for some of their policyholders. Historically, they would buy government gilts or blue-chip Triple A corporate bonds that would guarantee an annual return of, say, 5 per cent or so and repay the full amount of the gilt or the bond at the maturity date. So if Acme Inc. bought a million pounds, they would receive 5 per cent per annum during the term of the bond, and at the end the full million would be repaid.

Acme Inc. are happy to accept a moderate rate of return of 5 per cent because they know there would be no chance of the government defaulting; if they wanted a higher return, the investment would carry a higher risk, which would have more chance of going wrong. This type of investment would normally be looked at by a different department with different investment criteria. Now if we imagine that Acme Inc. bought £1 million of bonds issued by Big Blue plc yielding 5 per cent, their exposure would be if Big Blue did not pay the 5 per cent interest per annum, and of course they would have the capital repayment at the end of twenty-five years. The likelihood of Big Blue not paying the interest is minuscule as Big Blue are a Triple-A-rated company and considered to be an excellent risk.

Now Big Blue plc also pay rent to landlords on their various properties. Typically, they would have a twenty-five-year lease, with a rent review every five years. So, for example, they might pay £100,000 rent per year on an office block in Wimbledon, which is valued at £1 million, so the owner is getting a 10 per cent return on his property. In other words, safe-bet Big Blue is paying a 10 per cent return on a property investment of £1 million, rather than 5 per cent received from corporate bonds. The property investor has the added benefit that there is a high chance that the income will increase during the term of the lease by virtue of the five-yearly rent reviews.

So property investor Mr Trump Wannabe would like to buy this nice property in Wimbledon occupied by Big Blue plc but hasn't got £1 million. Our solution is to approach Acme Inc. and ask them to lend Mr Trump Wannabe the money. In return, he will pay them 7 per cent per annum on the money, 2 per cent more than they would typically get from Big Blue by buying their bonds, but there is one slight complication: Mr Trump Wannabe has not got the same credit rating as Big Blue.

In fact, the opposite is true, he is not even worth a million, so he is a bad credit risk. We explain that our client, Mr Trump Wannabe, will assign the rental income from Big Blue plc directly to Acme Inc. each quarter and will keep the 3 per cent surplus for himself, thus making Acme 2 per cent better off than they would be by buying bonds and the credit risk is exactly the same. Should, for any reason, Mr Trump Wannabe fail to pay his interest every quarter, Acme can simply repossess the property and collect all 10 per cent from Big Blue plc direct, thus be better off. Acme can't lose and everyone is a winner, including ourselves, since we would typically charge 1–2 per cent on each transaction, some of which were very substantial. This was how wannabe property investors only needed money for legal and valuation fees, stamp duty and of course our fee to buy a big commercial property. In that way, people could build a commercial investment property portfolio in no time with very little money. We were inundated, with queues of people who wanted to do business with us.

I, too, had bought a few properties myself for the proverbial rainy day. They were all 100 per cent funded. I just had to find my legal fees and my own fees, which I did fairly easily. I must have felt that there was a monsoon on the way because I accumulated quite a few properties. To be honest, there were times when I was even short of money to pay the legal fees so I'd borrow that from another bank. In these often over-regulated days it wouldn't be as easy to raise money as it was back then.

Opportunities were coming up thick and fast, and I began to think about what my next step should be. Was I going to do this for the rest of my life? Make money for other people? Run a business for somebody else? Or was I going to do something for myself? I had five or six years' experience not only of putting together the finance, but also of helping to restructure and refinance businesses and property, sometimes shutting bits of a business down or even putting some parts into receivership. At times I felt a bit like a gardener, cutting out the weeds that were clogging up the business and leaving those green shoots that, with a bit of nurturing, would soon begin to flower. People came to me with their financial woes and my job was to work out exactly how to resolve them. Maybe it was time to have my own garden rather than working in someone else's, for although I was doing very well, I was still some way short of becoming a millionaire, even including my home and some investments I had made.

Chapter Nine

Astra-nomical

A major turning point for me came in 1987. I received a call from a senior director of a small bank in the West End who told me they were second charge behind the Midland Bank on a bad loan and wondered whether I could do anything with it. I asked for all the details and it turned out it was a small public company, Astra Industrial Group, which had a Stock Exchange quote. Things didn't look too good; there were some assets but on the surface it didn't really stack up.

My contact said he had permission from the chairman and chief executive to approach me and had been given the authority to disclose everything to me; indeed he would be more than happy to meet with me and answer any questions. We met the following day. Although the main business was based in Birmingham, his offices were in Cardiff, so we met there. I would have preferred to have seen him in Birmingham, as I thought this might give me a better idea of how the business was faring. Once in Cardiff, however, he took me to a fabulous wine bar called Champers, which I still frequent whenever I'm in the city. The food and wine are great and it was here that I was introduced to Rioja wine, for which I have had a passion ever since.

Two days later I met him again, this time in Birmingham to review the businesses, of which there was an eclectic mix – an engineering concern in Birmingham, another in Lancaster as well as a leisure business, which consisted of a restaurant in Sutton Coldfield and a bingo and snooker hall in Aston. It was a real hotchpotch.

By this time, I was used to dealing with hospital cases and difficult deals and thought I'd come across most things, but this was a real eye-opener. He told me he had been with the company for less than a year and it was only when he stepped into the hot seat that he found he had been handed the tin-opener for a can of worms. This was the first time I had really encountered, let's just say, misdemeanours within an organisation as opposed to businesses not doing well for reasons beyond the management's control.

I did the report for the bank, and said I felt there was half a chance they could get their money back, but it was going to take time. I felt new management was needed because the present management team seemed to have given up. They lacked passion, drive and enthusiasm. The business needed a serious hands-on approach. The bank thought my report was backable and asked me when I could start. Their offer came as a complete surprise; up to then I'd simply been doing my usual job. Suddenly, instead of refinancing a company, I was being given the chance to run it. I wasn't sure what to do, but I knew I had to give serious thought to moving on.

In those days, Friday night was boys' night out. It was the Thatcher years, the Filofax era and mobile phones had just arrived – the size and weight of house bricks. We would hit the champagne bars, and if the boys at work hadn't made lots of money by doing deals, we'd mock them mercilessly. It was a real sales-driven operation.

Just a few days after being offered the job to turn round Astra and before I'd made any decision, we went out on our 'normal' Friday-night binge. I can remember being pushed in a shopping trolley down Bond Street, much to the disgust of a member of the local constabulary, who decided that he would give us a stern warning. We were all suited up, but I doubt we looked too smart. This was not the sort of behaviour appropriate for someone who was possibly going to head up a public company. But it was a case of work hard, play hard.

My first thought when I got home that morning at six o'clock was that Mrs P was going to kill me, especially as I hadn't called. She knew I worked most nights but not until six in the morning, so I crept up the stairs very, very quietly. I didn't put any lights on in the bedroom and had started to take off my suit when Mrs P turned her head towards me and opened one eye. I began putting my trousers back on.

'What are you doing?' she asked.

'Shh, I'm going to work. I'll give you a ring later,' I replied. She turned over and shut her eyes, so I carried on dressing.

Then she said, 'It's Saturday. You've just come in, haven't you?'

Cover blown, I ended up going to bed for a few hours, expecting some earache at the very least. Later she came upstairs and brought me a cup of tea. I thought she'd forgiven me but she told me to get up as she had made an appointment to see a house. I commented that I hadn't realised we had agreed to move house, but she replied, 'Well, one of us is going to be moving, and if you're going to move with me, you're going to get up and you're going to come and see this house with me.'

I was still wrecked and when we got there the owner was in the garden and immediately offered me a beer. In the circumstances, I thought it best to decline. Mrs P had been going on and on about this house for weeks. I had already told her that we couldn't afford it, but she saw an opportunity, with me very much in the doghouse, to get what she wanted.

I felt cornered. It was a straight choice between getting a divorce or buying a house we couldn't really afford. I found myself buying a house we couldn't afford. Mrs P was also expecting our third child. It was clearly the perfect time to take a leap into the unknown with Astra.

The new house was in the same long street in Carshalton Beeches where we already lived. But we were moving from a three-bedroom semi to a five-bedroom detached. It was a sign that we were doing OK. But I liked the house we were living in and felt comfortable there. Living there also meant that I could reinvest any money I was making in property.

I was hocked up to the eyeballs but Mrs P was not aware of that. All she knew was that I was working eighteen hours a day, had a good job, we were having great holidays, I had a Porsche, and she had a nice Golf GTI, so things must be going well.

I had two loans on most properties I had invested in and any money I had made I had used to buy things. So the thought of buying a house at three times the price we were selling at was definitely not a good idea as far as I was concerned. But I couldn't go back on my word. So we bought the house and on 28 April 1987 our third child, Alex, was born. Now we had Dominic, Zoe and Alex. Later we had the twins, Hollie and Annabelle.

While all this was going on I was still trying to resolve my dilemma over Astra. Do I leave the comfort of the job I'm in, doing a few deals, investing here, there and everywhere, and earning the respect of my colleagues in a business that's doing well? Or do I go to Astra? The facts screamed that I should stay for at least another three years. Everyone I spoke to gave me the same advice: 'Stay, get the house-move out of the way and maybe sell a few of the properties to give you a bit of cash.'

Naturally, I took the job of chairman and chief executive of Astra! My resignation from Druce went down as well as a bacon butty at a barmitzvah. Steven took it badly, chucked me out of the office the next day and refused to speak to me. I had to deal with the company secretary. I also had to buy the rest of the car because I owned 25 per cent of it. The only problem was that I couldn't afford it.

I was at the helm of Astra Industrial Group for almost three years and it turned out to be one hell of a trip – a real roller-coaster ride, but an unbelievable learning curve. I didn't have a clue about what was required to run a public company. I knew a lot about little private companies and I knew about property finance, but public companies weren't even on my radar. I was told there was a Blue Book and Yellow Book that contained the official Stock Exchange rules, so these two books were my first port of call.

The shares were about a penny and that valued the company at roughly a couple of million quid, that's all. It had a load of awful businesses, some of which I did know about. In fact, I could identify with the crappy businesses; I just couldn't get my head round all that big City stuff, liaising with the Oxbridge types in their funny suits. But I knew they were no better or brighter than me. They were just working in the City, wearing braces.

When I arrived at Astra, they couldn't even pay me my salary because they were going bust. I was working for a public company that couldn't write a cheque that wouldn't bounce. My first job, therefore, was to negotiate with the bank to give the company an extension on an overdraft that was already over the limit; indeed that was a condition of my going in. I needed some breathing space, so they gave me a couple of hundred thousand quid so I could get an office, sort myself out, start work and slowly start paying a few people.

For the first three months I'd get up in the morning, drive the Porsche I couldn't afford to Birmingham and go straight to the engineering plant, which was just off the motorway. Then I'd visit the bingo and snooker halls, which were not far away in Aston, and call on the restaurant in Sutton Coldfield.

I managed to scale back the costs at the engineering business, which helped. Then, within a few months of taking over, I managed to sell the restaurant for £450,000 to Whitbread, a ridiculous amount of money. Despite being in a beautiful location in Sutton Park overlooking the lake, the restaurant was losing around £150,000 a year so to get close to half a million was a great result – even the bank couldn't believe it. I was able to use that money to pay back some of the loans that were outstanding.

I also paid attention to the bingo and the snooker, and stemmed the losses there too. Because things were now under control, I decided I could return to London and thus I needed an office. The company had been restructured and I reckoned I didn't need to be in Birmingham as I could handle things from London. So I took an office in Baker Street, which was about a quarter of a mile from my old firm in Manchester Square. I put in some partitions and some furniture, and hung a name over the door. I was up and running, but I was lonely and wondered how I could best take the company forward. I decided to do what I do best – set up a financial services business as part of Astra.

It wasn't long before the whole team from across the road at Druce had parked their arses in my new offices and were working for me once more. I was, after all, the person who had trained them. It didn't half upset everybody back at the old place. Not only that, some of the insurance boys who weren't on my team had come across. Steven Parnes, who ran Druce, was very angry and threatened me with plagues of locusts. There was nothing he could do. If people want to leave, they leave.

Once again the boys and I worked hard and played hard, and we became a very close-knit team. And the reason we were able to party so hard was because we were making a lot of money – it was the glue that held us together, as with lots of others in the heyday of the late 1980s. By now my team had grown to four and Jo had come across with me as well.

With the old part of Astra now on an even keel and the financial services operation in London making money, I began to realise that the people who would benefit most from this turnaround were the shareholders, and I didn't have many shares, just a lot of options. It looked like I had done it again – made the same bloody mistake once more. My pride and ego had got the better of me.

With hindsight, what I should have done was set up the business outside Astra, run it for a year or two and then sold it to the company. Instead, I had set up the new money-making business within the company, a company that I didn't own, and so watched everyone else get richer. Even if I didn't benefit from the rising share price, I was convinced I would be the blue-eyed boy if I got it right, and when your eyes are that colour other opportunities seem to fall into your lap. In effect, I was sacrificing the chance to make short-term money for myself to build a career and a reputation.

My next step was to sell the bingo and snooker hall for £1.5 million and, once again, no one could believe what a good deal I had managed to pull off. For the first time, we'd paid off all our debt and there was cash in the bank. Now all the company had was an engineering plant, which was now in profit, and the financial services.

The banks were happy and I was even happier, especially as I had received some good PR in the wake of putting the company back on its feet. I was beginning to believe in my own publicity. In fact, things were not quite as good as they seemed. After all, the company I had saved was only tiny.

I had a good team around me and it was full steam ahead. The

City was the place to be. Along with almost everyone else, we were making loadsamoney. I had a few private interests, mainly in the property field, that were doing well and the broking and finance businesses were going through the roof. We set up an insurance business and then a leasing business and the money was rolling in. It seemed we could do no wrong. That is until Black Monday turned everything on its head in October 1987.

For many people and many businesses, it signalled the end of the good times, but as far as we were concerned Black Monday wasn't a problem. People had borrowed money on the security of shares they had bought and now the value of the shares had dropped, they had to refinance. They didn't need to look much further than us.

Things were going well: Mrs P was happy in her five-bedroom detached des res. She had always dreamed of having a beautiful home – and now she had exactly what she wanted. Business was good and I even took on a chauffeur to drive me around in a big Jaguar XJ12, with leather interior, electric blinds and a phone. However, the first guy I took on, Roy, was to last only two weeks after he caused my very own Black Friday.

The night began in a bar in Paddington Street owned by the legendary footballer and drinker George Best. It was 200 yards from the office and on this particular night I had a few beers with a friend of mine, Bob Holt, who worked for Blue Arrow and was later to become chief executive of Tottenham Hotspur.

There were some girls there and there was plenty of banter when they came over to join us. Eventually we wanted to move on, so I told Mike Watkins, who was my number two, to politely get rid of them. But Mike was giving it large about having a chauffeur-driven Jag. The girls told him they lived in Stoke Newington so he suggested that Roy drive them home in the Jaguar and then come back for us. All I can say is that it seemed like a good idea at the time, but it went horribly wrong.

Roy took the girls off in the Jaguar, then returned promptly, and by three in the morning we were ready to go home. He dropped me off in Carshalton first and then took Mike on to Redhill. Rather the worse for wear, I walked through the door. Mrs P was on the sofa, with a few pertinent questions. Even in my state I could see she was seething.

'You know Friday night is boys' night. We've worked hard all week and it's a treat for the boys,' I told her.

'The boys, was it?' fired back Mrs P. 'Then who were those tarts in your car?'

She had telephoned the car and one of the girls had answered and made some inappropriate and drunken remarks. Roy had then taken the phone from the girl and spoken to Mrs P – so she knew she'd definitely got the right number.

Just then the phone rang and Mike told me he had just sacked Roy. Mike was furious that Roy hadn't had the balls to tell me in advance that my wife had called on the car phone and that the girls had given her some lip. Roy had told him that my wife hadn't sounded happy. 'Not happy,' I said. 'She's standing in front of me in her curlers with her rolling pin at the ready!'

Despite the explanation, I was definitely in the doghouse. At least I was used to it, having spent many hours in there during our years of marriage.

Fortunately, Roy's successor, Jim Carpenter, did much better and remained my driver until he retired in 2004. By then he was sixty-five and had certainly earned his retirement, having put up with me for fifteen years. He was one of the nicest guys you could hope to meet, and would always be there whenever I needed him, even if I called him out at three in the morning.

Jim was ex-military. He says he was in the SAS – I think he meant Saturdays and Sundays! He didn't think for himself, he just took orders, which I suppose was down to his military background. One day, for example, we turned up at the offices of Capel-Cure Myers, the stockbrokers in Holborn in central London, at about eleven in the morning. I didn't know how long I was going to be, so I told Jim to wait for me. We were thrashing out a deal and the negotiations dragged on for about twenty-four hours. I completely forgot about poor Jim, but when I looked out of the window at about six o'clock the following morning, he was still there. He hadn't moved, apart from dashing in to go to the toilet once or twice and going to buy some food from a sweet shop. That was typical Jim.

And, of course, he had every army story going. As soon as anyone saw him coming, they got out of the way – there is only so many times you can hear the same story without your eyes glazing over. He said he'd had a metal plate inserted in his head, he'd nearly died a thousand times, and I lost count of how often he'd stormed machine-gun posts single-handedly, but everyone loved Jim.

Chapter Ten

I Splash out and lose the lot

After a year or so at Astra, thanks largely to the share options that had grown in value as I'd turned the company round, I was a millionaire on paper. All my hard work was beginning to pay off. But then in 1988 Jeremy Porter came into my life, and caused more havoc than anyone else I'd ever met. He had spent time at Her Majesty's Pleasure for VAT misdemeanours as one of the few unfortunates who got done for not declaring the VAT on tips received by the staff he employed, so he told me. Two years in an open prison had apparently done him the world of good. But he was well educated and could certainly talk the talk. His family used to own a hotel group, which included a very famous and hugely successful hotel, the Bear in Woodstock. Eventually, he and his brothers sold it to a big catering group and they became millionaires on the proceeds.

By 1988 Porter was in his mid- to late-forties. He was the archetypal older yuppie, a multi-millionaire with a beautiful house. He was also charming and personable, a very, very nice guy. I knew that he had plenty of cash and invested in lots and lots of companies, but what I didn't realise was that he didn't do as much homework as me on the companies he was buying into and that he was easily influenced, so he could be sold

Theo Paphitis comes into the world on 25 September 1959, but as I subsequently found out, neither the date nor the name was correct.

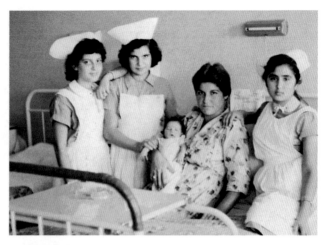

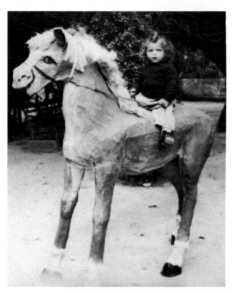

Playing in the park as a curly-haired baby. Mum was desperate for a little girl.

Getting into trouble again on the beach, aged five.

Having crushed my hand in a grate earlier in the day, I was
unable to hold the candle at my uncle Sissos's wedding.

My brother Marinos and I pose with our parents on the jetty in
Venice during our 'banana boat' journey to a new life in England.

My youngest brother, George, sits on Mum's knee, while her mother, Elathe, had come to visit us and help look after the children (above). So did my dad's mother, Xanthi, who we are sitting with at home (right).

Marinos and I check out the wrestling in our home in Manchester (left).

What might have been. Dad, Marinos and me in our first band – and our last!

The Directors of
Stenhouse Reed Shaw London Limited
Stenhouse Reed Shaw Marketing Limited
Sten-Re Limited

request the pleasure of the company of

Miss D.A. Stocker

Cocktail Party at the Elizabeth Suite, Barrington House,
~~~cham Street, E.C.2

~~ 7.30 p.m.

Happiness night of my life

I met ♡ THEO ♡ !
x x x

He took me home, and I asked him if
he wanted to see my Christmas Tree
he Said 'Yes' and raised his eyebrows,
So I told him to cross the road
and he could see it from the window
HA! HA! HA! HA!

Debbie shows her sense of humour on the back of the invitation for our first date,
after she left me standing outside. The photo we took in a Tube station picture
booth at the end of the night (right).

Me and Debbie on a very early date in Regent's Park.

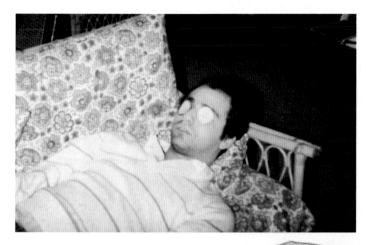

Getting some well-deserved rest!

More than thirty years on, I still have the advert for the job I got selling watches on Bond Street.

E STAFF

TYME
(Quartztronics) Limited,
One Old Bond Street, W.1

Having settled into our magnificent new showroom we now require additional

SALESPEOPLE

These vacancies are permanent and progressive, being ideally suited to those with experience of luxury retailing. Knowledge of the watch business is preferred but as full product training will be given the prime requirements are a congenial personality and the desire to become a member of a successful team. If you feel you meet these qualifications and would like to discuss the position and terms in more detail, please contact Mr. D. JEEVES on 01-499 1331.

Here I am with Anne Stocker, Debbie's nan, and Jim. Nan not only put me up before we got married, she provided the money we needed to help us move into our first home together in Peckham. Remember what I said about Jim's nose?

With Mrs P on our wedding day, 28 January 1978.

Learning to play golf on an Imperial
Life weekend away.

My Clintos Eastwoodos impersonation.

Part of my birthday present from Mrs P, while working at the Surrey & Kent Associates office. But Mrs P was there to take the picture.

Proudly showing off the Porsche I bought soon after joining Druce.

One of my first ever publicity shots, when I was at Astra.

At home with Mrs P – there's never been any question who
rules the roost in our house.

Sailing with Mrs P.

businesses he should probably have avoided.

Porter had a stake in a company called Pavilion, which had bought the bingo and snooker hall from me in Aston. I don't think he had ever heard the homily about a fool and his money. When we sold the bingo and snooker hall, my friend Sean O'Neil went to work with Porter at Pavilion. It all looked like good fun, but it didn't seem quite right. Porter had money, plenty of it, probably too much for his own good, but I could see that the decisions he was making were not the brightest, and the £1.5 million he had paid Astra for the bingo hall confirmed that.

One day he invited me to lunch with a stockbroker and put a proposal to me about a publicly quoted company in which he had taken a significant stake. The company was called Splash, and its main claim to fame was designing and manufacturing souvenir T-shirts. They had a chain of thirteen stores across London selling policemen's hats, clapping dogs and singing flowers. There were four or five of their outlets in Oxford Street alone and they had a manufacturing plant in Swindon, which in truth was a collection of sheds and warehouses.

They had the licence for Garfield and Batman, and these designs were on Splash-made T-shirts. But the company was badly managed, so I thought there was an opportunity to mount a takeover. Porter and the stockbroker felt I was the man to sort things out and they were willing to support such a takeover, putting their shareholdings behind the bid. It was takeover time in the City with deals being done all over the place and I began to get really excited at the prospect of turning round another ailing operation. I felt I could do no wrong. Anything I touched turned to gold, so why should this be any different?

I went to see one of the directors of Splash for a preliminary off-the-record chat to see if there was a deal to be done and how they felt about it. He agreed to give it some thought and said he would come back to me. I left the meeting feeling happy at the way things had gone, but next morning, before I had even got to the office, I had a call to say that news had leaked that Astra had made an approach for the company and the share price had gone through the roof.

This was a major lesson. Assume nothing, trust no one and don't be naive. It was my first experience of dealing with the Takeover Panel and I had to make a statement. They wanted me to clarify the situation, to know whether or not I was going to make a bid, and thus bring some order back to the share price. Under Stock Exchange rules, if I didn't want to make a bid now, then I wouldn't be able to make another bid for a year, but if I did want to make a bid, I had to go ahead and make it immediately. They were putting a gun to my head. We compromised and I said I wasn't sure whether I was going to bid or not. The Takeover Panel appeared to be satisfied with the statement, but that didn't stop the shares from continuing to rise. I was in all the papers and lots of flattering things were being written about me.

I agreed to meet Porter and the management team again, but this time the mood was different. They said they weren't going to give me any more information apart from what was on public record. We scrutinised the figures available and then, through my advisers, Astra made an all-share bid for the company. The upshot was that Porter and his cohorts accepted the offer, but the management did not. We still went on to win the bid, however, which came as a surprise to me.

There was no cash involved. Through our advisers we agreed we would raise £4 or £5 million via a rights issue for working capital and to pay down debts that Splash owed to its bank. The deal went through, which left the existing directors of Splash owning quite a slice of the new combined company, which had changed its name from Astra to AT Trust.

As soon as the deal went through, the Splash directors sold

large chunks of their shares on the market, which had the effect of sending the AT Trust shares plunging. It put the rights issue in grave doubt, especially as the institutions were still feeling cautious about investing in the aftermath of Black Monday. All this wouldn't have happened if our advisers had carried out the agreed plan, which was to place the Splash directors' unwanted shares with the institutions, thus creating a stable market for the shares. But Black Monday made it very hard for them to do this.

I was caught in a pincer movement. I had bought the company, our share price had collapsed and I couldn't raise any cash to pay back debts that had to be repaid – I felt like one of the hospital cases I had been feeding off for years. It wasn't a pleasant feeling, even though I was confident we could trade our way out of trouble.

As I got more involved in the business, I found that I had not bought what I thought I had bought. We had based our bid on the publicly available information – the reports and accounts that companies have to publish every year. But there were aspects of the balance sheet that were absolute nonsense. For example, a large part of their stockholding was in fact old stock that had now gone out of fashion and was consequently worthless.

I had gone from chairing a company that was making profits and had cash in the bank to a company that was in debt with no cash reserves and a pile of stock that was complete rubbish and needed to be written off. I ran around at a rate of knots trying to plug every hole. But for every hole plugged, I found another one. It was like sailing the ocean in a colander.

I had a small management team and we were really being stretched. Our share price was almost down to nothing and my brokers had pretty well given up in their quest to raise money. They were having problems of their own and the whole of the City was merging and consolidating, trying to save their own skins following the collapse in confidence in the financial markets.

If our brokers had been able to place the shares and raise the cash we might have been OK, but they couldn't and we were abandoned with only some horrendous trading figures to keep us company. We were under tremendous pressure from Porter and his other shareholders, who between them owned a large chunk of the combined company. My relationship with Porter was becoming more and more strained by the day. I was trying to get some explanations from Splash's auditors about the books.

At that stage, Porter came to see me and revealed that he knew some people who were very liquid and were interested in taking a stake in the company. It seemed to be a positive development – investors were exactly what we needed. I met them, went through everything and their response was immediate. They would inject £500,000 into the company straight away and a further £5 million down the line. Things were starting to look a lot better.

But when I started to check out Porter's investors, I began to feel uncomfortable. I was getting a bit nervous about whether I wanted to be in business with them – and whether they had the ability to put in the rest of the money they had promised. I didn't believe that they were the real deal. I felt they were trying to take advantage of the situation and wasn't sure they could turn it round.

We had a meeting of all the major shareholders, including Porter, and much to my surprise these new investors told me they didn't care what I thought because they wanted to take control and had the full support of Porter and his associates. I would no longer be required. This was a bolt out of the blue.

I agreed to step down, but whichever way you look at it, I was being booted out and for the first time in my life I was unemployed. One minute I was chairman of a public company and the next minute I had no real reason to get out of bed in the morning. I found it very difficult to cope with. I couldn't get to grips with not getting up and going to work in the morning, with having to explain to Mrs P that I was no longer gainfully employed. My confidence was shattered and I had no idea what the future held for me.

With nothing else to do, I had plenty of time to reflect on some of the decisions I had taken off my own bat and others I had been coerced into taking. I quickly came to the conclusion that some of the decisions had been pretty poor. I also felt terribly let down by the City. During the takeover the advisers had been very bullish, massaging my ego at every opportunity. They had earned hefty fees from the deal, but when I needed them to help me maintain my position, they had vanished into thin air.

It was the first time in my life I had suffered such a reversal in fortunes. I was well on the way to being one of those rising stars of the late 1980s boom who had fallen out of sight into obscurity – a classic case of boom and bust. All those paper assets I'd had that could have made me a millionaire had pretty much disappeared and I was almost back to where I had been when I left Hanover Druce almost three years previously.

Chapter Eleven

Back in the game

I was back where I had started fourteen years ago: looking for a job. I still had few formal skills or qualifications, but this time I had a wife, three children and debts I had stupidly accumulated by borrowing money from the bank to buy shares in Astra in order to show confidence and further support my own position.

Stockbrokers were always telling people to buy shares to show confidence in the company. I didn't have huge wealth, but I borrowed hundreds of thousands of pounds to buy shares that I now couldn't sell. They were worthless bits of paper and I had secured this massive bank debt against my new house in Oxshott, Surrey, a beautiful property with an indoor pool, gym, snooker room and electric gates. It was mortgaged to the hilt.

I was becoming persona non grata; most people wouldn't even return my calls. I was yesterday's news, but not as interesting. I was running out of names to call in my little black book – the City was a very fickle place, especially when you were down on your luck. The people who might have been willing to help were having problems of their own. Interest rates went up to 15 per cent for a short period and Lloyds' insurance market and the stock market had collapsed. After initially feeling I could ride out the storm and come out the other side dry and warm, I was starting to feel unloved and unwanted. I entered into a spiral of depression but knew I had to get out of it. Feeling sorry for yourself does not put food on the table or pay off the rapidly rising bank debt.

I had always preached that cash is king and always had my 'walking the street' money. The best decision I ever made when things were going brilliantly was to put aside a sum of cash in case I was ever poor again. So I had between £75,000 and £100,000 stashed away for a rainy day – and the weather was so bad that it would have sent Noah down to the local timber yard. Even if I had given all my spare cash to the banks it wouldn't have gone anywhere near paying off what I owed. But it did give me a stake to get back in the game – if I could find a game that would give me a seat at the table and that was the difficult part.

During one of the lowest points in my post-Astra/Splash life I went for a drink with my old friend Adam Phokou from Imperial Life. He had just sold several properties that he and his wife had owned in central London and bought D'Oyly Carte Island – an island on the Thames at Weybridge. There was just one big house on the island, which was to be his new home. He had taken on some debt and it couldn't have happened at a worse time as, unsurprisingly, property was crashing along with the markets.

Adam and I were now near neighbours and we met up often. I enjoyed the river scene and dipped into my 'walking the street' money to buy a boat, which Adam allowed me to moor off his island. It was a ridiculous thing to do, but as I couldn't get into any big-time business game, I thought I might as well chill out on the boat. I found myself going there almost every day. I read sailing books, did DIY on the boat and went fishing.

It was like the summers spent with my brother at Hampstead

Heath Ponds twenty years earlier – fishing and listening to cricket on the radio. It could have been utterly depressing, but it was quite calming. When life gets tough I am always drawn to water – probably because I feel like jumping in and drowning, although I've never tried it.

I still had my brick-size mobile phone but the only time it ever rang was when Mrs P wanted to know when I was coming home. I said I was working on the boat, even though it was brand, spanking new and didn't need working on. I was anonymous and would go on day trips up and down the locks. I even had a portable TV and forgot all about work and business. My only challenges were the number of locks I could go through during the day, how many fish I would catch, and finding out whether England were getting a hiding at cricket. I'd stop off and have a drink in a pub on the river – and no one knew who I was or my past.

High finance had totally disappeared from my life and I just couldn't relate to it any more. I kept my frustrations and depression to myself. It was my secret, nobody else's business. But my cash stash was getting lower and even if I could get some City action, I wasn't sure I'd have the necessary money.

Then one day I was on my boat when I got a phone call from a friend who worked for a bank. He said Astra had gone into administration. The rest of the promised money hadn't materialised, which is exactly what I had predicted. It didn't ease my sadness at hearing this news to know that I had been proved right. I certainly didn't want to dance on the company's grave. They were my friends and former colleagues.

Next morning, instead of heading for the river I started working the phone. I wanted to try to sort something out. The various parts of the company were going to be sold off piecemeal by the administrators. I had always been keen on the retail side, which had been part of Splash, but that was snapped up very quickly. It was never offered to me, which was a big disappointment as I wanted the chance to have a go at it.

A few days later I got a call from Ian Childs, who used to work for Movie and Media Marketing, which was another part of Splash. When he joined, we had launched a subsidiary, Movie and Media Sports, which specialised in selling perimeter advertising around sports grounds.

The guys who ran Movie and Media Marketing were part of the Porter set, but Ian had carried on running Movie and Media Sports. He was distraught. He had left a fantastic job nine months earlier and now the parent company was going bust and he was terrified his credibility was going down the toilet. I said we should meet up at my house. I was on the boat at the time and he arrived before I did; I told him I had been at a business meeting. He had a mortgage to pay, a family to support, and existing contracts and commitments with a host of people. His reputation was on the line and I really did feel for him. I suggested he bid for Movie and Media Sports from the receiver, which he did but the receiver quoted silly numbers.

Ian was in turmoil, worried sick that his rivals would snap up the company he had created from under his feet and that he would lose his job. We agreed to meet several days later in a London wine bar near our old offices. I told him I would be prepared to invest in the business and then handed him an envelope containing a banker's draft for £30,000. I told him to offer the money to the receiver, but not to show him the envelope until the price had been agreed. I didn't want to show my face at this stage because the price would have shot up.

I waited with the lawyer in the bar across the road and told Ian we could complete the deal by the end of the day. He went in and started negotiating; but the receiver said if Ian could show he had £50,000, he might be interested – he was £20,000 short. He came back to the wine bar and pleaded for more. I produced another envelope, this one containing a banker's draft worth £10,000.

'That's it, Ian,' I said. 'I don't have any more. Tell them to take it or leave it.'

What I didn't tell Ian was that I had put up my last £40,000 – except for the £10,000 that was in my back pocket! But I had to make Ian believe £40,000 was the final offer. He went back to the receiver in a very emotional state and explained that £40,000 was all he could raise.

I was sitting by the window and saw him run towards the bar. He raced through the door and knocked my drink all over me. When I asked him where the money was, he said he'd left it with the receiver. Even the solicitor couldn't believe it, but it worked in our favour as we only had to draw up a simple contract. We bought the name and the tools and equipment required to carry out the business – two desks, two chairs and a filing cabinet, the sum contents of Ian's office. We didn't even have a typewriter.

Then we had a good old drink to celebrate the fact that we were both back in business. Actually, I was in business. I don't think in all the euphoria Ian realised that I had bought the company with my own money and owned exactly 100 per cent of it. When I pointed this out to him he looked at me ashen-faced with disappointment. I laughed and worked out a deal on the basis that as and when I was repaid my investment, I would transfer 50 per cent of the shares to Ian and we would run the company together. After all, that forty grand was my 'walking the street' money and I didn't know when I was going to need it again.

I knew this was a small deal and was never going to make me a fortune, but Ian reckoned that if his forecasts were correct he would be able to repay me in six months. When Ian and I struck our original deal there was no documentation, no letters. It was all done on a handshake.

We found an office and bought a third desk for the secretary. We knocked up some letterheads and Movie and Media Sports was reborn. We were the classic two men and a dog – only we hadn't hired the dog yet. But what really mattered was that I was back at work with a will.

The company sold perimeter board advertising at sports grounds and we had some incredible contacts. Pretty soon we renewed an existing deal with the Welsh Rugby Union. The way it worked was that we would guarantee the WRU, say, £500,000 over the season for the rights to the perimeter advertising at the National Stadium – and then we would go out and sell that advertising 'space'. Obviously, we had to bring in the initial £500,000 before we started making any money ourselves. It was a high-risk enterprise but we were confident we could pull it off.

Sport was becoming a really good medium for sponsorship and advertising and we did well. Every year we gave guarantees to football and cricket clubs for their commercial rights around their stadia.

Pretty soon I wasn't just an investor, but was spending a lot of time in the office and enjoying it, particularly as we were making a decent profit. I was getting up each morning, putting on a suit and going to work, something that hadn't happened for a long time. I was back in the West End, dealing with respectable blue-chip companies and major sporting bodies, seeing people, networking, doing lunches and beginning to envisage other opportunities. I was well and truly back in the swing of things. There was no time for messing about on the boat and I put away my fishing rod.

I'd spent most of my 'walking the street' money investing in Movie and Media Sports but the company paid me back my £40,000 even sooner than Ian had predicted – within three months. Ian got his 50 per cent equity in the business and we were proper partners, especially as I was working in the business, which hadn't been part of the original deal. The business was growing and making money but couldn't sustain the sort of salary I needed and I was still living on my savings.

It became clear to me that I needed a completely new opportunity. All my capital was tied up in our massive house in Oxshott, which seemed to have about 523 rooms. I could sense that there were opportunities out there, but I badly needed cash in order to take advantage of them. I took the decision to sell the house, pay off all my debts and buy a more modest house to enable me to top up my cash reserves.

After a good lunch one day, I went home, took my tie off, and sat down with Mrs P.

'Look, I don't know how to tell you this, but this beautiful dream home that we've built together is most, if not all, of our worldly worth. Everything else, I'm afraid, darling, I've either lost or reinvested. Cash is scarce and it really would make an awful lot of . . .'

'Sense if we sold the house?'

Mrs P wasn't upset or angry or even shocked. She said she'd never really been content there and would be happy to move into more of a family house. She could see that the cash flow would enable me to do what I wanted to do and was right behind me.

It only then dawned on me that the house had been built for me. It wasn't built for her or for the family; it was built for my ego. It was part and parcel of something I'd dreamed of as a kid. We put the house on the market and started looking around. We sold it for just below the asking price and found a lovely house on an estate in Cobham. It was tiny compared with where we had come from. My driver, Jim, described it as a doll's house.

Our new house was a NatWest Bank repossession and needed quite a lot of work doing to it. We quickly set about refurbishing it, but I could see what was going through the minds of friends and acquaintances who came to visit – they all felt we were on the verge of bankruptcy! The most important thing, though, was that I now had some cash and could get back into business. All I needed to do was to find the right opportunity. I didn't have to wait long.

Chapter Twelve

Upwardly mobile

In 1992 I heard about somebody in the telecoms business who was looking for investment. I knew very little about the telecoms industry other than that I had a mobile phone. Movie and Media Sports had also worked with a company called Rabbit, which was part of the giant Hutchinson group that was launching a new telecommunications system in the UK. We worked for them on the branding and placed quite a lot of signage round rugby grounds throughout the UK.

From rabbiting to Rabbit, I soon discovered that the telecoms business was awash with money. They were far and away our biggest clients, spending millions on advertising, and an industry that can spend that sort of money on advertising must be upwardly mobile.

I met up with Tony Kleanthous, a Cypriot lad just like me, who ran a company called NAG Communications. I went through his business with him and it soon became clear to me that the business was insolvent. He had three shops selling mobile phones, but had over-expanded, had very little capital and was close to bankruptcy. He was young and inexperienced but he was bright. But bright as he was, he wasn't prepared to acknowledge that the company was under-capitalised and over-trading and in danger of going bust soon.

He was also reluctant to release any of the equity in the business, even though he needed the money. There was no point in forcing the issue, but I told him I would be interested in investing and sent him on his way. I heard nothing for several weeks and assumed he wasn't interested in bringing me on board. I carried on meeting other people and looking at other opportunities.

I looked at some nursing homes, which I got quite excited about, but the investment needed a lot more capital than I could muster because it was property-based. I looked at hotels; I looked at the whole market really. But I kept coming back to telecoms because it was almost drowning in a sea of cash and I knew this was for me.

Everyone wanted a mobile phone so I was quite pleased when Tony finally got back to me several months after our initial meeting. Things were getting fraught for NAG – the bank had stopped honouring their cheques and it had finally dawned on Tony that he was seriously under-capitalised and about to go bust. We hammered out a deal and reconstituted the company. I took a majority stake in return for an investment, putting in about £50,000. Because I was working very closely with Ian, I gave some of the equity to him so that he could be part of it and could help out even though he was quite busy running Movie and Media Sports.

NAG had three stores in London – one in Holloway Road, one in the City and one in Mill Hill. But the only one that had a proper lease was Holloway Road. It was a bit of a shock – maybe I should have been a bit more diligent in my due diligence. I thought that if we were asked to leave those two stores we would be able to find alternative premises quickly, but there wasn't much time as both landlords wanted us out.

Although Tony was very bright, he had some rather insular

ideas about how a business should be run. We didn't see eye to eye on a lot of things. I knew I was right because I had the business experience and he didn't, but it took a while before Tony agreed that I should be more hands-on.

I found another store in Wimbledon, which was closer to my home, and managed to buy the freehold of the building with Ian. We opened a NAG shop at the front, and converted the back to offices, moving Movie and Media Sports out from central London. That way Ian and I could run Movie and Media Sports and NAG from the same building. We even had space for a small stockroom to supply Holloway Road, which Tony was running.

Working with Ian on Movie and Media Sports and with Tony on the new NAG venture, I was back to putting in sixteen- to seventeen-hour days in two different fields that were quite exciting. Couple this with a few other investments and I was fully occupied again.

The sports marketing business was absolutely fantastic because we could go to all the big games in the UK and around the world – put our jeans and boots on, wear our official passes, walk round the touchline, look after our boards and watch the games for free. There wasn't a sporting event we couldn't go to – in a 'working' capacity of course. I spent quite a lot of my time watching football and rugby and some cricket. It was fabulous and I was making money from sport; it doesn't get much better than that.

The telecoms business was going well too. It wasn't like it is now with half a dozen mobile phone shops in almost every high street. To ensure our name was known, we spent quite a bit of money on advertising and marketing, using any excess boards around the various grounds to promote NAG. We opened another shop in Harrow and were back to three shops again, all nicely kitted out, and so our reputation began to grow. We advertised in the *Evening Standard* and on Capital Radio and ploughed the profits back in to stimulate long-term growth. Tony had other ideas: he wanted to see some of the fruits of his labours. It was always a bit of a strained relationship, but we managed to get through most of our disagreements and, more importantly, the business continued to thrive.

There were only two phone networks back then, Cellnet and Vodafone, until a third player joined the market, One to One. We used to call it One to No One because the whole network was launched in a hurry, using Sellotape and string to keep it all together. It only worked in London; they hadn't rolled it out to the rest of the UK. We dealt with Cellnet and our service provider was Securicor, who owned 40 per cent of Cellnet (the remainder owned by BT).

The mobile phone industry was like no other business I had ever encountered. Normally, if you're in retail, you buy a product for £1 and sell it for £2 or £3 and your profit is the difference between what you paid and what you got from the customer, but the mobile phone industry didn't work like that. You bought a phone for £100 and sold it for £50, so automatically you were selling at a loss. You made up the difference through the connection commission you received from the network. That would vary on a monthly basis depending on how aggressive they were in obtaining connections. Some months they'd pay you a £75 connection bonus, so you'd make £25 profit, while in other months they would pay you £150. It was incredible, but you never knew until the beginning of each month what the commission bonus would be.

We were very aggressive and Securicor became more and more generous with regard to commission rates, marketing support and other help. Eventually I became a lot more comfortable with this concept of selling at a loss. It really boiled down to a negotiation every month with the service provider as to how much commission they would give you.

Some months they would just chuck cash at us because they'd made so many connections and you could end up making £125 or even £150 on each sale. It was all about how badly the service provider wanted the business and how hard you wanted to push them. We never agreed with them on their first offer every month, we'd always try to get an extra £10 or £15.

If I had negotiated a great deal on commission I was able to drop the price of a phone from £50 to £9.99, which caused pandemonium across the industry. But it got us noticed. In such a competitive environment, any way of distinguishing yourself from the rest had to be of benefit.

It was a wonderful industry to be in, but it was a bit like the Wild West as there were lots of people involved who were totally inexperienced. It seemed that everyone who had jumped ship after the recession had made their way into telecoms, with the result that the quality of personnel varied dramatically. There were some incredibly bright, honourable, professional people and then there were some absolute rascals taking the industry for everything they could squeeze out of it. I was determined that we would be seen as a professional operation and we did everything properly, but it was very frustrating sometimes having to deal with people who had been promoted way above their level of competence.

The industry is mature now but back then I was astonished at some of the decisions being taken, the feast and famine of the commissions paid, and some of the ridiculous expenditure and costs incurred. Nevertheless, I wanted to make sure NAG got its fair share of the cash that was flying around and I attended lots of functions and got to know everybody.

I think the reason the two companies were doing so well, when plenty of others were falling by the wayside, was because I stuck to my business principles. Even though NAG and Movie and Media Sports were sunrise industries and there was loads of cash out there, we didn't just scoop it all up and spend it. While other outfits opened expensive offices and ran big expense accounts and even bigger cars, we made sure we kept costs to a minimum. I suppose I was still hurting from the Astra debacle and was determined not to let it happen to me again. We had no showy offices like the ones I'd had at Druce – this time it was my money at stake.

I'd lived through a time when money was coming in so fast you hardly had time to count it, but I'd also seen the bad times. Now I was a lot more conservative when things were going well again and thought it couldn't last for ever. I had recovered financially and was probably once more a paper millionaire, but I made sure we were well positioned in case the worst should happen. I believed that when the inevitable downturn came again, only those people running their businesses professionally and properly and taking into account the basic fundamentals would survive. And so things might have continued, had I not gone to see *Sunset Boulevard*.

Chapter Thirteen

Ryman reason

In the autumn of 1993 I got a phone call from Nigel Russell, Securicor's marketing director, inviting me to the theatre. He had organised a table for ten people to eat at the Savoy Hotel plus tickets to see *Sunset Boulevard* at the Savoy Theatre. I had no idea that the evening would shape the rest of my life. It was here that I met Malcolm Cooke, the marketing director of Ryman the stationer, where Mrs P had bought me a dictionary all those years ago.

Ryman had starting selling mobile phones through Securicor – simply because Nigel lived in the same village as Malcolm and they met at the local tennis club. But the stationery firm wasn't exactly geared up for selling mobiles and was finding it difficult to be competitive.

While we were wheeling and dealing with Securicor every month on the commissions, Ryman couldn't get their heads around selling a product at negative profit. So Securicor said they would give them £10 or £15 for every phone they sold. While we could make up to £150 on a phone, Ryman made £15. Malcolm and I got on well, but I didn't see him again until many months later.

It was March 1994 and Manchester United were playing

Aston Villa in the League Cup final at Wembley and I had promised to take my son Alex. With all the corporate hospitality I received, it was much more fun going to watch a game as a normal punter. It was great buying the tickets, getting on the train and the tube, getting to the stadium, smelling the pungent aroma of the hot dogs and onions outside the ground, watching the crowds go by and enjoying the day like a proper fan. It was better for Alex to see a game this way rather than from a hospitality box or from the touchline if I was working with the advertising boards. And as we squeezed on to a tube at Baker Street, who should be sitting opposite me but Malcolm from Ryman. He was a big United fan and was going to the game with his nephew. His nephew was no little kid, however, but a six-foot two-inch bloke who lived in Holland and was a mad Manchester United fan who would travel all around the world to watch them. So I had my six-year-old son and he had his thirty-something nephew with him and we started to chat. When we got to Wembley, we found we were sitting on opposite sides of the ground, but I agreed to give him a call.

A few weeks later I called Malcolm and arranged to have lunch with him. I must admit to having had a simple ulterior motive. I had concerns about the mobile phone scene and the monthly uncertainty about how much commission you were going to make. To open a shop I had to take a fifteen- to twenty-year lease and had to pay a fixed rent each month. I also needed staff. In a good month we sold between fifty and seventy-five phones a month per store, which was fine when you were making £100 profit per sale, but wasn't so acceptable when you were making £10. It made me wary of expanding much further. I started looking at advertising and selling off the page, as opposed to having retail stores.

The plain fact was that whether my business was going to be profitable or not was out of my hands – it was down to individuals for whom I didn't have much respect and who, in many cases, didn't have a clue what they were doing. The lesson I'd learned from my days at Druce was the importance of having a good business plan, yet here I was, having to commit to relatively high fixed costs with no certainty about my income. Although the business had worked well for me so far, I wasn't blind to the potential dangers.

If I wanted to expand, I needed to find ways to do so without facing high fixed costs. And this was where Malcolm, and Ryman, came in. I knew from talking to him and other research I'd done that Ryman weren't selling many phones. My plan was to persuade him to give us a concession within Ryman, especially as they had some great sites in central London, including Great Portland Street, Oxford Street and Marble Arch. I thought this would be a quick way to increase our reach and exposure without having to take on massive leases and expend huge amounts of capital fitting out stores. Ryman would benefit, too, as I was sure I could give them more than they were making on each sale at the time.

So I put the proposal to Malcolm and suggested we took some space – a few hundred square feet – in the bigger outlets. Instead of him selling five or ten phones a month, we could sell 200 or 300 phones a month – and I could afford to pay him either a rent or a commission. But more importantly for Malcolm, through advertising, I'd be driving customers into the stores. So Ryman would get rent or commission that they were not getting at the moment and I'd be sending customers their way who would, hopefully, buy other items.

Malcolm is an incredibly bright person and quickly saw the advantages of my proposal. We did a deal and soon opened up six 'NAG at Ryman' concessions and began advertising. Very soon we were selling phones as quickly as we could get them into the stores. It seemed that Malcolm had backed the right NAG!

It was at this time that Malcolm started sharing some information about his business with me, and talking about some of the pressures he faced. The main problem was cash flow. Not enough was flowing in the right direction and Ryman was often unable to pay its suppliers on time, which meant it wasn't getting the right stock in and the business was suffering as a result.

One of the reasons for this was that Ryman was part of the Pentos Group, which owned several different chains, including Dillons the booksellers and Athena, the cards and poster business. In addition, Pentos had bought an office machine business called Wildings, a bad buy that they amalgamated into Ryman, and which was causing them a lot of grief. The parent company was struggling for cash so it was ripping it out of Ryman at every opportunity and spreading it around the other parts of the business. So from being reasonably healthy, Ryman was starting to look quite sick.

Pentos was refinancing but they were keeping the Ryman directors in the dark about what was going on. Instead of running the business, the Ryman management was spending more and more time writing reports for the banks and all the other people involved in the group. Of course, the Pentos problems didn't affect NAG – we were selling tons of phones and must have been one of Ryman's biggest profit-earners, if not the biggest.

I was getting to know the Ryman business quite well and could see that a lot of the decisions being made were damaging the company. It wasn't my business, but nevertheless I was frustrated by what was going on. I got to know the staff, especially in the West End stores and they were becoming more and more demoralised. In fact, the only ray of sunshine for them was the fact that NAG was creating a buzz of activity in their stores. I could see things were not as they should be – they were frequently out of key items of stock. They were even fresh out of paper clips. How can a stationery store be out of paper clips? It's like a pub with no beer.

I'd speak to Malcolm and come up with various suggestions as to how they could improve things. But I was only telling him what he knew already. He was in no position to change things. He was reliant upon the half-wits at Pentos who were taking their cash away, making rash decisions and sending in consultants. The consultants were borrowing their watches to tell them the time, taking up their time to learn about the business and pointing out the obvious. Malcolm was as frustrated as his staff.

My main concern, however, was that Ryman was a key part of our business. Most of our sales came through Ryman, and we were in around forty of their stores. If Ryman went under, we could be in a difficult situation.

One day Malcolm said to me, 'You seem to have all the answers. Why don't you buy Ryman?'

While he said it flippantly, it really bugged me, and the thought stayed with me. I couldn't imagine how many noughts there would be on the end of the price, or how I would find the money. By this time my reputation as a turnaround specialist was practically restored and I was even getting some column inches in the press again for my prowess in reviving failing businesses, which led to my being offered various non-executive roles in a number of small companies, including a small plc. Malcolm couldn't understand why I wouldn't have a go at Ryman. My contention was that I had my hands full and didn't want to relive the Astra scenario where I was stretched to breaking point.

Enter stage right Dick Towner, who was the lawyer on the other side in the ill-fated Splash deal. Although he had been a member of the opposition, so to speak, I got on well with him.

He was quite amusing and would break into song halfway through a drafting meeting. Later I offered him a non-executive directorship on the board of Movie and Media Sports. There was only a small fee, but plenty of tickets for the big games, and Dick liked the arrangement although not the small fee!

I met Dick, who was now acting as a consultant, for dinner one night and told him I thought Ryman could be bought. I told Dick I didn't know how much for and that I hadn't got a lot of money, so he would have to introduce me to the right people who would back an equity purchase. He was really positive about my idea so I decided to take the plunge.

Pentos had just parachuted in Bill McGrath as chief executive, who had previously occupied the same position at Wickes, to sort out the mess. I contacted him and explained that I would like to meet him to discuss the future of Ryman. I rang Dick, very excited, and asked him to come along as well.

I thought taking Dick with me would add weight to my argument as well as providing some moral support. At McGrath's office, a lady opened the door and I was just about to announce myself when Dick and this woman kissed one another on the cheek in greeting. It turned out that this lady, who was McGrath's secretary, used to be secretary to Captain Bob Maxwell and that Dick had been a non-executive director of one of Maxwell's television companies and had acted for him as a lawyer.

Dick had spent a lot of time talking to her because you could never get hold of Captain Bob and everything was done through his secretary. Well, it broke the ice and I took it as a good omen. We were shown into a meeting room where there was a table, six chairs and a flip chart on a tripod. We were having coffee when, being the nosey so-and-so I am, I flipped up the flip chart and – to my amazement – there was an analysis of the Ryman business and a valuation.

They had clearly discussed selling Ryman at the last meeting held in that room, so I knew the business was for sale and I even knew roughly what they thought it was worth, which was way above the figure I was prepared to pay. McGrath came in, we had our meeting and I tried not to look at the flip chart. I felt guilty that I'd seen it and found my eyes kept drifting towards it as I was speaking to him. But then I began to suspect a conspiracy theory and decided he must have left it there on purpose in order to set the expectation levels. After all, we were in the room a long time and we couldn't help but take a look at it. I was convinced we'd been set up and wasn't listening to a word he said.

We had a long discussion and I agreed that I'd put in an offer, even though I knew he was looking for a lot more than I was prepared to pay. I had a couple of phone conversations with him and by this time I knew from Malcolm, and from the papers, that things were going from bad to worse at Ryman. What's more, Pentos was forced to put Athena into administration.

All I could do was wait it out and hope that whoever bought Ryman allowed NAG to stay there. I was quite relieved when eventually Pentos went into administration, which put Ryman into administration as well, and I decided to see if I could buy the business from the administrator.

I knew I would be taking a huge risk – both financially and in terms of my reputation. But I felt that it was the deal that would take me to a completely new level. I reckoned if it did go wrong I had some assets that I had ring-fenced and would be able to keep body and soul together. But if I ended up slithering down one of the snakes instead of climbing the ladder, it would be a major setback.

I started working on it day and night, trying to get as much information as I could. Obviously, I had quite a lot of local information because of the business we were doing with Ryman through NAG. I knew several of the branches and knew roughly what some of them were taking, from discussions with the managers.

I continued to dig out more information and started to put a business plan together, which took several weeks, but showed that if I bought Ryman I could turn it into a profitable concern. I had turned it round on paper – all I needed now was the money to buy it so I could turn it round in practice. How hard could it be?

It was a lot harder than I envisaged, even getting to first base. When I approached a couple of banks, they told me to bugger off and not darken their doorsteps again. Retail was not flavour of the month. They couldn't get their corporate heads around it. Ryman had endured such bad publicity and retail was going through a very difficult period. We were still in the depths of the mid-1990s recession, and banks weren't lending a lot of money. I visited Dick at his office and told him that I'd got the business plan sussed. I asked him if he had any ideas on the money front.

Dick has never spent a penny in anger in his life. Getting him to buy a drink is an achievement and he bangs his head on the ceiling when he gets out of bed in the morning because he keeps all his money under the mattress. I didn't expect for one minute that he would offer to lend me the money, and he did not disappoint, but I knew he had some good contacts.

I thought I had good contacts with the banks but they were turning me down. Normally when I was looking for a loan, I only applied when I was confident the loan would go through. After all, that's what I did for a living once upon a time. Banks are great at giving you an umbrella when the sun's shining and taking it away when it's raining. Of course, one of the stumbling blocks was that I couldn't even tell them what the purchase price was going to be because I didn't know myself.

Dick got his little black book out, organised some introductions and together we went to see a few people. One was a small finance boutique, which shall remain nameless, and was run by some very clever corporate financiers who had known Dick for some time. I went through the presentation and they looked quite interested in what I had to say. I thought we were getting somewhere. I started to relax a little and was confident I was making a good pitch. In fact, it was an excellent pitch, the best pitch of my life, utilising all my turnaround experience.

They asked me a lot of questions, were getting an understanding of the business, and when I'd finished my presentation, they went off for a little chat amongst themselves. It was sounding good. I turned to Dick and got the thumbs up.

Twenty minutes later they returned. They said they'd spoken to one of their partners, and praised the great job I'd done analysing the business. They'd liked the presentation and the business plan, and they were very interested.

It sounded like job done. And then one of them turned round and said, 'But you do realise if we do put up the money to buy this business, we'll want a big stake and, of course, we'll want to put our own management in.'

It was a kick in the cobblers. I could understand they might want some equity but they also wanted their own management. I couldn't work out what part I played in all this. When it became clear that my role would be negligible, I got up and thanked them for their interest, their time and their coffee. I'd wasted three and a half hours of my time. If anyone was going to run Ryman, it was me, not some half-wit with a double-barrelled surname who was well known on the cocktail party circuit.

That evening I went for some drinks with my old friend Sean O'Neil, who mentioned another bank – the Israeli-owned Mizrahi Bank – that had funded various retail deals in the past. Sean put me in touch with the bank, I managed to get an appointment and enthusiastically went through my presentation with them. They seemed receptive to what I had to say and asked me to leave the paperwork with them. I didn't have high expectations, but saw this as another iron in the fire. It was time to get in touch with the receiver, KPMG, and register my interest.

The Ryman story was all over the newspapers and all sorts of prospective buyers were mentioned, except me. As well as registering my interest with the receiver, I got Dick's firm to send them a letter, formally stating my interest, confirming that I was a client of theirs and listing all of my considerable interests. But I didn't have the money and Dick's letter didn't actually say I did.

To my surprise, the people at Mizrahi got back to me and said they'd be interested in funding the deal. Instead of asking for equity, however, they wanted a remuneration to reflect the risk that they were taking and they said they would be looking for a very large fee. I didn't know how much they were going to lend me because I didn't know what the price would be, but I knew roughly what I wanted to pay and what I needed to borrow. I reckoned I needed about £3 million.

The arrangement fee they wanted was £500,000, which seemed a huge amount for a loan of £3 million, but they knew I had few options. However, as I knew I'd be able to repay a million of it very quickly, I began negotiating on the fee – all this before I'd even started talking to the receiver. In the end we came to a compromise. They would charge me £500,000, but that would be reduced to £250,000 if I paid them back £1 million in the first six months, which was perfectly possible if my business plan was correct. It was still nearly 10 per cent but we were at least getting somewhere, and I wasn't going to have to give away any equity.

I arranged a meeting with the administrator, but felt he didn't treat me seriously. I had indicated the sort of amount I would be looking to offer for the business, but we were still a long way apart. I felt they were just humouring me in allowing me to continue.

Several days went by and I didn't hear back from KPMG. When Dick rang me one afternoon I told him that there was nothing doing. I pointed out that the papers were coming up with all sorts of names apparently offering far more than I could afford. But Dick reminded me that if they hadn't actually got the money, it was all talk. We agreed to get a letter from the bank, which my lawyers would quote in a letter to the administrator, saying that their client was very keen and had got his funding in place. That should put me in a much stronger position.

KPMG's reply was like a very polite 'Get lost': 'We acknowledge your letter, thank you very much. If we deem it necessary to come back to you, then, of course, we will.' I'd made my mind up that it wasn't going to happen and I'd been reading in the press and hearing from Malcolm that so-and-so had visited and had a look round and interviewed the staff. I asked Malcolm whether anyone had got a deal and he couldn't tell me. All he could say was that Ryman wasn't saying anything.

While all this was going on, it was a busy time for Movie and Media Sports. In March 1995 Arsenal were playing in Europe and we had sold the rights to the advertising boards for their game, so we had to go and put all the boards up, something I always enjoyed doing. The Gunners were away in France and we were going out there mob-handed, leaving at lunchtime the day before the match – I had time to pop into the office in the morning.

The phone rang and my secretary said, 'It's someone from KPMG. Shall I tell him you've left?'

'Don't you dare,' I said. 'Put him through.'

Not having heard from me for about ten days, he said he assumed I was no longer interested in the business. I told him that, having read the papers, I thought the business had been sold for some ridiculous sum. But he told me not to believe everything I read in the newspapers. He went on to tell me that he had been in negotiations for the past thirty-six hours to complete a deal but it had fallen through. All I wanted to know was whether he would sell the business to me – and at what price. My offer was still on the table, but there was a lot of detail to be ironed out before I could have a deal.

When you buy from a receiver, you don't actually get legal title to very much. You get the goodwill and assets, but because the company's gone bust you have no legal rights to anything like the store leases. You have to get those reassigned to your company and some landlords might not be interested. The receiver can't sell you things he doesn't own, just a commitment to help you acquire it.

But despite the problems that I knew lay ahead, I was so excited. It was as if a huge weight had been lifted from my shoulders. I told Ian Childs that I thought I could do a deal on Ryman and that they had asked to meet me at their lawyers' offices in the next two to three hours. I had to cancel the trip to France and concentrate on putting together a team to do the deal.

With Dick and his legal team, we set off to meet KPMG's lawyers. The first meeting lasted about two hours but, having spent several days negotiating with other people, they were very precise and knew all the obstacles they had to surmount. In fairness to them, they put all those problems on the table in order to clear them up first. I was so keen that I was willing to live with most things. So they suggested we got down to heads of agreement, and started the legal work.

In my enthusiasm to get there, I hadn't informed the bank that we were now in negotiations. It was quite late in the day, four o'clock or something, so I quickly got on the phone to the bank and told them that they needed to get their lawyers over to where we were meeting. They thought it was a ridiculous request so late in the day and reminded me that they had only given me an indicative letter. I told them I thought we had a deal and that in receivership situations things were liable to move pretty quickly at any time of the day or night.

Half an hour later, the guy at the bank rang back to say that one of the partners and an assistant were on their way and that the rest would join us when they could. Now it was beginning to feel like a deal. We negotiated through the rest of that day and through the night and were still there in the morning. And every hour the lawyers were there was costing me a fortune. I was worried that if the deal didn't happen, I would probably have wasted £100,000 in legal fees. It was coming together, but it was happening in slow motion.

The amendments to the sale purchase agreement took an age to complete; it was as if there was only a one-fingered typist in the building. I felt like saying I'd type it myself because we were just hanging around, and the more you hang around, the more you start worrying about things you'd agreed to and commitments you'd made in the negotiation.

By four o'clock in the morning, we were all getting very tired and stressed – there was a lot of risk involved and we had to satisfy several sets of lawyers. But we had pretty well agreed the deal when the receiver reminded me it was the quarter date in ten days' time and that this could be a problem, as the rents had to be paid then. I said they would be my responsibility and that I was going to pay them. He was concerned that the landlords might come after the receiver if I didn't pay the rent, as it was unlikely the leases could all be transferred to me in time. And as I would be taking the shop receipts, the receiver could be out of pocket.

Because of this, the receiver wanted me to pay the rents to them, so they were in the clear – the only problem was, I didn't have the money as I'd used it all up in buying Ryman. My plan had been to use the takings to pay the rent. This is a great example of why cash flow is so important.

It all made sense to the receiver, because it would mean there'd be a further three months in which the paperwork could be done to assign the leases. I then asked how much rent would be required – it was about a million quid. It felt like a punch to the solar plexus. I asked for half an hour and sat down with Dick. The whole deal was in danger of collapsing, so I asked Dick to go in and argue about anything, anything at all that we'd agreed in the documentation that was contentious, that we'd given in to. I needed him to buy me some time.

And my strategy? It was simple: I was going to go home, have a shave, put on a clean shirt and go and find a million quid. At that moment I was unshaven, I smelled, I was tired and I was a million quid short of a deal.

Dick went into battle, while I slipped out the back door and went home. It was six in the morning and Mrs P was just getting up to get the kids to school. As she got out of bed I got into it. When she got back, she woke me as if from the dead – I was completely shattered. I got in the shower, shaved, put on a clean shirt and headed back into town, on the mobile all the way, and went to see the bank.

I sat down with them and hit them with my little predicament. I had to push the point that they were going to make a lot of money out of the deal, that we were on the verge of making it happen and that the only thing we were short of was a short-term million quid, which I could repay in ten days' time – as sure as eggs is eggs.

I persuaded them that this was a good risk to take and I thought I had them on board until one of them pointed out that because of the size the loan had grown to, it had to be cleared by Israel. They got on the blower to Israel, sending paperwork backwards and forwards, and eventually they got the go-ahead.

I was like a dog with two willies: I've done it, I've done it! I rushed back to the lawyers' office. The lift took for ever to get up there. My heart was pounding. I burst into the big meeting room to see about eight or nine dishevelled individuals, one of whom was Dick. He was the only one awake and still talking, bless him. He'd bored the pants off them. I quickly made enough noise to wake everyone up – they'd never even missed me. I called the receiver into a private office and told him we could now guarantee to pay the rents up front.

'Well, we can't complete. Your lawyer, Dick, he's changed everything again.'

'Oh, don't worry about him, I'll sort him out. We'll go back to what it was.' And we did.

By now it was late afternoon on Friday. Even though we'd agreed everything, documents were still going to and fro, and the bank's lawyers wanted to change this, that and the other. It dragged on until one o'clock on Saturday morning and then the deal was finally done. All I had to do was pass over a nominal £1 coin and then the rest of the money would be passed over by the solicitors.

Even once I'd signed everything and the receiver was just about to sign, we hit another snag: in the heat of the deal I'd forgotten about the insurance documents for the shops, the warehouse and the stock. Once again the deal hung in the balance. I might have to wait until Monday to get the insurance and that would mean I'd lose the weekend's takings and so perhaps struggle to pay the rent a few days later. Fortunately, the receiver's insurers were available, as they have to be in case a company goes into receivership at any time. Because they were already giving the cover, they agreed to do exactly the same for me – with the small proviso that they'd take an extra 25 per cent premium until I could get my own insurance set up.

The insurance sorted, we completed, I handed over a pound, we signed all the papers, and I was the owner of Ryman the stationer.

Well, I was the owner of the name, the assets, the goodwill and all the equipment and stock, but the leases still needed to be assigned. Some of the stock, which hadn't been paid for, belonged to other people who would soon be starting to claim it back or demand payment. I knew I had all sorts of fights ahead of me, but these were issues to be dealt with in the cold light of day. It was quite an anti-climax in the end and we all went home – there were certainly no champagne celebrations.

I'd been invited by Cellnet to their box at Twickenham to watch the rugby later that day and I couldn't even remember who England were playing. Mrs P was astonished to hear I planned to go, but I'd had a few hours' sleep and was ready for it. I told her the news would be on TV, so she put it on and, right on cue, they announced that Ryman the stationer has been saved by Theo Paphitis – and that's when the phone started to ring.

But I wasn't changing my plans. Off I went to the rugby and as I stepped into the box there was a round of applause from the group of people with whom I did business. It made me feel good. I watched the game, where England secured the Grand Slam against Scotland, got absolutely wrecked and went home and caught up on my sleep.

The following Monday was one of the most exciting days of my life. I couldn't wait to get to Ryman's office in Hayes, which was strange because every time I'd visited before I'd thought what a horrible, dark and dingy place the reception area was.

When I arrived, the receptionist barely acknowledged me and suddenly I didn't know what to do. Should I go up the stairs and take control, or sign myself in and wait for somebody to come and get me? At least I knew one thing was going to change quickly: I was going to have to sort out that uninviting reception area.

Then Malcolm arrived and we went upstairs to meet some of the staff. I started to look for somewhere to park my butt, and the only place was in the middle of the main office. Someone had been made redundant by the receiver and had obviously left in a hurry as all their personal belongings were still in the desk drawer. I decided that this was to be the control centre. I didn't want to chuck people out of their offices because I hadn't decided who was staying and who was going. Well, I had, but it wasn't the right thing to do there and then.

Now it was just a little matter of putting the business plan in place! All the theory had to become reality, and as confident as I was when I was out there pitching for the money, I can honestly say I was as nervous as a kitten. I owned Ryman, but I was in debt up to my eyeballs, had loans and guarantees out there far in excess of anything I possessed, and if it all went wrong it wouldn't just be the small house that would be going – we'd be living in a tent.

I'd gambled heavily on this one and there was no question whether it would work or not – it simply had to work, there was no other option. And as nervous as I was deep inside, I showed a massive outward confidence with everybody, because my job, as always, was to persuade them all to come along with me on a journey of recovery.

The first step was to do a lot of reorganising and to win the hearts and minds of the staff, who were totally demoralised. They had had their wages cut, their privileges cut, their budgets cut, their facilities cut. There was hardly any capital expenditure and morale was on the floor. We had to work very hard – and very quickly – to put these matters right because one of my great beliefs is that your biggest asset is your workforce. My main challenge was to make sure that the staff bought in to what I wanted to achieve. But I managed to pull the workforce along with me and along came the profits.

Second, I knew that one of the keys to the recovery was sorting out the suppliers who were owed money by old Ryman, though not by new Ryman. At first they didn't want to supply us, but I explained that supplying us would give them a chance to earn back some of the money they had lost. I pointed out something that must have been starkly obvious to them – if they didn't supply us, one of their competitors would and, without exception, they began to supply Ryman again. With the credit they gave us, I was able to start the company's cash juices flowing again.

Third, I rationalised the company's outlets and stock range. Ryman originally consisted of about 120 stores, but we quickly shut down thirty-three loss-making sites. The good thing about buying a business from receivership is that you can leave those stores behind as a liability for the administrators, so you don't have to take on the costs of shutting them down or get distracted by trying to turn them round. That left us with eighty-seven profitable stores, which were all making a contribution over and above their costs. That total contribution needed to cover the overheads at head office and leave a profit, plus pay off the rent and pay back the loan.

As well as focusing on fewer stores, we also scaled down the product range, taking it down from 3,500 SKU (Stock Keeping Units) to about 2,500, so we weren't carrying as much stock and didn't need to tie up as much capital. The profile of the Ryman business was always geared towards the small office, the home office and business. And that really hasn't changed very much. But you have to have the products that these businesses want. So we abandoned the experiments they'd been running with selling sweets, sandwiches, drinks and so on. These were not high-margin products. They filled up shelves but they weren't what people shopping in Ryman were looking for.

The fourth strand of my strategy was to talk to the store staff and find out what our customers actually wanted. I firmly believe that most of the answers to problems people have in business are within the organisation itself, and that most of those answers are to be found at a very low level. Head office managers are often far too theoretical and detached from the reality of the business. So a fundamental part of all my businesses is talking to the people who work with the customers.

The final element was to make sure we got the stock into the stores on the right days at the right time and at the right price. It may all sound very simple, but that's what business is. With all these things in place, in our first year we moved from losing £8 million on a turnover of £35–40 million to making about £800,000 profit on a turnover of £25 million. NAG's turnover was £5 million, so you can see I had caught a much bigger fish when I did the Ryman deal.

I couldn't have achieved the Ryman turnaround on my own – I had a fantastic team around me, from the shop floor to the boardroom. And I had a good relationship with the team. My employees were not working for a faceless organisation. They felt I was approachable, that there was an individual in charge and they could see that I was there, in the buying department, in the warehouse, in the store. There was very little, if anything, that I didn't know about the business. We were one big, happy – and successful – family.

And as the head of that family, my finances weren't too shabby. Frankly, the Ryman deal had launched me into the financial stratosphere. But after about eighteen months I was lonely and bored again – where have you heard that before? I really was. I was sitting back having a cigar. Ryman had enhanced my reputation, no doubt about that, but now I wanted to do some more deals.

Chapter Fourteen

I'm in lingerie!

I soon realised that Ryman was too small a business to keep me fully occupied for long and by 1996 I was looking around for something else to buy. I was aware of Stephen Hinchcliffe, who had created the Facia group of retail shops including Salisbury, Sock Shop, Red or Dead and Contessa. Facia was a huge operation, which consisted of 850 shops employing 80,000 people, but Hinchcliffe was accused of being an asset-stripper. Eventually, he stripped a little too many of the group's assets and was given an eighteen-month jail sentence for fraud.

Not surprisingly, Hinchcliffe's group went into receivership, so I went to see the receiver with a view to making an offer for Sock Shop. I looked around the business and met all the key people involved in running it, but while I was doing this I got a call from another receiver, Ian, who was looking after another part of the Facia group. He told me that the business I should be looking at was Contessa, and suggested that I went over to Bracknell to meet him. I didn't even know what line of business they were in, but I was intrigued. When I found out it was lingerie, I wasn't sure it was for me.

Myself and Malcolm Cooke spent most of the day looking at

the business and then, at about four o'clock, the receiver announced that he'd arranged for the buyers to give me a presentation.

'I don't need a presentation.'

'No, trust me, you do.'

In trouped a line of ladies wearing Contessa lingerie. My number two, Malcolm Cooke, and I didn't know where to look. I'd never shown any interest in ladies' lingerie before – only getting ladies out of their lingerie! We made jokes, mainly to cover our embarrassment, but it didn't seem to work. The buyers pointed out the details of the various products and we were 'forced' to stare at ladies' crotches and ladies' breasts that were ready to pop out of skimpy bras. I had gone from dealing in pencils and paper, moved on to socks and now here I was, surrounded by half-naked women.

Cookie dragged me away – rather slowly, I must admit – and we discussed the opportunity. At the time, Marks & Spencer completely dominated the lingerie market, but I could see it was a good market to be in, as women always need new underwear. Contessa was in trouble because it was badly run, not because of what it did. We reckoned their profit margin was about 33 per cent, and after playing around with a few figures over a cup of coffee, we reckoned we could get the margin up to over 50 per cent. I couldn't imagine Mrs P being impressed. Making money looking at women with few clothes on might make me popular with my mates, but I doubted it would have the same effect on her.

It was the world of Playboy-founder Hugh Hefner. I had visions of Hugh and me on the front cover of magazines. It just wasn't going to happen. And then Ian, the receiver, rang to tell me he was going to sell the business, that he had two offers already, and that I was going to miss out. He gave me until the end of the day, so I sat down with Cookie to look at the pros and cons. The only problem we could see was I wasn't comfortable with selling knickers and bras. So, despite all my misgivings, we put in an offer. The receiver said it was a little below what they were looking for, but that it would be worth trying to make a deal.

As the lawyers' negotiations dragged on I got bored, so I walked out onto the balcony and started looking into the other rooms. I spotted a man who I later found out went by the name Peter Ridsdale, who looked like he was in the middle of negotiations too. As he walked past our door later on, I decided to go and have a chat with him and found that he was negotiating to buy Sock Shop. I saw it as a chance to wind him up and started making things up about what was wrong with the company, but he didn't take a blind bit of notice. He went ahead and bought Sock Shop anyway.

Meanwhile, we were still negotiating. I thought I would use the old banker's draft routine that had proved so successful when I purchased Movie and Media Sports some years earlier. I told the receiver I couldn't come up with the price he wanted and all I had were the banker's drafts in my pocket. I gave him a choice – take it or leave it. I pulled out the draft, hoping that I'd picked the right one, otherwise I was going to end up paying more than I wanted.

We had spent twenty-four hours in these offices and it wasn't pleasant – what with the smell of sweat, stale cigarette smoke and old sandwiches. Finally, and rather dramatically, the receiver reached out and took the envelope. The deal was done. It was Sunday 3 June: Father's Day. I walked out to my car, which was parked in the street – I had been feeding the meter all that time – and drove home. I was exhausted and my senses were shot to pieces. Even turning the steering wheel didn't feel right. When I finally made it home, Mrs P didn't look like she wanted to help celebrate Father's Day. I realised she had no idea what I'd been up to, so I broke the news: 'I've just bought a lingerie business.'

'What sort of lingerie business?'

'Contessa. You might know it, there's one in Twickenham and one in—'

'I know which one it is. There's one in Walton too. What the hell are you doing? What do you know about lingerie? What lingerie do I wear?'

'I don't know. It's a business, a retail business. Retail is retail and that's it. If I can sell pencils, I can sell lingerie.'

But I was soon to discover just what a pig's ear of a business I had purchased. They had no warehouse and they had the stock delivered directly to the stores. There was no stock control and the margins were crap because they weren't buying properly. The first thing we did was to consolidate the business by shutting down about thirty stores straight away, and keeping the seventy best stores. My own managers went into the stores we'd closed, stripped them out and sent the stock back to the Ryman warehouse, where we sorted it out and sent it to those stores we had kept.

For years, the staff in the Ryman warehouse in Hayes had been used to dealing with pencils and paper. Suddenly I had everyone – the secretaries, buyers and warehouse staff – working overtime re-boxing and sending out underwear. The girls thought it was great, dealing with girly stuff rather than stationery.

The margins were easily sorted. Because Contessa had no warehouse, they had required their suppliers to deliver small numbers of items to each individual store. The company had therefore been getting poor discounts on the retail price. Now that the suppliers could deliver everything to my warehouse, they agreed to give us much better terms. We were now buying at a 50 per cent, rather than 35 per cent, discount on our retail price.

Next, we looked at stock control. Once the lingerie from the closed stores had been sold, we began to buy more stock. With a decent IT system, we were able to manage our inventory much better. Instead of each shop getting ten of one particular bra, as might have happened in the past, we could send them just two or three, and if they sold them we could quickly replenish the stock. What had happened in the past was that one shop might sell all ten items, and then be unable to sell more because they had run out, while another would struggle to sell any. We reduced our overall stockholding by about half, and thus reduced our cash requirement to pay for it all.

But the biggest challenge was to make sure the staff, who had been downtrodden and demoralised under the old regime, bought into our dream of making Contessa a successful retail entity. So I spoke to them to find out what their problems were and why they were unhappy. Some complained that they had to pay for tea and coffee in the workplace; others mentioned that there was no fridge or microwave in the staffroom so they couldn't store or heat up anything for lunch. They now get their drinks for free, and each shop has a fridge and a microwave. I encouraged them to let me know if there was anything else they felt the stores needed. These things cost almost nothing, but they transformed the mood of the staff. I also set up an incentive scheme, giving them a chance to win an exotic holiday.

You don't need to bring in consultants to find out what is wrong with a business – just ask the staff. They'll know the answers. That's all consultants do. We made Contessa successful, and within a year it was profitable too. It was as simple as that.

By 1998 my reputation for turning round businesses was growing. The success of Ryman and Contessa attracted interest. I was contacted by a business broker about a company called La Senza, also a lingerie chain that I knew well and felt was under-performing. The broker was working on behalf of Laurie Lewin, the chief executive of the Canadian group that owned a majority stake in La Senza. They wondered if I would be interested in becoming chairman of the plc, and were prepared to offer me a big salary, plus free equity and lots of share options.

But I felt wary. I'd had my fill of public companies and liked being the master of my own destiny. I was not going to make the same mistake of working for someone else again. The broker pointed out, however, that not only was I already the chairman of a public company (Millwall – which was true – but more about that later), but the two lingerie firms worked very differently: Contessa sold branded products, while La Senza sold its own products. The business had its issues, but it was a publicly listed company, with thousands of shareholders.

I decided I had nothing to lose so I went to see Laurie Lewin in a tired old sixties office block in Gray's Inn Road. It wasn't quite what I had expected. Laurie told me he originally came from Romford, but had lived most of his life in Canada. He explained how he had become chief executive of the company, developed the La Senza concept and seen it grow very successfully and become a public company in Canada. They then brought it to the UK, opening up between twenty to thirty shops, and eventually floated it on the stock market in the UK to raise extra cash. But it hadn't worked for them over here.

Some of the problems were due to having an absentee owner, but I also think it takes someone very special to open a business in a country that isn't their own. I think it shows a lack of respect for the retailers already operating in that country to think you can just walk in and beat them at their own game.

Many companies fail when they go to other countries to trade and, in my opinion, the best way to 'export' a business is to franchise it. That way the people who live in and know the market in a particular country are the ones to own and run the business. You can't force North American culture on to a UK public, you have to adapt. Transplanting a heart or a kidney doesn't work without anti-rejection drugs. Transplanting a business brings similar problems, and franchising overcomes this.

La Senza failed to transplant their business idea to such an extent that by this stage they were haemorrhaging cash at a rate of nearly £10 million a year – about £800,000 a month. I'd had an experience of one reason why this was the case.

Two days before Christmas I was shopping in London with Malcolm Cooke. It was five o'clock in the afternoon and being nosey, as any good entrepreneurs should be, we tried to go into the La Senza store. They had locked the door – at five o'clock, two days before Christmas. We just couldn't believe it. Even the notice on the window said they were open until five thirty and that's still way too early in my view so close to Christmas.

I banged on the door. This girl looked up at me rather disdainfully and carried on doing her paperwork behind the till. I wasn't having this. I banged on the door again. Slowly she came to the door and said, 'Can I help you?'

'Yeah, I'd like to buy something.'

'We're shut.'

'You can't be. It says five thirty on here.'

'I've got to do my paperwork.'

'You've got two blokes here, two days before Christmas. We could be spending hundreds of pounds in your store.'

'Right, what do you want?'

'Forget it.'

I knew there and then that this business was going nowhere. It was a lesson I was never to forget.

I told Laurie that I couldn't become an employee, I couldn't become chairman or chief executive of the company. He wasn't surprised at what I had to say, but he wanted out. They were losing a lot of money and they had to consolidate those losses into their Canadian accounts. Their share price was suffering in Canada so he was prepared to do a very soft deal with me to sell the shares.

Even as the majority shareholder with a 60 per cent share, I'd still have 40 per cent owned by other people who'd give me grief and I'd have fund managers crawling over me like a rash. All this for a company that was losing £10 million a year. It didn't seem to add up, but when he suggested that the shares might be sold for a nominal one pound I realised we might have something to work with. As the shares were then trading at 5p each, I wondered about buying out the rest of the company at that price, but Laurie was worried that his company's reputation would be damaged if they sold out at such a low price – especially after they'd taken the financial hit of selling their stake for a pound.

But I knew my negotiating position was strong. The Canadian company couldn't afford the ongoing losses, and they didn't want the distraction of all the regulatory requirements involved in being a public company any more than I did. But we carried on talking and eventually I agreed to become chairman and chief executive and buy 60 per cent of the company for one pound, which would trigger a full-blown takeover. I would then have to bid for the remaining 40 per cent.

I asked Laurie what he would be happy with me offering for the other 40 per cent, and he came up with a figure of 10p. It would cost me £1.5 million. There was no guarantee, of course, that those shareholders would accept, even at 10p, because a lot of them had paid 80p or so for the shares when they'd originally been issued. On the other hand, it was double the price they were currently trading at and there was no prospect of the price going back up. I remained worried though that my offer wouldn't be accepted by enough shareholders for me to take full control.

I spent the rest of the day with the accountants trying to understand the business and all that it involved. I then returned to my office and continued looking at things until about one o'clock in the morning. The figures seemed even worse than I'd expected, but I believed that it could work. I understood the business and could see a way forward as long as my offer was accepted. I reckoned that once I announced the real figures, people would be happy to take the 10p.

I woke Laurie up at about half past one in the morning, and told him he had a deal. We arranged to meet at his lawyers' offices in the City in a couple of hours and he was going to get his executives in Canada ready as well, since the time difference meant they'd still be about. The negotiations dragged on for hour after hour, with people coming in and whispering to others in the room. I was used to these things taking time, but I felt uneasy about all the whispering. And then he dropped a bombshell. There was another bidder. I was furious. I'd spent a lot on legal fees and had been working pretty much non-stop for sixteen hours.

'No, no,' he said, 'calm down. We're very honourable people. We're in this room to do a deal with you. That's why we're here. There always was another bidder, but we will forsake that other bidder to complete the deal with you on the terms we agreed.'

And it was one of those rare occasions where someone said, 'We're honourable people,' and actually turned out to be honourable! He'd been negotiating with a guy called Peter Ridsdale (remember him?) for three months but things had moved slowly, because he'd had to work with venture capitalists, so I had been able to nip in ahead of him, even though our final offers were essentially the same. Once again, the advantage of being private was clear.

So Laurie, who subsequently went on to *Dragons' Den* in Canada, kept his word and we stayed there until we'd done the deal. I bought 60 per cent of La Senza plc for £1 and became its majority shareholder, chairman and CEO.

The following day I went to their head office and stood on a chair to address the staff. 'I know things have been tough, I know you've had difficulties communicating with the people over in Canada, but we're an independent business now, we're nothing to do with Canada any more. I've bought sixty per cent of the business and my intention is not to keep it as a public company. This is one of the few companies I've bought that isn't bankrupt. It would have been if I hadn't bought it, but it's not.'

Then I remembered that the last company I had purchased that wasn't bust, I'd lost my shirt on. I finished my speech with my usual call for everyone to buy in to my dreams and ambitions. I told them I wanted them to be the flowers in my garden. 'Anyone who doesn't want to be a flower in my garden and wants to be a flower in somebody else's garden, well, I'll shake your hand, we'll have a leaving drink, and we'll part as friends. If you don't want to be part of the future, you can go right now.'

I was just about to go on to my next bit when half a dozen people picked up their coats and left. I must admit it caught me by surprise as it had never happened before. It turned out that among those to leave were the buying director and various other key members of staff.

Not only had I broken my rules about investing in public companies, but people were taking me literally at my word and rather damaging the positive impression I'd been trying to create. It was another lesson learned. As it turned out, the people who left all had other jobs lined up and, in fairness to them, the company had been struggling for a long time. I don't blame them for looking elsewhere, just for not believing in me.

Shortly afterwards I got all the management and store managers together in a hotel in central London, and who should be on the front row but the manager at that branch I'd visited before Christmas. She had great big, red plastic high-heel shoes on – I call them Essex specials – and a tiny mini-skirt and she was full of herself. She kept crossing and uncrossing her legs. She knew exactly what she was doing. It was like that scene from *Basic Instinct*.

Cookie was due to speak after me and as he got up to give his talk, I warned him about the woman in the front row. But he completely ignored my advice and the first thing he did when he stood up was look down – and he totally lost what he was going to say!

I stepped up to give the group my normal pep talk and asked them whether they were all behind me. The response was positive and even the girl in the mini-skirt was giving it some. I then said I was going to tell a story about something that was never going to happen again. I related the Christmas incident and the girl in the mini-skirt sank lower and lower into her chair. You could see the shock on her face. She knew I was talking about her. 'I'm not going to tell you which store it was,' I said, 'but you know who you are. I don't think you're going to be a flower in my garden.' She quit the following day.

I was informed by those that remained that I needed to sort out the warehousing and the IT – the same problems I had encountered and solved at many of my other companies. I told them I would take the warehousing in-house, exactly as I had done with the others, although I had no idea where I was going to put all the stock, and promised to deal with the IT as well. Previously La Senza had used a third-party warehouse set-up with some disastrous IT systems.

In these circumstances, when everyone is worried about what the new boss will do and whether their jobs will be safe, it's important to be up-front and honest and not to make grandiose claims. I know I'm good at organisational, detailed stuff, but what I couldn't guarantee them was flair. I told them that was where I would rely on them.

I saw as many individuals as I could and quickly parted with the managing director and other senior directors. Some left when we moved the entire operation out of London to Hayes, which they perhaps felt wasn't suitably glamorous when compared with the previous headquarters in Gray's Inn Road. They had a vision of a Sloane Square boutique-type business and not my mass-market model. The entire operation was now run out of Portakabins in the car park at Hayes – the people who worked there did so because they wanted to be part of something, not because they wanted to be in a fancy office. Of my key members of staff, I think I was left with one in merchandising and one in the buying department.

I don't want to say, 'I was right and they were wrong,' but my mass-market ideas turned a £10 million annual loss into a £10 million annual profit and I later sold the business for more than £100 million with a fair chunk going to the staff that remained and made it happen. I set them targets, difficult targets, but not unachievable ones. If you set people unrealistic targets they will fail and they won't believe in you again. If you set them targets that they're unsure about but manage to achieve then they will trust you. The targets have to be such that they can be achieved by mere mortals working lots of hours, not only by superhuman beings. This rewards hard work and instils a good work ethic.

To achieve all this, we started by building more floors on to our existing warehouse to accommodate the additional stock. We then installed a new IT system, which, as with Contessa, meant we could manage by holding less stock than before, and so helped our cash situation.

Then when we were good and ready, we attacked Marks & Spencer. I looked at their profile and saw that they were struggling. M&S weren't giving their customers what they wanted and I was determined to fill that gap in the market. I wanted to sell lingerie that was good quality and fashionable, but not outrageously fashionable like the products the Canadians had offered, as that would be a step too far for many of our target customers.

I didn't want it to be too sexy, either. We don't do sexy very well here in the UK. Basically, I wanted to dress the Mrs Ps of this world and widen our appeal into the mass market, where a mother and daughter would be happy to shop together in a La Senza store. Rather than being a store where women would go when they wanted something really special, and so perhaps visit only once a year, La Senza needed to be the place they'd go whenever they needed some new lingerie.

Had they wanted to, M&S could have killed me off at birth, if they'd got their stock package right, but they let La Senza off the hook and allowed me to flourish. I was delighted when an M&S supplier rang and told me that he'd asked their chief executive if he thought La Senza was a threat. Apparently he wasn't that aware who we were. The supplier thought I might be insulted, but I was ecstatic as the longer it took for them to recognise that I was snapping at their heels, the better it was for me. This allowed me to do what had never been done before in the history of UK retailing – set up an independent seller of own-brand lingerie and beat M&S at their own game.

There are two reasons why an independent lingerie business had never previously made it work in the UK. Firstly, Marks & Spencer is so dominant in the market, and secondly, property costs are so high in the UK compared to the rest of the world.

When I took over, La Senza was operating out of high-profile sites like Lakeside and Brent Cross, paying sky-high rents, selling their own-brand products. We were up against the monolith of M&S, but they allowed me a window to establish myself. Once we rebuilt the business with passion, drive and ambition, we prayed every single day that that great retailer Marks & Spencer would not wake up until we were strong enough to stand up to them. We established our own customer base operating out of nearly eighty stores and by the time M&S got their act together it was too late.

One way in which we appealed to our customers was by making them feel special. An M&S customer would take something off a rack, queue along with everybody else, have their bit of lingerie popped into a plastic carrier bag and then walk out of the door. In our stores, customers would come to the till where we would take the item off a hanger, fold it in tissue paper, put it in a gift box with some beautiful-smelling beads inside, wrap a ribbon around it, and hand it over in a nice bag. You walked out of the store having spent ten quid but feeling like a million dollars. At M&S, you left feeling like you'd bought a sandwich.

When I'd suggested this approach, some of the managers pointed out that it would take extra time, and we'd probably have to take on more staff and increase our payroll budgets. I thought this was fine, because the extra costs would be small compared with the extra revenue and profits we would be making.

Another way of making customers feel special was ensuring that they felt they got a good fit when they bought our lingerie. There were several ways that this could be done. Before I took over, most La Senza pyjamas had a thirty-four-inch inside leg, because the longer the leg, the more elegant an item looks. But most women have much shorter legs, so the pyjamas didn't fit properly. We changed the length.

Because so much lingerie is designed to look good on models, rather than ordinary women, it rarely fits on the bottom, because models are so skinny in that area, so we changed the dimensions to suit 80 per cent of women on the high street. And finally, we made our sizing generous, so that a woman who was in danger of becoming a size 16 would definitely fit one of our size 14s. No woman wants to believe she is a bigger size than she feels she should be. When I spoke to the women on my team, the main reason they gave for choosing a brand of underwear was often not the fancy name, but because they liked the sizing.

We also made sure that customers felt La Senza was a special brand by putting our logo on everything. Astonishingly, the previous owners had often put their labels on only one piece of a two-piece outfit.

The final element of my strategy was to expand the chain. We opened a lot more stores, eventually taking us up to about 120 stores around the country. By being bigger, we could compete more easily.

In the meantime I bid for the remaining 40 per cent of the shares that were still in private hands. Once the appalling trading figures from before the takeover were announced I received 95–96 per cent acceptances, which cost me £1.5 million, and that left about 4 per cent, which under law I could compulsory purchase. Then I privatised the company. I didn't have any spotty fund managers to worry about.

I now owned the whole company. The original 60 per cent had cost me the pound I had handed over to Laurie plus the price of two packs of Benson & Hedges, which is what my driver went out to get Laurie during the night we spent negotiating. Come to think of it, Laurie never did pay me back for those fags, but I love him dearly and forgive him.

Chapter Fifteen

Expanding the Ryman empire

By the end of 1999, with La Senza, Ryman and Contessa all running successfully, I was looking for a new challenge. I'd noticed another stationery chain, a public company called Partners, and thought that if I bought them, I could consolidate things and make both companies more profitable. I believed that Partners was failing for three main reasons – poor management, over-expansion and under-capitalisation. It was too small to sustain a big public company structure and the people running it weren't as focused as they should have been.

They were living well above their means – I call it the 'ivory tower syndrome'. The chief executive's office, for example, was the size of the Oval Office in the White House. Every floor of their offices, depending on the status of the employees who worked there, had better furniture, better carpets, better fittings, until you got to the third floor where the bosses swanned around. I compared it to Ryman, where we were all working on top of each other and we were profitable.

I contacted the management through their stockbrokers to see if there was an opportunity for me to buy the business. They thought it seemed like a good idea, but a few days later got back to me to say the management were too busy to see me as they were sorting out their back-to-school stock.

As we were in July I wondered how they could be busy with back-to-school. Normally, back-to-school stock is bought by the previous December, arrives in April, May at the latest, and is out in the stores in early July. Either the management were all working in the stores or they didn't want to see me. Despite the negative signs, I told the stockbrokers that I could be interested in buying the company.

To cut a long story short, they wouldn't see me. But I kept visiting their stores, in the same way that I used to visit La Senza stores, and comparing them with ours. I could tell they were not doing that well. I made another approach. And again I got the brush-off. The company's share price went down to about 5p, and I decided not to contact them again.

I later discovered that they thought I was the Grim Reaper. From what I understand, the mere mention of my name gave the chief executive palpitations. When the name Paphitis came up at two subsequent board meetings after that, the chief executive had to go home and have a lie down. He didn't want to be in the same city as me, let alone the same room. As soon as I was mentioned, people thought it meant their company must be in trouble.

Eventually, the inevitable happened, and Partners went into receivership. I rang the receiver, who was expecting my call. He told me that there was a huge amount of interest in the company and I agreed to meet him in Crewe the next Monday morning. It was the twins, Annie and Hollie's, birthday party on the Sunday, which was to be held in a restaurant in Cobham during the day, and I decided to drive up there that night so that I could stay in a hotel in Crewe and be there bright and early for the morning meeting.

On Monday, I made my way to Partners' offices, which were

in a new building with a huge warehouse behind it. I met the receiver, who by this time had made most of the management redundant, but I had access to those who were left and started my due diligence.

The one thing I insist on about the businesses we buy is that I do my own due diligence. I do it all in-house with members of staff, my accountant or my assistants. We don't employ other people to decide whether we should waste our money or not.

I spent the whole day there seeing people and then sat with the administrator for an hour while he gave me the normal stuff about there being lots of interest. He sounded more like an estate agent than an administrator as he tried to drive up the price, partly on the back of the smart new offices and warehouse. I pointed out that the company didn't own them, were paying a huge rent and that the offices were too big, which was actually a liability.

The staff that I had spoken to all believed that the warehouse and offices were the reason behind going bust. The company had used up all its cash on a warehouse that could accommodate 300 stores when they'd got only 120. The staff also believed it had distracted the management from the real business. Because of the lack of cash, the company struggled to pay for their stock, which meant they found it hard to get stock into stores, which meant they had little to sell, which meant they were short of cash – the whole thing had become a vicious circle.

I continued to lay it on thick about how much of an albatross the offices and warehouse were. In fact, I was fibbing! They were more attractive to me than anything else. I was rapidly running out of office and warehouse space at Hayes. I had La Senza, Ryman and Contessa all operating out of one warehouse that just used to service Ryman and there was no more room for any more Portakabins, and I knew their set-up would be perfect for what I needed.

Having completed my due diligence, I went home late that Monday evening and was back in the office on Tuesday. I knew there was a deal to be done, but because I'd established a reputation, I knew they were going to try to work me to get the best price, so I had to seem as indifferent as possible.

As interested and as excited as I was about what I saw, it was a particularly badly run company that was over-structured, had too many layers of management, had facilities three times bigger than they needed and a cost base that had gone through the roof. They had opened twenty-five shops in quick succession because they had promised the City that they would – and that's what happens when you're a public company; you make commitments to the City and you have to stick to them even when they're wrong.

The management haven't usually got the guts to turn around to the fund managers and admit that they've made a mistake and that stores shouldn't be opened. And even if they do, that's the moment the fund managers lose confidence in the company – it's another vicious circle. They had carried on down what was clearly a blind alley. They hadn't read the warning signs, or if they had, they'd ignored them.

But beneath the surface, the core business was good. If we could re-utilise the warehouse and office space, halve the costs by sharing them with somebody else and shut the new stores that were haemorrhaging cash, there was the basis of a very profitable business. But I wasn't going to tell the receiver that. I was being Mr Cool.

That week Mrs P was going into hospital for a minor operation and I'd promised to go with her. I thought I would take the Partners' paperwork with me and read it at the hospital while I waited.

Worrying about Mrs P gave me a sense of mortality. I began to ask myself, Do I need another business? Do I want a business in Crewe? Do I want to bust my arse again turning around another business? My enthusiasm began to wane and I didn't ring them back. On the Friday, four days after my trip to Crewe, I got a call from the receiver.

'You were going to ring us with an offer.'

'Well, things have changed since I've come back.'

'No matter. We're going to sell it to someone else.'

'Give me until Monday.'

It's always a good tactic to keep them hanging on.

Monday is our trading meetings day and I got engrossed in the meetings and forgot to ring him. At four o'clock the receiver rang again to tell me he was going to sell the business if I didn't make an offer. The fact he kept calling made me feel I was in a stronger position than he'd wanted. So I sat down with Cookie and discussed the situation. Did we want to try to turn round another business, especially at such a distance?

I was also wary because I had tried to buy this business so many times before and it hadn't worked out. If you've got to push that hard it's likely you're going to do the wrong deal. Whenever I've done so, with the Splash deal, for example, I've realised later that I should have walked away. I told Cookie that I'd got that feeling again, but I rang up the guy anyway and put in a silly offer. I could hear the disappointment in his voice but he didn't tell me to clear off.

However, I knew he was getting near the rent quarter, which meant he would have to find money for the rents by the next week, and as the receiver hasn't got any money of his own to play with he would want to do any deal before then. In the Ryman deal, the rent quarter had been my problem; this time it was the receiver's. We digressed and started talking about other things, like football. That was when I knew he had problems. If he'd had a decent alternative available he wouldn't have been wasting time chatting. Clearly, I was his only option.

I told him what price I was prepared to pay and said if it wasn't a million miles away from his figure, he should tell me, otherwise I would expect to read in the papers tomorrow or the next day that he'd sold the company to someone else.

Half an hour later he was on the phone asking for another £150,000, which was neither here nor there. We agreed to complete the deal the next day in his lawyers' office.

I duly drove to his Birmingham lawyers and we stayed there until the following morning, Valentine's Day. My money was already transferred to their lawyers' office when right at the end, with the deal almost done, they decided to change the terms.

I'd invested twenty-four hours of my life, a lot of effort and considerable costs. I stuck to my rules, shut my folder and gathered up all my papers. I got everyone else to pack their papers up too.

They tried to change my mind with talk of how I'd made such a success of Ryman, Contessa and La Senza and how I was sure to do the same with Partners. They only wanted another couple of hundred thousand quid. But my response was that I was well overdue a failure, having had so many lucky breaks. My gut feeling was that this might be my Waterloo and when my gut tells me that I listen. I wished them luck and suggested to my lawyers that they be sensible when generating their abortive fees on the basis that if they were too high, I wouldn't use them again.

We left the boardroom and were at the top of the stairs when a member of their team came out and asked us to come back, on the terms of the original deal. We went back in and we completed the deal, and that was my Valentine's Day gift.

Once again, I was keen to go and see the staff, so despite not having slept all night, I went back to Crewe the same day to tell them the good news and to share my plans. I then contacted the landlord of the warehouse and told them that I'd be moving everybody out, down south, and they could have their warehouse and office block back, in the middle of Crewe, empty. It was far too big for us, I told them.

Unsurprisingly, they weren't very keen on this idea so they offered to reduce the rent, which was a good deal, but what I really wanted was to buy the building. So after they'd reduced the rent I pointed out the usual multiple on rent to give the value of a property and made them an offer, which they accepted. I then proceeded to extend the warehouse by at least 50 per cent, put in two mezzanine floors and moved La Senza there. The lingerie business had been growing at a rate of knots and all we'd had was temporary warehouse space all around the country. I consolidated it at Crewe, which immediately halved the costs for Partners.

As usual, we found there were outlets that weren't working, so we shut down twenty-odd stores, all the ones they had recently opened. They were beautiful stores but were leaking cash by the bucket load. Very soon we were back in profit. We got stock back into the stores, motivated the staff and put everybody on bonuses.

And then I turned my attention to the final stationery chain, Stationery Box, who were trickier than a weasel in a sewer. To me it was like a game of Monopoly only the stakes were real. I had two of the properties I wanted, but I needed a third in order to build hotels, if you get my meaning. My business brain never remains stationary for very long – excuse the pun!

Stationery Box was a discount stationery retailer with about 130 stores, run by a private equity outfit. It was struggling – one year it made a profit, the next year it turned in a loss. It had similar management techniques to those employed by Partners, with similar poor results, and competed with Partners' outlets in many locations.

I approached the owners to see if there might be an

opportunity to do business, but what I didn't know at the time was that Stationery Box had not long before been negotiating to buy Partners but hadn't been able to raise the funding. Had those two linked up to form a super stationery chain, they might have caused Ryman all sorts of problems.

Of course, a Stationery Box–Partners amalgamation might not have worked. Putting two loss-making businesses together often produces one business that loses even more money. But, in any event, the proposed merger had fallen to pieces and Partners had gone straight into receivership, which is when I stepped in to snap up the company.

Stationery Box was forced to soldier on alone, and a couple of weeks after I bought Partners, the management of Stationery Box was removed en masse and a new management team was parachuted in by the private equity people. They had seen all the merger paperwork and thought that the deal should have happened.

That's when Stationery Box's new management contacted me. I had only owned Partners for about eight weeks when their new chief executive, Alan Gaynor, called me with an offer he thought I couldn't refuse: he would buy Partners from me for £5 million more than I'd paid for it.

It would have been the quickest £5 million I ever made, and if it hadn't been for Ryman I might have been tempted. But the way I saw it, there were three major independent stationery chains in the UK: Ryman, which I owned, Partners, which I'd just bought, and Stationery Box. Ryman's core activity is 'business' stationery while Partners is more geared to the ordinary 'consumer', just like Stationery Box. Even though I knew how stretched they would be to buy Partners, there was a chance they could turn it all round and become a threat to Ryman. In short, by taking £5 million then, I could lose £50 million if they ended up forcing Ryman out of business.

However, his logic was right: Partners and Stationery Box were natural partners. I just wanted it to be me in charge, not Alan Gaynor. So I made him a counter-offer for his business. I offered £5 million but he wanted three times that amount. There was no way I was going to pay £15 million for a business that wasn't making any money. I told him that as the dominant player, I'd be buying it for nothing at some stage. I warned him that he couldn't succeed, that he had only enough money to carry on trading and hadn't got enough financial backing to attack me in the market. He felt sure he could turn it round, because his team were experienced and had good backing.

After that first time we sat down with them and started negotiations on three separate occasions, but each time when we did our review of the business we felt they wanted too much money and we pulled out. I made one last-gasp attempt about eighteen months before they eventually went to the wall and I offered them £10 million. But they turned me down. I knew I was overpaying, but I also knew I could get a lot of cost savings by merging all three stationery businesses. In this instance, I'd learned my lesson from Splash, when I should have walked away. Here it was a question of simply biding my time and waiting for the chance to buy the company; I can be a very patient person when it comes to business. The only danger was that someone else might step in, but this was a business that it really only made sense for me to buy, because I had Ryman and Partners. Anyone else coming in would have had my companies to contend with.

In the meantime they found another mug backer who put more money into the business. But eventually, several years later, they went bust and in January 2007 I got the company for £3 million – that was £7 million lower than my last offer and £2 million less than my first offer over five years earlier – and in the interim they had ploughed millions of pounds into the business. Plus for my £3 million, I got £1.5 million of stock. I'd call that a pretty good deal.

At the time of writing, we are in the process of re-branding all of the stationery businesses into the Ryman brand across the whole country. We've already merged the buying departments and our property side, and everything is based in Crewe. I have a small office in Wimbledon, consisting of myself, Kypros Kyprianou (my number two), Ann Mantz (the company secretary), Caroline Williams (personal assistant to both Kypros and me) and Anne Watkins, who assists Caroline. Malcolm Cooke, who was my number two in London, is now based in Crewe, where he runs the stationery businesses. Cookie is from Manchester originally so it's like going home for him.

One day a fortnight I go up to Crewe and I go round the stores myself – I'm rarely in the Wimbledon office. Our trading meetings are done through video conferencing every Monday; they're in the boardroom in Crewe and I'm in my boardroom in Wimbledon and it all works well.

The two lingerie businesses I used to own have completed their re-branding. I sold La Senza in July 2006, and Contessa was sold to the same people in December of the same year. The businesses are now all under the banner of La Senza, which is run from Hayes in Middlesex. And I still own 10 per cent of the new group.

As well as these major businesses, I've also been involved with Peter Jones in Red Letter Days, and with various *Dragons' Den* investments as well as a number of property investments. I also spend a lot of time monitoring companies, up to twenty-five at any one time, sometimes for years before I will try to acquire them. I look out for brands in particular, as it takes time and money to build a reputation. Even when that reputation has been damaged, as was the case with Red Letter Days, the name remains familiar. Taking it over, we didn't have to spend time telling people what we were or what we did, though it did cost us a small fortune to retrieve its reputation.

My real talent is not so much for being able to turn businesses around, as most of what I do is pretty simple, but in deciding which companies to go for in the first place and then getting them at the right price or at the right time (which is when being patient comes in handy). The one thing I have realised is that some firms, no matter what you do to them, cannot be saved. Doing any deal creates a lot of work, so there has got to be a good reward at the end of it – the company has to have the potential to be turned around and to give good returns, otherwise you just end up a busy fool.

Chapter Sixteen

My rock, Mrs P

No book on me would be complete without a chapter about the fabulous Mrs P and all she has shared with me over the years. It may sound like a well-worn cliché, but it was love at first sight. I loved Debbie almost from the moment we first met and she felt the same way about me. Our relationship was rock-solid right from the start and because of that I was able to focus on trying to improve myself. I was never a young playboy. I even enrolled for night classes to re-take my O-levels, which was a big mistake. After all, I couldn't wait to get out of school so going back was the wrong thing to do. I did it for three months and then realised it wasn't for me.

Before we got married, Debbie lived with her grandmother, and I lived at home. She was in south London, I was in north London. We'd spend most weekends together and I would stay over at her place and then go back home on a Sunday.

Debbie's nan was called Anne Stocker. Debbie's grand-father had died many years before and Anne had gone on to marry a local man called Jim Taylor. The pair of them lived in south London above Harry's, The Greengrocer, up two flights of stairs. Anne had suffered a stroke and was partially sighted but she was a very strong-willed lady and managed to go out to the shops every single day. Jim was a painter and decorator. He was very, very thin, not much fatter than one of his paint brushes. But the really strange thing about Jim was that he had no nose. I kid you not. He spoke in a peculiar sort of way, which wasn't surprising, and watching him eat and drink, which I tried to avoid at all costs, was even more bizarre.

Anne didn't seem to mind – or maybe she didn't notice because of her eyesight problems – but she had really fallen on her feet with Jim, who decorated the flat twice a year. He was semi-retired and did the odd job here and there. But his biggest job every six months was the unpaid one of painting and decorating the flat.

When I was staying at Debbie's nan's I was supposed to sleep in the front room. There was a mattress, which I pulled out from behind a wardrobe each night and put it away again each morning – even though I never slept on it! We had to go through this charade for months and months until one day her grand-mother pulled Debbie to one side and said, 'I'm a bit worried about that boy. He's not changed his sheets for months.' I think that's when the penny finally dropped.

I spent more and more time with Debbie, and her nan would even do my washing, so it very much became my home for about a year before we decided to get a place of our own. We started looking around for somewhere to rent and spent weeks and weeks after work or at weekends getting on the tube to view different properties. We wanted to rent a room because we couldn't afford to rent a flat or share a house. It didn't matter where. We looked as far out as Essex, but despite scouring the *Evening News* and *Standard* every night and listening to Capital Radio, which used to run a flat-share scheme, we couldn't find anything.

Then Debbie's nan came up trumps. Because of her poor eyesight, she couldn't watch TV, she spent hours listening to the radio and one night she heard that Southwark Council were giving 100 per cent mortgages to first-time buyers. I didn't think buying was an option for us because we had no money and wouldn't be able to get a mortgage, but the 100 per cent thing stuck in my mind and next morning I asked Debbie to ring the council and ask them to send us the papers so we could find out what it was all about. I thought that her nan had probably misheard.

Debbie phoned and a few days later Southwark Council sent us a pack through the post – and Nan was dead right. They were offering 100 per cent mortgages to couples who wanted to buy a property in the local area at a fixed rate of 9 per cent, I think. We had no money for a deposit, so we decided to apply for the full 100 per cent. We didn't even have the dosh for the stamp duty or legal fees and no idea how big a mortgage we could get. Very soon we got an offer in principle for £9,000, so we started looking around to see what we could buy.

We came across a flat on the main Peckham Road, next to the fire station and the sausage factory – no concerns about safety if the sausages burnt! About 400 yards from the town hall, it was pretty central and the number 12 bus ran into the West End. It was a big Victorian house that had been converted into eight flats with a side entrance and a roof terrace where you could hang out your washing. It reminded me of the roof terrace back in Cyprus where I'd played as a little boy, though of course this one had safety rails all the way round it.

They wanted £9,250 but accepted our offer of £9,000. We found a solicitor by knocking on the door of one in the high street in Clapham but, to our horror, he told us that the legal fees and stamp duty would run to £780. Of course, we didn't have that much spare and neither did my mum or dad. Although I was earning about £100 a week at the time, I knew it wasn't going to be easy paying the mortgage, let alone finding this extra money. We went back home and told Debbie's nan that we had fallen in love with this flat but had come up short as far as paying the fees.

I couldn't get that flat – and our cash problem – out of my mind for the whole of the next day at work and I was no nearer to finding a solution when I arrived back at Debbie's nan's next evening. As I walked through the door Debs said that her Nan wanted to see me. She was in the back room and when I went in she handed over an envelope. Inside was £750! It was like manna from heaven. Both of us were astonished.

'Where did you find that from?'

'I went into the building society and took it out.'

'We didn't know you had that sort of money.'

'It's my peril money. I might be in my seventies, but I've got no intention of dying for a few years yet and you can pay me back when you become a millionaire.'

It was the nicest thing anyone had ever done for us. We bought the flat, moved in at the end of November 1977 and started scrabbling around for furniture, borrowing some from friends and family. For Christmas, Debbie bought me a tool set from her nan's catalogue, paid monthly, obviously. It was a Black & Decker and cost £25 and I used it to make some high cupboards – an idea I had seen on TV – to keep all the tools in. The cupboards were so high I had to use a step ladder to get to the tools, but each one had its own hanging place. It took me days and days but I was very proud of my handiwork when I had finished.

I decorated the flat from top to bottom while I was working at Watches of Switzerland. When I worked Saturdays I had a day off during the week – and that became my decorating or building-project day. I found I was actually quite good at it and would save up for the materials or scavenge for them.

The mortgage was about £100 a month, so we didn't have a lot of money, but we did go to the pictures, the theatre and exhibitions. I felt I was a little bit more sophisticated than your average north London boy who had been to a comprehensive.

We'd already got engaged, while I was still at the tender age of seventeen. When I told my office manager Bernard the news all he could manage was a sort of smirk. He was very concerned and gave me the fatherly chat about it being a big step to take and that I had to be sure I was making the right decision. He told me Debbie was a great girl, which I already knew, but he wanted us to delay getting engaged. He wasn't exactly trying to put me off. I think he was just shocked that I was taking such a momentous step at such a young age.

But I wasn't put off and went and bought a ring for about £18 from Bravingtons in King's Cross. It was a little solitaire ring – a gold band with a tiny spec of white-coloured stone which was apparently a diamond. Debbie was very proud of it, showing it off all round the office. For my part, £18 was a big spend.

Debbie and I didn't have an engagement party because we didn't have the money for one – it was as simple as that. In fact, the response to our engagement was a bit like the family reaction to birthdays and Christmas – there was none! We were very much alone. Debbie wasn't close to her father or mother, who had separated. Although my mother and father were reasonably supportive, they were always busy and we were left to get on with it. We told my parents about our engagement and then told Debbie's parents, but nobody seemed to show much interest. I wasn't exactly showered with congratulations.

Debbie wasn't career-minded but I already knew and accepted that and it made for the perfect relationship. I was a forceful and impulsive individual, and she wanted to settle down and have a family. So I set out to make enough money to make Debbie's dreams possible. And that's the way it has been ever since: I concentrate on the business side of things, while her focus is on being a mother and keeping house. The arrangement works incredibly well because we both do what we do best.

Debbie has never once moaned about the time I spend out of the home trying to achieve my goals. She accepted from the start that I would have to work all the hours that God sends – and a few He didn't – in order to build a career. It has made a difficult task a little easier. Some relationships crumble when one partner is out all the time. In our case it has made our partnership stronger. We both knew that this was the way it was going to be if I was to turn myself into a success story.

Debbie always sends me out looking immaculate – and the house is always spic and span. I love the fact that she is fastidious around the house and wants everything clean and tidy with the children turned out neatly as well. She puts me in mind of my mother, who always wanted things at home to be just so.

But that is where the similarity ends. Unlike my mother, who is volatile and has a bad temper, Debbie is calm and measured most of the time and is always prepared to be the less dominant partner, something my mother could never accept. It doesn't mean that Debbie is a doormat. In fact, as soon as I step on the doormat each evening, there is only one boss in the house – and it isn't me. I am in charge outside the house, but she is clearly the governor inside those four walls and I always have to accept what she says and where she has decided we are going that evening or that weekend.

As far as I am concerned it is a perfect arrangement – all day I work my butt off with my brain in overdrive and then I come home and all is sweetness and light. There is absolutely no nagging because she knows her job and trusts me to know mine. That way I can come home and be able to switch off. It is a real blessing. Had Debbie and I both wanted control in the same areas, it just wouldn't have worked. She is exceptional at what she does, looking after me, the children and the house, and I am good at going out and making money.

Of course, we never actually sat down and discussed this strategy and our individual roles; it just evolved naturally, which made things so much easier. I think that sometimes if you sit down and work out a strategy then one of you has to adapt and that can make life difficult.

We tied the knot on 28 January 1978; I was eighteen and Debbie was twenty. I bought a new suit and Debbie bought a new suit. Deb's nan laid on a spread in her front room and we invited just our close family. It wasn't a major exercise or a major expense because we couldn't afford to turn it into one. In fact, the most expensive thing was hiring a car to take Debbie to the Register Office and back. There was no build-up, no antici-pation, no excitement and no planning. It was just another thing we had to do. We didn't go away on honeymoon; we just got married, had a couple of days off and then went to work on the Monday and that was it.

A few months into the marriage and things were going quite well – I was earning about £5,000 a year and Debbie a little more. We weren't spending much, so we decided it was the right time to try for a baby. After all, it was what Debbie wanted; it was the logical next step in our new life together.

We knew that once Debbie stopped working, my salary alone wouldn't be enough, but we decided to cross that bridge when we came to it. Once Debbie was pregnant, her nan and my mother were really helpful. One week one would buy us a pram, the next week the other would get us some baby clothes, and we reckoned that by the time the baby came along we would have virtually everything we needed.

I was making extra money by selling as many 'yellow sticker' products as possible, but it still wasn't enough when Debbie's salary finally dried up. That's when I stepped into the unknown with Imperial Life. For the first six months there I was guaranteed a salary of about £800 a month and then after six months it was commission only. But I did have that initial safety net. I had to make money or we would all starve – and that included baby Dominic who arrived on 5 April 1979, fourteen months after we got married. (Mrs P insisted I put that bit in, by the way.)

Because Debbie was suffering from high blood pressure, she had to go into St Thomas' Hospital for four weeks before Dominic finally arrived. She was also suffering from pre-eclampsia and eventually they decided to induce the baby. He didn't respond, however, and we became more and more concerned. All this time, I was on my own at home. Everything revolved around our unborn child and it was a very emotional and worrying period.

Debbie was in labour for about thirty-six hours and still the little bugger wouldn't make an appearance! In the end, they took her into theatre and she had an emergency caesarean section. When Dominic did finally see the light of day his face appeared to have been damaged; he looked a bit battered to my untrained eye. They were even concerned that he might have been brain-damaged.

After a week, Debbie was allowed home, while Dominic remained in intensive care. We went to the hospital every day to visit him. We weren't prepared to accept that he'd been damaged in any way and were convinced that he'd be fine.

Actually, Dominic is seriously dyslexic and has struggled all his life. We think it's got a lot to do with that difficult labour although we will never know for sure. His coordination was poor and he had a terrible squint and a speech impediment for which he has had to have speech lessons and two operations on his eyes. But he has fought hard and overcome his difficulties to build an independent life for himself.

One evening when we had just returned from our daily visit to see Dominic, we got a phone call from a nurse at St Thomas' who said she wanted Debbie to go back to the hospital. Obviously, we feared the worst – something must have happened to Dominic.

But, in fact, it had nothing to do with him. It was Debbie's mum, Pam, who had been taken into St Thomas'. We were informed that she was dying from cervical cancer. When her parents split up Debbie went to live with her mum, who went on to have other children, and Debbie ended up, at the age of twelve or thirteen, as a housekeeper and nanny to the other children, while her mum went to work. What's more, her mum's partner was an alcoholic – it was a far from ideal environment for a young girl. At fifteen she couldn't stand it any more and left to live with her nan – and she had not spoken to her mother since the day she walked out.

I hadn't seen Debbie's mum until I set eyes on her in the hospital. A day after we saw her, Debbie's mother passed away and twenty-four hours after that Dominic was finally released into our care. It was a traumatic time in our lives and the start of a difficult period for the pair of us. Debbie was stuck at home with a baby who was screaming 24/7 and I was coming to the end of my six-month buffer period at work, which meant I had to work six or seven nights a week to bring home a decent wage. It was clear that our little shoe box of a flat wasn't big enough for three. Our one bedroom contained our bed plus Dominic's cot as well as enough baby stuff to fill a branch of Mothercare.

I came home one night and told Debbie we couldn't live like this any more. I was slowly getting into the swing of things at work and was beginning to maintain my salary – I wasn't earning a lot more than the £800 a month I had started on, but my income seemed reasonably secure.

We began searching for a bigger place and soon found a house in Mitcham, a two-bedroom 1960s-style property that we both liked. I secured a mortgage but just before we were due to exchange, the vendors pulled out of the deal and we found ourselves on the wrong end of a gazumping.

We had buyers for our flat, and didn't want to lose them, so we completed on our flat and moved back into Debbie's nan's front room. It was quite a shock to the system going back there with all our furniture in store and our hopes of a bigger house crushed. We were back where we started, but this time with the addition of a baby, who was still crying non-stop.

After about four months, we came across a small two-up, two-down two-bedroom house, a little end-of-terrace cottage that hadn't been touched since the 1940s. It had been owned by an elderly couple; the husband had died and the lady of the house had been taken into a home. It was on the market for £21,500, within our rather limited price range, so we bought it. It needed a complete refurbishment plus central heating, but that didn't put us off – nothing did.

I saw an advert in the local paper for a company that would deliver all you needed to install your own central heating system, including the boiler, radiators, pipes, pumps and the thermostat along with step-by-step instructions, for just £299. I took them up on their kind offer, paid them the money, and all this plumbing stuff was delivered and dumped in our front room. I then started to teach myself plumbing. Most evenings I was at work so I installed the central heating at the weekends, and then I started decorating the house.

The first Christmas we were there the kitchen was diabolical. It only had a cooker, nothing else, not a single cupboard. We had a bit of a set-to as Debbie couldn't see how she was going to cook Christmas dinner and we couldn't afford to go and buy anything to improve things.

That evening, when Debbie had gone off to bed, I went out to the old-fashioned lean-to next to the house where there were two solid wood wardrobes, which we had removed from our bedroom to give ourselves more space. I got out my Black & Decker circular saw attachment and set to work. I stayed up all night and by morning I had built her a kitchen. It was a real DIY job but it served its purpose for about eighteen months, before I could afford to buy some proper units and install them.

Mrs P wanted a second child as quickly as possible and Zoe came along on 30 September 1981. We were ecstatic; we had a boy and a girl, we were the true suburban family.

I was still working for Legal & General at the time and by now the house, as well as the family, was really beginning to take shape. I had completely refurbished it, the central heating was operational, the kitchen had been improved, I had sorted out the lean-to, decorated the rooms and painted the front of the house. And I was relishing the job and the fresh challenge at Legal & General.

The staff mortgage at a preferential rate meant we could sell our little cottage and buy a three-bedroom semi about half a mile away. There wasn't much planning and decision-making behind the move, once again it was a natural progression.

It was a far better house than anything we'd had before. We had a big kitchen, two toilets – one downstairs and one upstairs – and an extension. I bought Mrs P a dishwasher for Christmas. We had a nice front room and a nice sitting room, but I wasn't happy. I thought there had to be more than this. So after about six months of feeling like the lord of the manor, I decided to set up on my own in business, giving up the guaranteed salary, company car, cheap mortgage. With hindsight, I am not sure I should have done it, but I felt the time was right.

From an early age it was clear that Zoe had a very different personality to Dominic. She has always been very theatrical, a bit of a drama queen, and she drove me absolutely bonkers when she was a child. She is self-opinionated, very bright, but terrible at taking advice. Some say that she reminds them a little of me. She's a very pretty girl but as stubborn as a mule.

She went to Claremont Fan Court School in Surrey, where she did her O-levels and A-levels, of which drama, unsurprisingly, was one. I tried to persuade her to go to university, but she wasn't having it. She announced she was going to become an actress, without even going to stage school.

One evening we had a long chat, and eventually I wore her down and she accepted that her best option if she wasn't going to university was to come and work for me – even though I reckoned I would probably try to kill her in the first week. Clutching at straws, I thought I could get her to learn something, maybe she would become a buyer or go into merchandising or operations. After all, she could turn her hand to anything and you only had to tell her something once; she was very capable, very with it, coordinated and clear-thinking. Finally, she agreed to come to the office and work for six months in various departments to see which one she liked best.

I very proudly went up to bed that night and told Mrs P that I'd got through to our daughter at long last, and went to sleep quite content. The following morning I got up and went to work but I was deeply unhappy. I realised I'd done a terrible thing. Zoe had been determined about her dream of becoming an actress and I'd killed it stone dead. What if she could become an actress and could make a career out of it? Maybe she wouldn't starve even though I had convinced her she would.

I felt terrible. I phoned her from the office. 'Zoe, do you remember the conversation we had last night?'

'Of course. I remember it all.'

'Well, do me a favour, forget the whole lot of it. I was talking absolute rubbish. If acting's what you want to do, you give it your best shot, and we'll be right behind you.'

She started crying, and so did I. She left school, started going to auditions and managed to get herself a small part in a soap opera on Sky called *Dream Team*. She was in it for about two years, but it was very much a bit-part and she decided to leave and move on. She felt she wasn't getting anywhere and she was earning an absolute pittance. You certainly don't make a lot of money being a bit-part actor in a soap opera.

By this time she thought it might be better if she moved out of the house and went to live on her own, so she got herself a flat in Kingston by the river, where she still lives. The acting roles dried up but she did do a few adverts. She did the cover and the publicity shots for the film *American Pie*, which was a bit of an embarrassment to me because it was a picture of her torso with her ample bosom in a bra made out of an American flag. It was on every poster site in London and I could hardly drive anywhere without seeing my daughter's boobs! She was also on the video covers, even though she never actually appeared in the film.

Her acting career appeared to have come to an end so she went and got a full-time job working for a firm of estate agents. After several years she decided that this wasn't for her and left to join a newspaper group in their advertising department.

Dominic is totally different to his sister. Where Zoe is strong and driven, he is quite sensitive and emotional. All his health problems as a baby made it very difficult for him as a youngster. Most of his problems have been ironed out now but they were difficult to cope with at the time. He really struggled with growing up and people found it easy to take advantage of him, knowing who he was and that he came from a reasonably wealthy family. Often he allowed himself to be used because he wanted people to like him. His teenage years were particularly difficult. He is very affectionate and loving but doesn't like stress.

Our third child, Alex, was born on 28 April 1987 and he is different again – strong, athletic, a very good sportsman and dyslexic just like Dominic and his dad. Alex is one of those scallywags who could charm the birds out of the trees. But at around fourteen, he was cheeky and argumentative. He argued constantly with his teachers and they eventually decided he would be better off at another school. He ended up at a boarding school in Romsey for his last two years before GCSEs, which was traumatic for us, not having him around. Moving schools, however, was probably the best thing that could have happened to him because he passed his GCSEs, which he had been told he would never do.

From an early age, Alex loved football, as I do, and started playing for the local team at the age of six. I would say this, but Alex was talented, especially at football, and there was a time when I thought he might be good enough to turn professional. We'd go to football every week, we'd go to internationals at Wembley and even as a small child, at the age of four, I'd take him to football and have him on my shoulders. It was great fun and reminded me of my youth, when I used to bunk off and go to Old Trafford. Alex absolutely loved it; he was just football-mad. And for me it was fabulous, a great excuse to go to every sporting event going.

Finally, after a long gap, we had the twins, Hollie and Annabelle, who were born on 23 January 1996, and for the first time I got to do the feeds. By the time they came along I was a far more relaxed person. When the other three children were born I was still out there trying to make it and very focused on being successful in my career. But by the time the twins were born I had already bought Ryman and we were doing well so I had more time. I even did the morning school runs when Mrs P was pregnant with the twins, although she did the afternoon shift. Having the twins was like having a second family.

Annabelle and Hollie were always begging me to get them a dog but I kept putting them off. This went on for about three years and eventually they registered with the Dogs Trust. At about the same time I got a call from a television production company asking whether I would do a programme about dogs. I was already on *Dragons' Den*, and when I heard that the programme was in association with the Dogs Trust I spoke to the production company. They were very keen to have me and explained that I would be filmed attempting to train a dog.

I asked for time to think it over and at dinner one evening I said to the girls, 'I've been asked to do this show with the Dogs Trust, taking a stray and training him in front of a live audience, but I've said no.'

'Right, that's it, we're never talking to you ever again.'

They got up from the table, threw their knives and forks down in disgust, and went upstairs. Debbie looked at me and said, 'Why did you say that? You're going to have to do it now.' I went upstairs to the girls' bedroom and told them we'd at least have a look. In the end I told the production company I'd do the series on one condition: that I got to keep the dog at the end.

I went to the Dogs Trust with the production people to choose a dog. The girls were at school and had instructed me to choose something small. While looking round the kennels I came across what looked like a black donkey. It was very skinny, its fur was matted and it was a right mess. It turned out to be an Afghan hound that had had its fur cut badly. The trainer told me how difficult they were to train because 'they're as scatty as a bag of jelly babies.' So I walked on and found a smaller dog, which seemed a better bet – until it snapped at me. I didn't want it doing that to the twins so we went back to the Afghan/donkey, whose name was Claudia. She was so soppy and her coat was so soft, but she was a big old thing. I sat with her outside, just holding on to her lead, and found that I quite liked her.

My mind was made up, despite being advised I'd never win the competition. But that wasn't why I was doing it. So I sent a photo to the girls, who were dubious until we went back the following day to have a look at her. She was such a gentle, lovely dog that they immediately fell in love with her. She was a bit disobedient because she hadn't been trained but her whole demeanour was very ladylike, even to the point of shaking her head if she didn't like something. We decided she'd make a great family pet. All I had to do now was train a scatty donkey of a dog in front of a live studio audience.

I had as much chance of winning this competition as I had of being picked to run for Cyprus in the 100 metres at the next Olympics. But I worked hard with her for about a fortnight and got her to a certain level, but when she'd had enough, she'd had enough. She would only train for fifteen minutes a day and then she would decide that she didn't want to know. In the show, the cameras racing along on rails had a terrible effect on her – one minute she was standing obediently by my side, the next minute she was chasing the camera around the studio!

In rehearsals she had a faultless round, but on the show itself she turned in a terrible performance and we were booted out in the first week. Getting our marching orders so soon was a godsend – there was no way I could have stayed in that show for six weeks, training that dog every day.

It was as big a commitment as *Strictly Come Dancing*. In fact, the reason I didn't do *Strictly Come Dancing* when I was asked was because I couldn't afford the time – and because I dance like an orangutan with piles! It's a family trait. We clench our buttocks and shuffle – not a pretty sight. In effect, I had turned down doing the number one TV show in the UK to do a dog show on BBC2. But we still finished as winners – we ended up with the lovely Claudia.

The Dogs Trust told us that Claudia had been found in

Glasgow and it was felt, looking at her, that maybe she was a breeding bitch who was no longer able to give birth and had been abandoned. I told the story on air and a few weeks after the show we got a letter from a family in Scotland who told us that she was their dog Tinsel, who'd gone missing some months previously. They enclosed her pedigree certificate and photos of her with the family. And, indeed, when I called out 'Tinsel' her ears popped up and she got up and came straight to me. But she's staying as Claudia – the name that was given to her by the woman who found her and thought she was elegant and looked like a model.

Once we had been living in our house in Cobham for ten years, and had extended it so many times we didn't remember where the old house ended and the extensions began, Mrs P decided it might be easier to move and we started looking for our next home. Each spring we went in search of somewhere new to live, or at least Mrs P did, as my heart wasn't really in it – I liked where we were. But then in June 2006, she rang me, sounding very excited about a place she had found. I was quite fussy about exactly where I lived, and although it was close to where we already were, it was somewhere I didn't particularly want to live.

But it was another one of those weak moments when I had Brownie points to make up so, as always, I tried to play the political game and agreed to have a look. I pulled up in front of the house and couldn't see why she liked it. But then again I'm never there so it's about her and it's about the family. The minute the estate agent opened the door I knew why she liked it. It was her kind of house. She was strolling around as if she already owned it. In truth, it ticked very few boxes for me, the only attraction being that it had a smashing gym and pool complex. But by the time we had finished our tour of inspection I knew she had to have it. I was going to have to compromise.

I agreed to buy the house and we live in it today and she was absolutely 100 per cent right. She has turned it into a home that the family can feel comfortable in. I was probably still looking for a house, while Mrs P was searching for a home. There's a massive difference between the two.

In January 2008 Debbie and I celebrated our thirtieth wedding anniversary. Even now, I do DIY round the house myself and I still get ordered about by Mrs P to get things done. I sometimes feel like turning around and saying, 'Do you know who I am?' But I don't say anything of the sort. I just do as I'm told. She is still very much the head of the household, as she's always been.

Chapter Seventeen

Into the Lions' Den

Football was a game I loved as a kid, although I was never any good at it. When I did play I tended to be stuck in goal because I didn't have the stamina to play anywhere else. But I loved to watch the game and, as I said earlier, I used to visit Old Trafford as a kid and then Highbury when we moved to Finsbury Park, which was so close to the Arsenal ground that we had to put dustbins out at the front of the house to stop people parking in our space. I don't think I missed an Arsenal home game the momentous year they did the Cup and League double in 1971. I think it was a shilling to get into the schoolboys' enclosure – what a bargain that was. But my first passion was always for Manchester United and those glory years of Best, Law and Charlton.

As much as I loved the game, I never expected to be involved in football. But then in the summer of 1994, after I'd moved to Cobham, a friend, Alan Smith, who had coached Walton and Hersham youth team, came to see me. Walton was our local non-league team, playing in those days in the Isthmian League, then sponsored by Diadora, and the club chairman was Nick Swindley, who had been in charge of the club for many years. Like so many football clubs, they'd run out of cash. They had just been promoted to the premier section of the Diadora League and needed some funding. Alan said, 'I'm going to put about £5,000 in; if you could put £5,000 in, we could both join the board and have some fun. Why don't you come in with me?'

I went to the ground in Stompond Lane to watch them, and almost before I knew it I'd put my hand in my pocket for £5,000. I'd joined the board along with Alan and became a director and started going every Saturday, home and away. It was great, as the ground was about two minutes away from home. The average crowd was a couple of hundred, and it was good fun. We had a small clubhouse with a boardroom attached and we'd have curled-up sandwiches after the game and a few beers and then sit in the clubhouse until about ten o'clock drinking with the fans. It was a great way to spend a Saturday.

All the team had other jobs. They played because they loved the game, but that's not to say they didn't want paying. The average wage was about £100 a week, which wasn't a lot even then, but it was if the crowds were only two hundred. The players were very passionate and would join you in the bar after the game and you'd put the world to rights. We became quite a close-knit unit and before I knew it, a year or so later, Nick left and I ended up being 'promoted' to chairman by default.

I had bought Ryman by then and when the next sponsor of the league – a company called ICIS – went bust, Ryman stepped in. I knew the chairman of the league, Alan Turvey, and he was a big fan of Ryman. I got on well with him at league meetings, which I attended regularly as a club chairman. I think I was one of the few who talked any sense and he came to see me and before I knew it not only was I chairman of Walton and Hersham, but by 1997 I was sponsoring the Isthmian League as well.

Now my team was playing in a league that I sponsored. I was beginning to have an influence. The club continued to lose money, but it was only a few thousand pounds a year, which wasn't a problem, as I was happy with my involvement. I'd take the kids there and Alex would be playing on the five-a-side pitch with the other children and even when the main match started, they would carry on playing their own game.

There was a real family atmosphere. Even when my little girls were born I would take them to the games in their car seats at the age of six months. It really became a way of life for us on a Saturday afternoon. You could leave home at half past two and arrive in plenty of time to say hello to the opposing chairman and have a drink.

Afterwards the referee would come into the boardroom, which obviously doesn't happen in the professional game, and you could tell them face-to-face if you thought they had had a crap game. You built up a relationship with the referees and could criticise them sensibly to their face. If you had something to say, you could say it politely, and give them the chance to answer back. Almost without exception they would have a good, honest reason why they took a particular decision.

Later when I was at Millwall, I never publicly castigated referees. If I had something to say to a ref I'd say it to him personally, just like I did all those years ago in the boardroom at Walton and Hersham. I recall one occasion when Mark Halsey, who is now a Premier League referee, was in charge of Walton's game against Aldershot. I thought Halsey had a shocker. We were 1–0 down and then had a player sent off after ten minutes, following a bit of argy-bargy during which an Aldershot player went down. The man Halsey sent off wasn't even involved. How can I be sure? Well, the guys who had the fight were six foot and white, while the player sent off was small and black, with dreadlocks. No wonder he looked amazed.

Fortunately, we came back and drew 1–1. Afterwards, I was talking to Alan Turvey, a respected ex-referee himself, when

Mark Halsey walked into the boardroom. I was almost speechless – well, not quite – about his performance. Alan agreed he'd had a bad day, but insisted he was one of the best referees in the league. What was more, he believed that with some more good marks, he could step up to the Football League, something he felt he truly deserved. In the circumstances, I was horrified. Eventually, Halsey came up and we had a drink and I let him know exactly what I thought of his performance and he very nervously said, 'I suppose you're going to be marking me down'.

'No, I'm going to give you full marks. I don't want you refereeing us again, you're bloody useless. The Football League can have you. In fact, I insist they have you.' And he got promoted that year, and went on to become one of the country's top referees. Shows how much I know.

What was incredibly funny was that in my first season at Millwall, in one of our early home games, I looked at the team sheet and whose name was there – Mark bloody Halsey! Anyway, he booked a few people, but I didn't have time to go and say hello to him because it was early on in my tenure and I was in demand for interviews and with people wanting to see me.

The following day, I was woken up first thing in the morning by the phone. It was Mark Halsey. He'd tracked me down from the old Isthmian League yearbooks, and he had a problem: he'd left his paperwork at the ground and needed to send his report to the league that day, and needed me to arrange access to the stadium that Sunday morning. When he got to the changing room, it was clean – the paperwork had been thrown in the skip. So he had to wade through all the skips until he eventually found it. In some ways, I thought I'd finally got my revenge for that game against Aldershot.

I came across Mark many times afterwards and one day at

Bristol Rovers I heard he wanted some bottled water. So I volunteered and took some fizzy water down to the referee's room. I banged on the door really hard, and as he opened it I sprayed him with it. I looked over his shoulder and the assistant referees were absolutely disgusted, but Mark took it as a joke. Once they realised that we knew each other, his two linesmen relaxed. It didn't stop Mark sending off one of our players, though, and booking God knows how many!

I'm sure I would have been happy at Walton had Ian at Movie and Media Sports not rung me in 1997 to tell me that Millwall had gone bust. He knew I'd gone to watch them in the days when I lived in Peckham. The fans were passionate about their football. It wasn't wonderful quality but they loved their team to bits. Unfortunately I didn't see a role there for me. A day later I got a call from Lee Manning of Buckler Phillips, who were the administrators of Millwall, trying to get me interested, but I didn't want to get involved.

A week later, Lee rang again and this time he managed to persuade me to have a look round the club. I must admit I was pretty well seduced once I saw the inners of the new stadium, but I still said no. I just knew how much money and time it would take, even though they were playing in what was then Division Two (now League One).

Then I got a call from another friend who said he knew Peter Mead, the chairman when the club went bust. Peter was a passionate supporter but, despite his successful business background, totally the wrong person to be chairman because he was so emotionally involved. Peter thought he could run Millwall like his businesses by having managers in there doing things on his behalf. But at Millwall you need to punch well above your weight to get an edge on your competitors. You've got to be hands-on – and you've got to be better than all the rest. Peter wasn't doing that, he was running it as a normal business, and he got beaten to the punch many times – so, in the end, Millwall went into administration.

The club was in disarray, many of the best players had been sold, a lot of the staff had been made redundant and morale was as low as the club's league position. The natives were restless to say the least – and the fans made that very clear. What you see is what you get with Millwall fans; they're right in your face.

I went to see Peter and we agreed that the priority was to raise about £10 million to pay off all the debts and have some cash in the bank. It was going to be a big ask. Someone suggested I see Reg Burr, who had been chairman for a long time before Peter took over. He was an astute businessman, who had had a colourful career in the City and then got involved with Luton and Millwall football clubs. He was quite influential on various Football Association and Football League committees and was one of the sharpest people I'd ever come across.

So I met Reg for the first time in his offices behind Manchester Square. He was in his seventies and was becoming a bit frail. I'd expected our meeting to last about thirty minutes. Well, that half-hour turned into three hours – and all I did was listen! I'd never come across a man with such a deep knowledge of football. Now and again, because of his age, he'd wander off the subject, but it soon became clear that Reg was somebody I needed to depend on. For a start, he had the knowledge that I didn't. If I was going to take over at Millwall here was someone who was going to have to play a part, even though when he left he was vilified by some of the fans. They must have had short memories because under Reg's chairmanship the club had been promoted to the old First Division for a couple of seasons at the end of the 1980s.

He ran Millwall with an iron fist and did the hard work behind the scenes that allowed the club to build its new purpose-built 20,000 all-seater stadium, which they moved into in 1993. He sold a lot of players for a lot of money to balance the books, but had developed those players in the first place and you've got to give him credit for that. Reg was going to be instrumental in helping me raise the money with the brokers, because he knew them incredibly well. After all, he was the man who had floated the club in the first place, which meant Millwall were the second football club to become a public company, the first being Tottenham Hotspur.

Post-Reg it was a bit like after the Lord Mayor's Show for Peter when he took over as chairman. He started brilliantly and by December 1995 Millwall were top of the league and scenting a possible promotion to the top flight, but by the end of the season everything had gone horribly wrong and Millwall were cruelly relegated on goal difference – closely followed in the next season by going into administration. It could only happen at Millwall.

Reg was quite scathing about what happened under Peter. He had built Millwall up and felt, rightly or wrongly, that Peter had let the side down. I'm not sure Reg was right. I think it was a combination of factors. As I've said, I don't think Peter's passion for the club helped, because some of the decisions that he took were more populist than businesslike. Also, I think in his world, people usually did what they said they would do, and I'm not sure he realised that football wasn't quite like that. But while you might question his decision-making, you could never question Peter's honesty and loyalty.

With time and money running out before the administrators folded the company, I realised I had to decide quickly. I went home, had a few beers, went to bed, and slept on it. Next morning I woke up and decided to take over at Millwall. I remember a great bit of advice from Brian Clough that went, 'Go to bed and sleep on it, and in the morning, if you still want to do it, you should go back to bed.' But I didn't go back to bed. Instead, I rang Lee and told him I'd step in.

I put some money in, and a few other people I knew put some money in, and then we raised some more funds in the City and, hey presto, we were out of administration. I joined the board and very soon became chairman of Millwall plc. I had well and truly stepped into the Lions' Den!

One of my first moves was to persuade Reg to come back on to the board as a non-executive director and Peter remained on the board as well. That meant I had two ex-chairmen on the board, which in retrospect wasn't a great idea because they both had their own opinions on how things should be done. But I'm a strong individual so I felt I could deal with them and whenever I felt they were out of order we'd have words.

Reg was by far the most helpful man around and another key person was chief scout Bob Pearson. In many ways he was a bit like old Reg – he couldn't half talk. Bob had made more comebacks than Lazarus and Frank Sinatra put together. He had been fired several times and I could see why. He was bombastic and self-opinionated and could drive you up the wall. He even walked out twice while I was at the club. But I knew I had to keep Reg and Bob onside if I was going to succeed in turning the club around. Bob's knowledge of players was superb and I got very close to him. I have to say that I trusted his opinion on players more than most of my managers; the good ones listened to what he said.

My first problem was appointing a manager, as John Docherty had resigned, and the name that kept on cropping up as his replacement was ex-West Ham star Billy Bonds. I went to meet him and was bowled over. So in May 1997 he got the job – and you would have thought I had brought in the devil to run the club. The fans who had loved me after I had saved the club, which had been minutes from extinction, were now outraged by my decision. I had committed the cardinal sin and appointed a West Ham legend to manage Millwall. Luckily, Billy was from south London and a lot of his family were Millwall fans and well known to a lot of our crowd. So enough supporters felt Billy had some Millwall in him and gave him a chance.

But he lasted only a season. I called him after the last game and told him he was out. It was very tough, but I think it was inevitable. We had only just avoided relegation, finishing eighteenth, just two points above the drop with no wins in our last eight games. Billy had introduced a lot of older players, some of them ex-West Ham like Paul Allen and Kenny Brown, to try to prop us up. But it hadn't worked as our season tailed off in the second half. In fairness to Billy we didn't have a structure to support him. And as much as I liked him as an individual, it was clear it was time to move on. An inexperienced manager married to an inexperienced chairman, no wonder we got divorced.

As his replacement, I decided to appoint Keith 'Rhino' Stevens, a Millwall legend who was approaching retirement after playing his entire career for the club, and Alan McLeary, another Millwall player, as his assistant. Not surprisingly these appointments proved very popular with the fans. I thought it wasn't just popular; it was the right thing to do. I felt we needed Millwall people in charge to bring back the passion that was missing under Billy's management. Although they also may have lacked experience, they did know Millwall and the passion it created.

Sometimes, over the years, that enthusiasm had spilled over a little and Millwall fans had gained an unsavoury reputation that followed us around like a bad smell. Eradicating that smell was probably my biggest challenge in running the football club. What I can say was that in all the time I was there, I never suffered any form of racial abuse or prejudice from anybody within our ground. I'd encountered it at other grounds, but not at Millwall.

Keith and Alan cleared out most of the older players from

Bonds's reign and we started 1998–9 with a host of young players. Some of the players Bob had scouted started to come through, like Tim Cahill, Steven Reid and Paul Ifill, who were talented youngsters but raw as hell. They had a lot to learn, and I was learning alongside them. In truth, we were having a very average season, but we made it all the way to Wembley. It might only have been the Auto Windscreen Shield (for teams in the bottom two divisions), but it was our cup final. Millwall had never made it to Wembley in their history, but now we were on our way to the famous old ground just before the bulldozers moved in to tear it down to make way for the new stadium.

Keith and Alan and I were all heroes in the eyes of our success-starved fans. Our average crowd was about 7,000, yet we sold an astonishing 45,000 tickets for the final. Where did they all come from? If only 40 per cent of them turned up every Saturday we would have had a full house every week and would really be going places – and not just to Wembley. It gave me confidence – wrongly as it turned out – that the club could grow because of this huge untapped fanbase. What had really happened was that everyone was bringing their friends and granddads and everyone else they could think of to a one-off Wembley final against Wigan.

Wembley was an unforgettable experience. I'd been there many times before, but going with your very own team is something I never thought would happen even in my wildest dreams. I rang my mother in Cyprus to tell her we were playing at Wembley and asked her if she would like to come over and sit in the royal box – and she jumped at the chance! On the day we had a coach leaving my house with about forty friends who had all turned up for a pre-match drink with everyone wearing blue hats and carrying blue flags. Then out came Mum with an outrageous hat and white gloves, who said, 'Well, if I'm going to see the Queen, I want to make sure I look my best.'

Unfortunately, we lost to a very dodgy handball goal in the last minute, which was a real body blow. Wigan were never lucky opponents for us. We had struggled against them in the past – and would do so again in the future.

The result apart we did everything properly. We had our suits specially made and in my wardrobe today there's a suit carrier with my final suit, shirt, tie and royal box tickets. It's still got the mud at the bottom of my trousers where I went on the pitch to applaud the fans at the end, in tears I may add, after we lost. There was also Wembley mud on my shoes, which I haven't worn since and never will. It was truly a one-off occasion.

My football-mad son Alex was our mascot that day. In fact, he took penalties against the goalkeeper in the warm-up and just before the referee cleared them off the field, the little bugger decided to dig up the penalty spot, which he's still got somewhere. So they played the whole game without a penalty spot because Alex stole it.

Despite our run to Wembley, it was during that season that the old Millwall hoodoo returned. We had a home game against Manchester City, who had been relegated to Division Two and had reached the lowest point in their history, and the crowd invaded the pitch. If it had happened anywhere else, not a lot would have been said, but the FA, the half-wits that run football, were under a lot of pressure in many areas and decided they would get some positive PR by hanging Millwall out to dry.

The result, a 1–1 draw, was forgotten because there was a pitch invasion after each of the goals, although I felt the encroachment had come from the Man City supporters. But it was our home game and we were held responsible. That was my first experience of dealing with the FA and I was in no doubt that they were probably the most incompetent people I've ever come across. After a two-day inquiry we were handed a suspended sentence but no points were deducted on the basis that we had done everything possible to prevent the encroachment. The bad press that ensued was unbelievable.

I think the fact that I had tried my level best to reinvent Millwall, to try to get away from the public perception of a violent club, held us in good stead. My hard work in that area and our work in the community were taken into account. But it was still a terrible time. We always took a big support away from home, but the police at several clubs had banned our fans from travelling and we were forced to show the games on a big screen at the New Den. It was so unfair as our fans didn't cause any more trouble than any other club's supporters.

The following season, 1999–2000, after finishing fifth, we qualified for the Second Division play-offs, where we met Wigan again, but lost out on aggregate over two legs. So after that disappointment, we had to regroup once again for the 2000–1 season. A lot of our talented youngsters were getting rave reviews and, after failing to go up, there was a danger we might lose some of them. I was determined this wasn't going to happen and worked very hard to keep them. In fact, we started off badly. After one particularly painful defeat, Keith and Alan were absolutely slaughtered by the fans as they left the pitch at the end of the game.

It was then that I knew, as much as I loved the two boys – and it was my decision to turn them from players into the management team – that they had taken the team as far as they could. I invited Keith and Alan to my home, and gave them the bad news. They took it like men. They knew it was on the cards. Millwall were in thirteenth place in the league, but were treading water. It was in danger of turning out to be a nothing season. Alan was to return to Millwall as youth coach a few years later, because we always got on well, and Keith emigrated to Australia and we still chat over the internet.

They were very inexperienced on the management side and I

tried to help them by appointing Ray Hartford as first team coach. Hartford had worked with Kenny Dalglish at Blackburn when they had Alan Shearer up there and won the Premiership. I persuaded Ray to come in on a temporary basis, but it was obvious almost from the off that it wasn't going to work. Maybe if Keith and Alan had taken a little more notice of what Ray was telling them they might have done a bit better. I asked Ray if he would take the team temporarily. He agreed but made it crystal clear to me that he didn't want to be the manager on a permanent basis. He knew full well that if a new gaffer came in he would have a clear-out and appoint his own number two.

I'd busted my backside to keep this young team together and I was determined to halt the revolving door culture where a new man would come in, get rid of the backroom staff and the players, and start again from scratch. This happens so often in football and seems bizarre. In any other business, if the basic structure was sound you wouldn't change the whole thing. I knew the players were good, I knew Ray was a brilliant coach and I knew whichever manager I brought in would have to agree to some interference – from me! I wasn't going to have somebody come in and wipe everything out overnight so he could make his own mistakes. There was nobody within the club I could promote to manager, but I wanted to keep Ray and Steve Gritt, who were doing a good coaching job.

I make no apologies for deciding to stick with most of the staff who were already there, and simply change the manager. People say I interfered, bloody right I interfered. I'm not stupid and just because someone was a professional football player once upon a time it doesn't automatically make him the best manager in the world, the best wheeler-dealer, the best financier, the best motivator of men, the best planner.

I was still searching for a manager and there were two hot candidates. I was leaning towards one of them when I got a phone call from an agent, which is rarely good news in my book, but this time was an exception. He suggested another name to me – Mark McGhee – who had been out of the game for a couple of years. He had done superbly well at Reading, with the support of John Madejski, went to Leicester for a few games, then jumped ship and went to Wolves where he stayed for three years and didn't do that well, even though he had quite a lot of backing. But because he left Leicester so abruptly he was considered a bit of a risk. However, I was persuaded to see him for forty-five minutes.

Mark came to the office and the forty-five minutes ended up more like four hours! But it only took ten minutes for me to realise that here was someone bright and intelligent, someone I could work with. I made no secret of the fact that it would be unlike any appointment he had had in the past where he would be allowed just to get on with the job. I said I couldn't afford him to make mistakes at my expense, which is what happens so often. Managers come in; they get it wrong and are paid off. Football is one of the few industries that rewards failure in this way.

He looked at me in disbelief because no one had been that straight with him before. And while I didn't want him to be my puppet, I explained how I wanted him to keep the coaching and backroom staff in place. Rather than worrying that he couldn't bring in his own people, he was pleased to hear my confidence about the staff and left even more anxious to join us. Instead, I told him to come and watch the side take on Oxford – Ray had promised me a win for my birthday and I was feeling good after we'd beaten Ipswich at home in the first leg of our Worthington Cup tie.

By now I had decided to hold off my appointment of a manager, because I was impressed with this guy, even though I'd made my mind up on one of the two other candidates. Mark agreed to come and watch the game, as long as he could sit in

Dominic, our eldest son.

With Zoe, our second child.

Alex, our middle child, tries to take my wig in his stride.

The twins, Annabelle and
Hollie, identify themselves.

Debbie, Zoe and Alex
take the twins swimming
in May 1997.

Relaxing on Father's
Day after completing
the Contessa deal.
There was lots to
celebrate!

The girls get their first experience of Millwall.

Celebrating our promotion to Division One of the Football League in 2001, with Big Ben looking on. (Brian Tonks)

Dennis Wise and I embrace after we'd beaten Sunderland 1–0 in the FA Cup semi-final at Old Trafford in 2005.

The entire squad celebrates Millwall making it through to the final of the FA Cup for the first time in the club's history. It wasn't a quiet night that night, I can tell you

(both pictures Brian Tonks)

Applauding our fans at the Millennium Stadium in Cardiff after losing the final to Manchester United – we still had plenty to celebrate.

With Dennis Wise, Ray Wilkins and the Mayor of Lewisham during the parade to celebrate our great FA Cup run.

With so many other pressures on my time, I had to call it a day at Millwall, but the eight years I spent with the club were some of the most exciting I can remember.

(all pictures Brian Tonks)

My first series on *Dragons' Den*, with (from left to right) Rachel Elnaugh, Duncan Bannatyne, Doug Richard, me and Peter Jones.

In the Den during filming. I decided to try to bring more humour to the show, so when I said to one hopeful 'I'd rather stick pins in my eyes than invest in you', people seemed to like it. (both pictures Steffan Hill)

etting prepared for another ession in the Den. (Steffan Hill)

During filming of the shows, I've undoubtedly looked up to Pylon Pete the most. But then, who doesn't? (Steffan Hill)

e and Peter Jones dressed as ldy bears with Imran Hakim the launch of the iTeddy London Zoo – for some son, Peter was reluctant to ess up like this.

The cast for *Dragons' Den* Series Three and Four. Deborah Meaden replaced Rachel, after the problems with Red Letter Days, while Richard Farleigh (right) came in for Doug Richard. (BBC)

The current line-up of Dragons, with James Caan (left) the latest recruit. (BBC)

the crowd, as he felt he'd draw too much attention to himself if he was in the directors' box, and then he would let me know his decision after the weekend. Already I felt so positive about the guy that I was affectionately calling him Mr McGoo. I put him at the back of the stand and, with Ray having got the team on a bit of a high and Oxford marooned at the bottom, I settled back to see what the lads could do to persuade him to join us.

We absolutely murdered them 5–0. Ray had got the young kids playing with confidence. They respected him; he was a brilliant coach, sadly to die of cancer a couple of years later. He was still coaching us when he got ill and passed away. It was a massive blow to everyone at the club. Not a lot of people realised how instrumental he was at Millwall. Against Oxford we were magnificent, the crowd was fantastic, and it was just wonderful after the fans had been getting at Keith and Alan and me. Neil Harris got a hat-trick and Sam Parkin, who was on loan from Chelsea, got two.

The next day, I decided to ring Mark to see what he thought. He was very keen to join us, but I was also pleased to hear him checking that Ray didn't want the job, because he knew he was capable of doing it and sensibly didn't want to be walking in to any resentment from him or Steve. I reassured him on this and we agreed he could start the next day. Amazingly, we'd got to this stage and not even mentioned money or contractual terms. I explained that, as a Second Division side, we couldn't afford big wages, but that I could offer him a two-year contract, with the security that he'd only lose his job if he was rubbish. And I knew he wasn't. In fact, we didn't sort out his contract until months later. He was as good as his word. He came because he wanted the job, not for the money. He was quite a wealthy man, having done well out of football. He played at the top level in Europe and under Sir Alex Ferguson at Aberdeen in the side that won the European Cup Winners' Cup in 1983, beating Real

Madrid 2–1. Money certainly wasn't the motivator for him, which also helped me.

There was a funny story that happened around then, too. I went into my office at Millwall, delighted to have secured his services, and asked the temp, who was covering for my secretary, to ensure no calls were put through to me as I needed to finish some paperwork. When I came out some time later, she told me there'd been a few calls, including one from someone called Ferguson, who was about to fly to Italy.

Now usually in football when that name is mentioned, people pay attention, but from her attitude it could have been anyone on the line. So I asked if perhaps his name was Alex, she thought it was. I wondered if he'd had a Scottish accent, by any chance. She seemed impressed that I'd guessed correctly. Barely containing my anger by now, for if Manchester United wanted to sign one of my players I knew that it would transform our financial position, I made sure that if he called again, she was to put him straight through.

Unfortunately, when he did ring it wasn't to offer us untold fortunes, but to suggest another name for the role of manager. When I told him I'd already gone for Mark McGhee, there was a pause and he simply said, 'He'll be good for you,' before hanging up.

Before McGhee took control of the team, he had another 5–0 experience, but this time it was a bad one. Ray was still in temporary charge of the team the next day for the second leg at Portman Road where the referee ended up insisting that one of our players who had been injured came back on, as we'd had two sent off and two got injured after we'd made all our substitutions, otherwise we'd have had only seven on the pitch. It was an appalling game thanks to an appalling referee. I felt gutted for Ray because in the first leg he did brilliantly, but in the second he got well and truly mugged.

After that, we went on a strong run and by December we'd topped the league for the first time, and more or less stayed there for the rest of the season. In the last game we beat Oldham 5–0, were crowned champions with ninety-three points, and were promoted to the First Division. Neil Harris, our talisman striker, whom we bought from non-league for about £50,000, scored twenty-seven goals and was the division's joint top scorer. I was actually offered £2 million by Preston for him towards the end of the season, but had not the slightest hesitation in turning them down.

I'd given Neil about five contracts from the time we signed him two years earlier because I started him off on bugger all a week and then made him the highest-paid player at the club. Not because he asked for it, but because I didn't want to lose him. And furthermore, he earned it.

So we kept Neil, got promoted and a couple of weeks after the season ended I went off to Cyprus to see my mother, who had moved back there in the early nineties, because she wasn't well. I got there about four o'clock in the morning, and went to bed only to be woken up by a telephone call from Neil to say he'd been diagnosed with testicular cancer. What do you say to a lad not yet twenty-four when he tells you that? He'd wanted to let me know first, because he knew he'd not be playing during the next season and was anxious learn what I was going to do. I tried to reassure him that he'd be back, and amazingly, he ended up playing more than twenty games in 2001–2, many of them as substitute, though understandably he wasn't the force he'd been the previous campaign.

However, at Watford on New Year's Day, Neil got one of his trademark goals, his first since the diagnosis, and everybody went wild. We won 4–1 and our players lifted Neil up on their shoulders and paraded him around – even though the game wasn't over. That's how emotional it was. I was so chuffed. I was with my son Alex, who was sixteen at the time, and was suited up and with me in the boardroom. The team was doing very well under McGoo, having got into one of the play-off places, and Neil was back. I noticed that Alex had a great big lump under his coat and he told me he'd picked up the match ball from the referee, who must have thought he was one of the Watford officials and handed it over. Alex, who was a big fan of Neil's, wrote, 'Watford 1–4 Millwall, Neil Harris is back,' on the ball. But Alex's conscience got to him; he knew who had to have it.

So at the next home game we went into the changing room and I called Neil over. Alex then surprised him and gave him the ball. Neil was so chuffed that the following week he gave Alex a signed picture of him being hoisted on the shoulders of the other players after scoring. Neil had had the picture blown up, signed and framed. It was a fair swap as far as Alex was concerned.

That season was massive for us because, having got into a play-off position, we managed to hold on to it for the rest of the campaign, quite an achievement in our first season in the old First Division. We had to play Birmingham City in the semi-finals, but we weren't unduly worried about meeting one of the big names in the division. We still had some great youngsters, but Steve Claridge took the average age up somewhat. However, his experience was invaluable and he ended up with seventeen goals.

As the season drew to a climax, we were suffering with injuries and managed to get another vastly experienced player, Dion Dublin, on loan from Aston Villa. We had to pay a six-figure loan fee to bring him to the New Den – and his wages were more than £20,000 a week, unheard of at the club. Dublin's signing showed just how committed we were to getting into the Premier League – and the gamble paid off big style when he scored the late equaliser in a 1–1 draw in the first leg at St Andrews. We were all over Birmingham in the second leg at our place when, in injury time, Stern John nipped in to score. It ripped our hearts out. Soon after John's goal, the whistle blew, and our dream – and our season – was over.

In the boardroom after the game there were a lot of solemn faces and I thought, I'm not having this, so I started doing one of my trademark motivational speeches to our directors and officials when one of them interrupted me, because trouble had broken out. There was a full-scale riot going on just outside our ground. I forgot all about the game; it just paled into insignificance compared with what I was seeing. Everything we'd all been working for in relaunching the club's image and the success on the pitch was disappearing before my eyes. We were this young team, playing fantastic, attractive football, we'd been in two play-offs and we'd been to Wembley. But none of that mattered now. I could sense every ounce of my enthusiasm and love of football just draining from me.

The riot scenes were being shown live on television news programmes all round the world. There were reports of petrol bombs, coaches being ambushed; they were even talking about dead police horses. Unfortunately, three horses were injured, but thankfully none had died. It made the front pages of practically every newspaper. Scotland Yard said that at about 10 p.m. fifty people began throwing missiles and fireworks, cars were set alight, police officers and horses were attacked. I think fifty policemen required hospital treatment. It was horrendous, absolutely horrendous.

I couldn't believe it of our fans, it didn't make sense and when I finally got home at four o'clock in the morning I was totally and utterly dejected. It was one of the worst nights of my life. Four or five years of hard work had literally gone up in smoke. There was no question that elements of our fans were involved.

What I didn't know, and found out much later, was that the riot had been orchestrated.

A lot of people who had nothing to do with the game had organised it and no intelligence had been picked up. We later learned that missiles and petrol bombs had been stashed behind garden walls and hooligans from all around London and the Midlands had come to the New Den for a dust-up. What was happening in the stadium was irrelevant to these thugs. We could have won the game and the riots would still have happened. This was a bunch of hooligans deciding that Millwall's patch was a good place to go and have some 'fun'. Unfortunately, a certain element of our fans, the sheep I call them, decided to get involved. But the vast majority didn't. And when the arrests were made about a year later, I think of the twenty-odd prosecuted – and some of them went to prison – very few were Millwall supporters. They were supporters from all over the place and it was disappointing behaviour.

Afterwards we met with the police and understandably they were very unhappy as many of their officers had been hurt. It was agreed that there were big gaps in the police intelligence-gathering operation and there were many lessons to be learned. However, what made it worse was when Deputy Commissioner Ian Blair threatened to shut me down, saying he would withdraw our safety certificate. I found him totally uncon-structive about a problem that went beyond our club. I told him I couldn't defend the indefensible. What had happened was atrocious and should never have happened anywhere, never mind at a football ground. It was our duty to make sure it never happened again. But I felt that shouting me down wasn't really helpful. That didn't deal with the issue, which I felt wasn't an isolated Millwall issue.

I met with the police all through the summer and in the end we agreed to introduce a membership scheme, which meant that if you weren't a member you couldn't buy a ticket for a game. That way we would know the identity of every one of our fans who attended each game. The fans didn't like it – at least a certain element of fans I didn't want to be associated with. They were banging on about it on bulletin boards blaming me for the new scheme. It was ridiculous to put the blame on my shoulders – the last thing I wanted was to reduce the club's income and the membership scheme would obviously have that effect. However, it seemed the only way forward, given the pressure the club was under.

We started 2002–3 with a massive hangover from the play-off defeat and the after-match riots. We had our unpopular membership scheme and there was one other problem facing the club over which we had no control: the collapse of ITV Digital. As if things were not bad enough off the field, we began with a terrible result in our first home match, a 6–0 thrashing by Rotherham. That result was a portent of things to come and we just about achieved mediocrity with a ninth-place finish, with the fans often on my back.

Ray Wilkins called me to say Dennis Wise was available, having just been released by Leicester City, and that I should give him a call. This I promptly did and the more I got to know him, the more I realised he was nothing like the public's perception of him – a lot like Millwall, I suppose. As he was available, I persuaded him Millwall was right for him and we agreed a very sensible salary. I rang McGoo to find out if he wanted Dennis, and when he responded enthusiastically we had our man. I signed Dennis Wise on my birthday, 24 September, barely five months after that fateful riot. Unfortunately, Dennis spent a lot of time out with injuries and towards the end of the campaign his fragile relationship with the manager broke down completely. Add in the fact that Ray Hartford finally succumbed to cancer and you can see it really was our *annus horribilis*.

For season 2003–4, Mark McGhee brought in another very experienced man, Archie Knox, as his number two to replace Ray, and Steve Gritt also left. But these changes didn't work the oracle and the players didn't take to Archie. So, after another poor home performance, against Preston in October, I called in McGhee and told him it was over. I was criticised by some because we were in the top half of the table and in no imminent danger of going down. It's just that I felt after all the earlier progress we'd made, we were now no longer going forward. I had high expectations and my expectations weren't being met.

The following morning, I rang Dennis at home and told him to come straight to the training ground. As he'd been given a couple of days off, he was surprised but agreed to do so when I told him the news about Mark and Archie Knox (who'd also gone). I even had a good way of keeping him around: 'After training I want you to come to the stadium. I've hired it out for my company conference, and I'll be there with about twenty women in a state of undress while they're rehearsing a La Senza lingerie fashion show. You come and see me afterwards. I want you at the ground, please.'

And he came over in the afternoon, right in the middle of rehearsals, and all these girls were prancing up and down the stage in their lingerie. I sat him next to me and said, 'Right, hope you don't mind but I want you to sit here for about forty-five minutes while the girls finish dancing. I've got to see this final rehearsal before tomorrow when we've got our conference.' He didn't mind.

I told him I wanted him to take over as manager, but we agreed we'd announce it as a temporary role as player/manager and that he should go out and find a good assistant. This way, if he found it wasn't working, he could step away without any embarrassment. However, before he'd even told me, I knew he'd ask for Ray Wilkins, as he'd been the one to recommend him to

Millwall in the first place, so I said he couldn't have the assistant he wanted – it had to be someone else. He kept on insisting, and I said no, with neither of us actually mentioning Ray's name.

In fact, I knew Ray quite well and I also knew football, and the last thing you want is friends working with you in management because one thing's for certain, at some stage, you're going to have to fire them. In the end, Dennis rang me the following day to confirm he wanted the job – but only if Ray came in as his deputy. I agreed, but only if I could talk to Ray first. I wasn't sure that having him work for me would be ideal as it might ruin our relationship. When Ray replied, 'I've been fired so many times; don't think I'm going to fall out with you over that. I've been fired by some really nasty people so being fired by you would be a pleasure!' I gave in and agreed to Dennis's request.

For Dennis's first game in charge, he wasn't 100 per cent fit but insisted that he came on in the second half – and within four minutes he got himself sent off! It was a bad decision in my opinion, and he was one of two players to be dismissed, but we won the game 2–0 and it was like a breath of fresh air. The crowd loved Dennis because he epitomised that will to win – that special Millwall brand of fight and desire burned within him. I loved him for that, and soon called him Napoleon, because he was small and wouldn't listen to any advice I might have.

But soon Dennis and I were talking a lot more because we were having an unbelievable run in the FA Cup. We beat Walsall and Telford in rounds three and four and Burnley 1–0 in the fifth round with a goal from Danny Dichio, who had been round the block and back and Millwall was his eighth club.

Dennis had wanted Dichio and initially he came on loan. After that we decided to make the move permanent, despite the fee of £700,000 (though we didn't have to pay it all at once) and our rocky finances. In retrospect, we probably did pay over the odds and eventually sold him at a big loss, but at the time I was chuffed with Dichio, and he did well for us that season. I felt we had been vindicated and Dennis was ecstatic.

However, suddenly we not only had an FA Cup run on our minds, we also had to take on Tony Blair's former spin doctor, Alastair Campbell. After his Burnley side had been beaten by us twice in a fortnight, he wrote in a column in *The Times* that our fans had been chanting racist abuse at one of Burnley's players, and that Dennis or I should have stopped the game to deal with it. After all the work we'd done, I was furious with what he had said – to me, it was another dodgy dossier to suit his agenda. What particularly irritated me was that this was a man who seemed happy to come into club boardrooms when following his team, and who had even asked to borrow my helicopter on a previous occasion, as he'd been unable to get a flight elsewhere. He claimed this request was a joke, but it didn't seem that way to me.

We then beat Tranmere in the quarter-finals and marched on to the semi-final against Sunderland at Old Trafford – we were just ninety minutes away from glory, having avoided being drawn against Arsenal or Manchester United. We won that momentous game 1–0 and Tim Cahill scored the fantastic goal that got us into the final for the first time in our history. And not only that, we were in Europe as well because Manchester United, the other finalists after beating Arsenal in their semi-final, were already in Europe.

Dennis was a hero and we had so much media coverage, all of it positive, I must say. But, looking back on those great days now, the biggest day was not the Cup final; the biggest day was that semi-final. When you get to the final, you've done the job, you're there. After all, we were in Europe whatever the result. I was a winner even if we lost. That day at the Millennium

Stadium in Cardiff was really fantastic and I relaxed and enjoyed it immensely.

But taking my team to an Old Trafford semi-final to play against a Sunderland side managed by ex-Millwall boss Mick McCarthy was something else. We had a big night of it in our hotel in Manchester and I didn't get to bed until about six in the morning – and at half past seven the kids were excitedly knocking on the door. I was absolutely blind drunk. Eventually, I dragged myself out of bed by about nine and managed to get dressed.

It was an early kick-off and I was late for the pre-match meal with all the great and the good from the FA. I couldn't have a conversation with any of them because I was unable to string more than a couple of words together. So poor Mrs P had to do the translating for me. It wasn't until kick-off time that I started sobering up and it was then that the enormity of the occasion began to hit me.

After Tim got his goal midway through the first half, I was convinced Sunderland was going to equalise and I was crossing everything. At the end, the BBC actually got footage of me counting down the seconds. That's how nervous I was. But when that final whistle went you should have seen me run down to that pitch and give everybody a big sloppy kiss. The players had just worked their knackers off for ninety minutes and here was the chairman slobbering all over them. There's a great picture that went all round the world of me and Dennis snogging each other.

It was the start of a party that lasted all night. We drank Old Trafford dry and then drank some more elsewhere. I can't remember what time we got home on the coach but we were drinking all the way there.

The match referee for the final was Jeff Winter. It was his last match on the list, but I'd had a spat with him a few years back in private, not in public. We had been 4–0 down at Burnley but came back to 4–3 and he disallowed a perfectly good goal that would have made it 4–4 and also turned down a perfectly good penalty appeal, so we could have won that game 5–4. Just as I was leaving Turf Moor I bumped into Jeff. I was fuming and knew that if I said anything I was going to get into trouble, so I was walking past him when he asked for my Millwall badge as a swap for his referee's badge. Apparently, he collected them. As mine was a special edition sterling-silver badge that I had made for the directors and the team for when we got to Wembley, there were only a few of them around, and I wasn't about to swap it for a ref's badge, especially after his decisions that day, so I ended up telling him to get stuffed.

For the Millennium final I'd had the same badge cast in an eighteen-carat-gold limited edition of about seventy, half of which went to the players and staff. They were all inscribed and numbered with the Cup final logo and proper gold lions and I thought I'd give one to him and to the other three officials as a memento. I think it showed how relaxed I was about the whole thing, so I went down to the referee's room and said hello to Jeff and spoke to the other guys, joking that they shouldn't be biased in favour of United.

We chatted for a while, then I brought out these four little bags and made a presentation to them. Jeff opened up his and commented, 'It's not a badge, is it? Normally we get a bag of cash and you bring us a bloody badge!' The whole thing was very relaxed. As it happened, Jeff refereed brilliantly and there were times when it all got a bit desperate and Dennis missed a few tackles on Paul Scholes. On another day he might have had to go but the ref kept it moving. Dennis still insists that one of United's goals was offside and the penalty was never a penalty, so he still holds it against Jeff tongue in cheek, but I think he did really well. We lost 3–0 but it was a fair result. We didn't really turn up.

We partied again afterwards as if we'd won the game and Dennis gave a speech that could not be repeated ever again. I'm often asked did we expect to win. And I say, no. Did we have one of the greatest times of our lives? And I say, yes. And we still had Europe to look forward to the following season.

By now chairing the club had taken its toll on me and I had resolved that 2003–4 was to be my swan song. Originally I said I'd do five years and now I was into my eighth and felt it was time to go. I wanted to leave after the Cup final, but there was no clear successor. We'd made a fair amount of money out of the Cup, but we'd started off with a deficit of £3 million and I had bought Dichio and a few others, so all we did was cover our losses. But I felt we had got through the dark days of the riots and even had an open-top bus parade for the fans after the final – so I got seduced into staying for another season.

I thought that by making it public that I wanted to move on, a successor would come forward, but I couldn't have got it more wrong. Anyone we did try to attract ran a bloody mile when they took a close look at the economics of football – and I didn't blame them. In the end, there was only one person on the board who was up for it, Jeff Burnage, whose father had been chairman many years ago. Jeff had been associated with the club since the year dot and had been on the board for many years. He wasn't a particularly wealthy man but was convinced he could run the club on a tight budget. I thought I'd stay on the board and help out. Because of my contacts with the banks and the City, it was possible I could do for him what Reg Burr did for me at the beginning. History has shown I was wrong.

Of course, staying that extra season allowed me to be part of Millwall's European adventure in the UEFA Cup. We went to the draw in Monaco and were paired with the Hungarian side Ferencváros, whose reputation makes Millwall look like a bunch of Girl Guides. The first leg was at the New Den and we drew

1–1, with Dennis scoring our goal. The away leg in Budapest was something else. On the coach to the game I had never seen so many paramilitary police in my life. At the ground we were stuck right in the middle of their fanatical supporters and it was frightening. Being in the official Millwall party, we were all dressed to the nines so we stuck out like sore thumbs.

We were easy targets and the home fans started throwing glasses of beer and Coke at us and spitting at us. It got very hairy. One guy took a knife out and mimicked cutting his throat right in front of me as if that was what he was going to do to me after I had the audacity to complain about being covered in beer. Mrs P, Zoe and Alex were with me and there were other women in our party. I was seriously worried for our safety.

The UEFA observer was nearby and he went and remonstrated with the officials after I'd complained. The next thing I knew we were surrounded by about forty cops and couldn't see the bloody game. Not that it was worth seeing; we didn't perform that night. Dennis scored our only goal in a 3–1 defeat – and he remains the only Millwall player ever to score in a European competition.

As if getting beaten and being knocked out of the UEFA Cup wasn't bad enough, after the game we learned there had been a number of incidents during the course of the day and that night, and several of our fans had been stabbed; three of them were in intensive care. We managed to get hold of the British Embassy in Budapest and they sent an official to the hospital to speak to the doctors, some of whom didn't want to talk to us because they felt that football hooligans deserved what they got.

That made us fear for the fans that didn't have any identification on them as all their clothes had been stored away. We persuaded the hospital to let us have access to their personal belongings so that our fans could be identified and once we were satisfied they were going to be looked after by the embassy, we got a taxi back to the airport. I felt disgusted by all the violence. We made a formal complaint to UEFA and Ferencváros got a massive fine and were sanctioned for the way they'd policed the game.

The season was stagnating. Once again, we were in mid-table, and everyone knew I was leaving. Dennis didn't get on with the chairman-elect and he made it clear he wouldn't be too far behind me out of the door. I didn't want to saddle Jeff with a deficit of £2.5 million. So at the end of the season I sold Darren Ward to Crystal Palace and Paul Ifill to Sheffield United for about £2.25 million. Tim Cahill had already been sold to Everton for £2 million before the season started because he was in his last year of contract and had made it clear he was not going to sign a new one, which meant he could leave the club on a free transfer at the end of the season. On top of that, I put in another £1 million of my own money to balance the books so the new chairman could start with a clean sheet. In fairness, I was chairman for that last season so the deficit had happened on my watch.

Once Dennis had gone, Jeff decided he was going to appoint a manager, but he did it without consulting the board. Of course, I had also made unilateral decisions when I was chairman, but I would at least back them with my own money. Jeff couldn't do the same. So the first I heard about it was when he rang me up to say he was holding a press conference the next morning to unveil the new man. And then he told me who he had chosen: Steve Claridge.

My heart sank. Now I love Steve; he's one of the nicest blokes I've ever met, and I brought him to Millwall. I had signed Steve and Tony Cottee during our promotion year because our two strikers, Neil Harris and Paul Moody, had been sent off and were suspended for our next match against Bristol Rovers. The only players I could get at such short notice were Steve and

Tony. Steve was about ninety-four and Tony wasn't much younger! But I loved both of them. Tony's contract negotiations had been swift and easy, but Steve took a different approach, insisting he would be our best player. He also warned me that Mark McGhee might not want him at the club, as they'd fallen out when they'd both been at Wolves, but he told me he'd talk him round.

So I rang McGoo, who was in Spain with the team as we had a week off because of internationals, to tell him I'd found a couple of strikers. He was surprised about Tony Cottee, thinking he'd moved into management, but when he heard the other one was Steve Claridge I thought the line had gone dead and then McGoo said, 'No, no way.'

I put Steve on to him and he persuaded McGoo to take him. In the end, he played for us for almost three seasons and worked his nuts off and became an icon at our place. He was probably the fittest person in the team for most of the time and became a good mate of mine.

Anyway, Jeff agreed to cancel the press conference to announce Steve as our new manager and we had a board meeting instead. Eventually he got his way and appointed Steve. Very soon things started going badly wrong. Board members were receiving phone calls directly from players, saying they wanted to go on the transfer list, and that they couldn't work with Steve.

His budget for the next season and his transfer dealings also caused me concern. In the end, he got the message and stood down – and once more we didn't have a chairman. I didn't want to take the chair but offered to help find another chairman, on the basis that I had supported Jeff for the job in the first place, so I was partly to blame. In the end, I did reluctantly take back the reins, but as I was also filming *Dragons' Den* at the time I had too much on to do the job as well as I would have liked.

One of my first actions once I was back in charge was to sack Claridge, basically because some of the players were refusing to play for him. He had lasted only thirty-seven days – and in that time we didn't play a single competitive game. I think it was a record at the time, although one manager was sacked recently on the day he was appointed.

I got stick from the fans for getting rid of Steve. They liked him, as did I, but they had no idea what was going on behind the scenes and I have no doubt his continued presence would have been detrimental to the club if he had been allowed to carry on much longer. I put Steve's number two, Colin Lee, in temporary charge.

Now we were looking for a new manager as well as a new chairman. Halfway through 2005–6 we found Peter de Savary, the well-known entrepreneur and yachtsman. In November 2005, he agreed to take on the chairmanship of both the football club and Millwall Holdings plc, at which point I resigned from the board. Later de Savary brought in Stewart Till to take over as chairman of the club.

Now de Savary has gone, some Americans have taken over, although Till is still there, and Millwall are struggling. With all the turbulence, at the end of the season when I left they got relegated to the Second Division so all that hard work getting them into the Championship had been wasted – and believe me, nothing saddens me more.

In retrospect, I did the right thing, however much I miss it. I was spreading myself too thin. On top of my role at Millwall, I was chief executive and chairman of Ryman, Partners, Contessa and La Senza. Our group turnover was now approaching £170 million with 3,000 staff and two head offices, in Crewe and Hayes. I was beginning to feel, as I had at Astra, that I was running myself ragged. It was getting to the point where I was doing something I had promised I would never do – allowing my business and other interests to detract from family life. Something had to give.

I had a choice: either get rid of some of my businesses and devote more time to Millwall or jettison the football club. It was a no-brainer really. After all, Millwall didn't make me a penny so choosing them would not have been very clever financially. I decided that my adventure with football would have to be curtailed for the moment. Maybe it's something I will pick up on again later. But I knew I couldn't walk away from the businesses. I had to make sure they were growing and expanding.

Chapter Eighteen

Dealing with Digital and the sharks

The previous chapter showed how difficult it was for a club the size of Millwall to compete on the pitch, and to keep everything on an even keel. I feel very proud about what we achieved, but none of this would have been possible without making sure the financial side of things worked out properly. There were two elements to this: how I ran the club myself, and how all the clubs in the Football League were run by that body. My role at Millwall wasn't just about what I did, it meant I was involved in various meetings with the Football League and the FA. Coming from a non-league environment at Walton and Hersham, I expected that the professional game would conduct itself, well, professionally. But I was very mistaken. In fact, I was absolutely staggered when I attended my first Football League meeting as chairman of Millwall to find it was like a throwback to the Wild West.

There were conflicts of interest at every corner. There were seventy-two clubs represented and there must have been an equal number of different opinions. Of course, football has always been highly politicised, never more so than when the Premier League broke away from the Football League. But I certainly wasn't expecting so many self-interests to be in evidence.

At the time of the breakaway, the Premier League asked the Football League to go along with them and be part of a joint TV deal. But the grey suits without the grey cells who were then running the Football League waved away the offer like a referee refusing a stone-bonking penalty. Not a good business decision as it turned out. There have been various rumours about what was on the table, but I understand that the Football League was offered between 25 and 30 per cent of the television money, though they didn't want it – they wanted to do their own deal. Looking at the sort of money the Premier League is getting now from television, it was a pretty bad call. The Football League felt they were being offered the crumbs from the Premiership table – well, even back then they looked like bloody big loaves to me.

I spoke briefly at the first couple of Football League meetings I attended, but nobody seemed to listen to a word I said because I had only been in the game two minutes, while some of them appeared to have been there since the league was founded more than a hundred years ago.

But I started to become really vocal when the league agreed to ITV Digital being their broadcast partner. We were told it would increase clubs' income enormously and that it was a fantastic deal with all this new money sloshing around. On offer was £315 million, spread over three years. For Millwall, this meant a good seven-figure sum each season. Therefore, for 2002–3, the first season it came into operation, we had allowed for all this extra income in our budget.

ITV Digital had been set up by the independent TV companies in a bid to rival Sky. The difference, of course, was that ITV was able to deliver via existing aerials, whereas Sky needed subscribers to buy satellite dishes and set top boxes. But ITV needed their customers to purchase digital boxes instead of Sky boxes so they were buying up sports events, just as Sky had done so successfully, to entice viewers.

Unfortunately, the business plan was flawed and it was no surprise to me that they went bust in their first year. This left Millwall, and other clubs, with a huge hole in our finances. We couldn't cut pay to our players, because of their contracts, and it was hard to sell any of them to cover our losses, because all the other Football League clubs were suffering too, and so had no funds to sign up new players. There was a real danger that Millwall would go bust, along with many other clubs. Thankfully, there was some interim assistance from the Football Foundation and that went some way to relieving the financial pressure. It gave us valuable breathing space to reorganise our finances.

The mistake ITV Digital had made was that they had forgotten that to make it work they needed to attract viewers – a lot of them. Now it should have been clear that for a large number of people, they'd always prefer what the Premier League had to offer. But that wasn't the only problem: crucially, the Football League had failed to get parent company guarantees. The deal was only with the subsidiary, ITV Digital, and not with ITV itself. All of a sudden our new-found wealth had disappeared down the tubes and we were searching desperately for a new broadcast partner. And the board was left with little option but to go back to the people they'd upset by ignoring the last time: Sky. They told us that their budgets had mostly been spent, and besides they already had the games that most people wanted to watch.

The incompetence of the negotiation team not to wrap up a parent company guarantee from what was a new company led to several court cases, all of which, predictably, the league lost, incurring further expense and humiliation into the bargain. The league claimed that a parent company guarantee was discussed and expected but the final document was never completed and nowhere in the agreement was 'parent company guarantee' mentioned. However, in court, ITV said they would not have provided such a guarantee even if the league had insisted on one.

Sky eventually signed up to show Football League matches, but at a fraction of the price ITV Digital had agreed, so all the clubs were faced with a massive shortfall in TV income. The new deal was bundled through with almost indecent haste. They said it was the best deal in town, but what was clear was that they had hurried it through in case it was the only deal in town. Given the failures in the original negotiation and the new deal, the club chairmen lost all confidence in our ruling body. As this was Millwall's first year in the First Division and we'd worked very hard to get there, we wanted our fair share of the riches, but when we got there those riches had disappeared.

You can imagine that those of us with an ounce of business acumen were quite vocal. I got more than my fair share of airtime because I was a new boy in the First Division and had plenty to say on what had gone wrong. Suddenly, I was invited to special meetings and there was the whiff of mutiny in the air. We'd already had one breakaway, with the Premiership big boys saying goodbye. Yet here was the First Division contemplating another one and the chance to do our own TV deal. In fact, much of the talk was a knee-jerk reaction by some of the so-called bigger clubs who had been relegated from the Premiership and were used to sharing TV income with the likes of Manchester United and Arsenal, not Rotherham and Rochdale.

I came from grass-roots football and believed the league should stick together, acting as a single, unified unit. And while there were a few very vocal people talking about going it alone, it wasn't practical, it wasn't realistic, it wasn't commercially sound and it wasn't morally right either, because it would have meant casting away the rest of the Football League. It would have been the end of the Football League as we know it. So, led by myself and a few others, including my good friends Simon Jordan from Crystal Palace (Millwall's arch-enemies) and Charles Koppel, who was public enemy number one even at his own club, Wimbledon, which he wanted to relocate to Milton Keynes, we fought very hard against some very experienced football people.

Now, while mentioning my very good personal friend Simon Jordan, I must mention the first time we played 'Crippled Alice' (Crystal Palace) at 'Shithurst Park' (Selhurst Park) after our promotion to Division One. He very kindly replaced my chairman's seat in the stand with a toilet pan and decked out his boardroom in the Grecian style, complete with a doner-kebab machine (too ignorant to realise this was a greek product), at the same time playing a video of me on the large screen in the stadium claiming 'I must be mad!' It did not seem to matter since we beat them comfortably and I had the last laugh.

At Millwall, we were on a different flight path to those who were struggling to cope in the Football League, having come up from the Second Division. We were used to working on a lower budget. Because I was passionate about staying with the Football League and trying to make changes from within, I became a sort of unofficial spokesman for the cause, with a lot of support from other smaller clubs. But I was rapidly becoming a thorn in the side of the Football League and, in an attempt to silence me, I was appointed to one of their many sub-committees, called the Review Panel. It was clear they had no intention of taking a blind bit of notice of me; I had been shunted off into a siding.

I called a meeting of the Football League through my membership of the Review Panel and was told that the new chairman, Brian Mawhinney, would be attending as an observer. I proceeded to give a slide presentation on the shambolic dealings of the Football League. I highlighted the deals they shouldn't have done but did and the deals they should have done but didn't. It was a wide-ranging and all-embracing condemnation of the organisation. The one slide showing their good points was left blank deliberately. Mawhinney, at the back of the room, must have been shifting uneasily in his seat.

The presentation received thunderous applause – even the three Football League first division directors were in agreement. It was agreed that changes had to be made and that this should include the re-election of the first division's representatives on the Football League board. So, together with David Sheepshanks of Ipswich and Sheffield United's Terry Robinson, I was one of the three new boys on the Football League board and FA Council.

I came up with various ideas about the structure of the league management, but I also felt we needed to re-brand and freshen up the league. As an example I said the First Division should change its name to the Championship. Subsequently, the league, as part of its reorganisation, paid a lot of money to consultants to come up with exactly the same name. I suggested looking for new sponsors and that we should increase our commercial activities to try to close the ever-widening gap between the Premier League and ourselves.

This took place at the same time as Brian Mawhinney was appointed Chairman of the Football League which proved to be pivotal. For the first time we had a talented and experienced individual who was far more commercial than his CV as a career politician would suggest. He presided over some incredibly tense board meetings, but in the end the breakaway by the First Division was avoided and a vital battle had been won. I felt all the hard work I had put into quelling the revolt had been hugely worthwhile. Brian, using all his political nous, allowed the First Division sides to have a greater say in league affairs without somehow alienating the other two divisions. It was quite a feat, but he managed to achieve it.

Eventually, when we did re-brand at the start of 2004–5, the First Division became the Championship and the Second and Third Divisions were renamed League One and League Two. We had a new sponsor as well – Millwall were now playing in the Coca-Cola Championship. In that first season, attendances rose by about 10 per cent to the highest level since the early 1950s, matching those of Serie A in Italy. Re-branding the Football League as 'real football for real fans' and getting back to the grass roots played an important part in the increase in popularity. That then enabled us to negotiate a new television deal with far greater rewards. Suddenly, the whole thing seemed to be in safe hands, and I felt I had helped move it there.

I think one of my biggest disappointments, however, was that having been elected to the FA Council, I never stayed on board long enough to make changes within that organisation. That said, I felt that I could have stuck around for twenty years before making any significant difference. But I wasn't going to sacrifice my life trying to change the FA.

So there was plenty of politics involved at boardroom level in running a football club, and the outcome of those negotiations could have a huge impact, as we have seen on all clubs. But at our own club level, there were more complications. Someone once told me that the finances of football are the finances of the asylum. I can't remember who, but I do remember he was involved in football and so, by definition, slightly mad. I didn't really appreciate the importance of what he'd said until I had been in football for a season and those words would constantly ring in my ears at every board meeting and every time we needed to announce our financial figures. Because Millwall is a public company, we needed to do this for the half-year and full-year results. As it was a rare occasion when we had the luxury of announcing a profit, it was always about containing losses.

I remember when I first got involved with the club after we salvaged it out of administration and I gave interviews to the media stating how I would run the club just like any other of my businesses and we would have to live within our means. Well, it took till the first time we sat down to cut the first real budget since taking charge that I realised what we would have to live with.

By this time, I had had a chance to talk to all the playing staff and many of the fans, and it became clear that the only way we could balance the books was by virtue of a consistent spell of success on the pitch, which would attract more fans. Even doing this was not an easy thing, when you take into account Millwall fans' terrible, but unjustifiable and unwarranted, reputation. The real measure of success was if we could gain promotion to Division One, where the Football League television award money was much greater than in Division Two. Just to give you an idea what a difference this would make, for every pound the Football League received in TV broadcast money, 80p went to the First Division, now known as the Championship, 13p to the Second Division, now known as League One, and 7p to the Third Division, now known as League Two. Beyond that, of course, was the Premier League, where the top sides can earn more in TV revenue than the whole of the Football League put together, a real imbalance of income.

As we've seen, when I joined, Millwall were in the second tier of the Football League, so we needed to move up one division if we were to enjoy a larger income. In addition to the basic awards, a club also receives money every time it appears on television, but the choice of who appears on TV is taken by the broadcasters, and they tend to choose teams doing well at the top of the respective divisions.

The other way to boost revenue was to have a good cup run, where the further you progress, the greater your share of the prize pot. Even more valuable than that, and having your cup tie shown on TV, was if you were drawn against a big Premier League team away from home. In that case, you would also enjoy in the share of the gate receipts for that game. Just to put this one into perspective, our share of the gate receipts at a cup game of one of the big Premiership clubs could be up to as much as our walk-up home gate receipts for the entire season.

So the business model was easy: all we needed to do was be successful and the money would roll in. There was one slight problem in executing this particular strategy, other than the fact that there were seventy-one other clubs trying to achieve exactly the same thing. When I looked at our income from gate receipts, TV money, commercial activities plus all ancillary income and then paid out all the minimum necessary expenses to run the club, including the stadium and youth academy, we had only enough money left to pay the wages of a small band of very average players and youngsters, who, far from getting us promotion or success, would probably get us relegated to the bottom tier of the Football League. This in turn would reduce our TV money and gate receipts, and we would enter a vicious circle spiralling downwards.

It became clear to me that in the world of football, our problem was not unique. It was one that was shared by most, if not all, the league clubs and obviously a normal model of running a business would not work. I looked to see if we could construct one that would be different, but as hard as we tried, we kept arriving at the one I was hoping to keep away from: running a negative budget every year to maintain a squad of players that will be capable of delivering success and hope this would in turn generate income and thus bridge the funding gap. In the long term, the target was to get to the Premier League, because once you reach that level the money generated can bring in the profits. Even if the club were to be relegated after only one season, the parachute money from the Premier League would still put us on a much better footing. The main problem with that model, of course, is it depended on us achieving success; without it, we had further losses to cover.

Every season we would start with a budget deficit of anything ranging from £1–4 million and no idea where we would end up in May. During the season, if things weren't going well, we would need to spend more money on players to avoid relegation (making our deficit worse than budgeted). On the other hand, if we were doing well, we would need to sign new players to give us a greater chance of achieving our goal of getting to the next level or to continue our cup run, which would generate more income.

Depending on our assessment of the playing squad, we would decide every season on how adventurous we would be. In real business, this would be known as the risk-reward ratio, something I'm very familiar with in my normal day-to-day business life. If we thought we had a chance of promotion, we would take the gamble. If not, we would try to contain our losses.

On those occasions we decided to go for it, we signed off the budget with a large deficit. When the gamble failed, we would then have to find the money to bridge the gap through loans from the directors or, more usually, by launching a rights issue to the shareholders, which obviously included the directors. The fresh capital from the issue of shares, coupled with a small amount of sustainable borrowings, would get us through the next season. Those seasons when we got to Wembley, the FA Cup final or won promotion were obviously good ones where we beat our pre-season budget. Achieving these things generated millions of pounds for us, which obviously went towards bridging some, if not all, of the deficit and meant we could start the next season without carrying forward any extra debts.

But even successful seasons caused us problems. Rightly, the fans are always ambitious beyond reasonable expectation, and they expect you to splash out big in the following season on the basis that you have banked a fair amount of money. They totally ignore the fact that you had to gamble and speculate at the beginning of that good season with a large deficit, so the rewards derived from the success simply went to cover the original wager. What a game!

I remember one occasion, the season after we got to the FA Cup final, we were well beaten by Wigan at home, and some of the fans began a chant of 'Where's the money gone?' to the tune of that famous 1970s hit 'Chirpy Chirpy Cheep Cheep' by Middle of the Road. So, in my naivety, I tried to explain in the following home programme the finances of the club and where the money actually went. This was very helpful to the minority that bothered to read it, but the rest just continued to sing 'Where's the money gone?'

The only other way you could deal with the financial problems was by buying and selling players. But, unlike any other business I've been involved in, if I sold a key asset I'd have several thousand people telling me what they thought of me on a Saturday afternoon, especially if we were losing. On the other hand, a popular buy and a win and I'd be everyone's favourite. The difficulty for any chairman is taking the right decision for the club, rather than the one that gets you the biggest cheer from the fans.

But at least the problems of budgeting and dealing with fans' expectations were an acceptable part of the business. What I found much harder to accept was salary inflation and the demands of agents. Now I will touch on those little devils known as agents later, but with players' pay it seemed no matter how much money we were able to raise from broadcast rights and commercial activities, all we and other clubs did was give it straight to the players and agents in our competitiveness to sign the best available talent. It was just uncanny. Football clubs seem to do this every time there is any smell of increased income. There was talk of a wage cap and one was actually briefly introduced for the lower division, but the bigger club chairmen were having none of it as they wanted to run things in the way they chose, without outside interference.

But all club chairmen had to deal with agents, and this aspect of the business was something that none of my previous experiences had prepared me for. I was totally astonished at how much money was leaving the game by virtue of payments to football agents. Obviously it was justifiable that they should get something, but the level was certainly not. One of the achievements I look back on with great satisfaction from my time on the League Board was the implementation of a league table for payments to agents published at the end of every season so we would have transparency and fans could see where their money was going. In fairness to Football League clubs, the biggest culprits were, and still are, the Premier League clubs where a million pound fee to an agent is not unusual.

One of the reasons I take issue with agents is because of the role of clubs in developing young players. At Millwall, as with most other clubs, we would take a boy from the age of eight and invest in him, train him and mentor him until he reaches the age of sixteen, when we could sign him as an apprentice. Then, between the age of sixteen to eighteen, he gets a chance to play in the youth team, reserve team or maybe the first team. Depending on his progress and performances, we would then take the decision to offer him a professional contract, the pinnacle of a very short football career, and the prize he has been working towards for more than half his life.

To celebrate this momentous achievement, we would invite his parents and family to attend a signing ceremony at the stadium, often people the club has known for years. In a lot of cases, the club would have supported them during difficult times, whether it be with financial or personal help. Usually, the boy and the family have shown respect and gratitude to the club for its efforts in looking after him. So all in all, this should turn out to be a very pleasant and enjoyable experience for all concerned.

Well, not always. One of the first times I participated in this event, it didn't quite go the way I expected. The morning before the player was due to sign, I received a phone call from a man who introduced himself in a very matey and familiar way. He then proceeded to tell me that apparently I had made an offer of a contract to one of his players, and he would like to come in and see me to carry out the negotiations, and of course agree a personal fee for himself in negotiating the contract. Now, I was new and inexperienced, but even I had worked out that something didn't quite sound right, because I had already been briefed by my academy team with regard to this boy. I knew that we had trained him at the club since an early age through our academy system, which happened to be a very large expense line on our profit and loss account but did produce some fantastic home-grown players. In some cases, Millwall would eventually transfer them to bigger clubs for a fee, which went some way to covering the cost of the academy.

Now I decided to play a little dumb and asked him how he had any claim on this young lad, as we held his registration and had done so for some years. What had happened was this inarticulate chancer had been hanging around outside the training ground watching the kids come out of training and befriending them. He would then try to impress them with his car and the number of well-known people he was connected to, repeating stories of great deals that he had negotiated with other clubs for his players and how he could do the same for them if they agreed that he could represent them. Suddenly, what should have been a happy occasion for all concerned had become a battle.

After having my patience stretched to breaking point, within a few years I had adopted a new name for the profession of football agents, 'scumbags'. Not very flattering or polite, I know, but I had just had enough. There were three main reasons that drove me to give up football and my beloved Millwall. Pressure on my time; the half-wits that run the FA; and lastly, the scumbags that represent players, called agents. Not everyone engaged in the so-called profession of football agent was in fact a scumbag, but I must say the majority I had to deal with definitely fell within this category. Of course, some agents acted professionally and realistically and in the best interests of their clients, and those we affectionately called 'nice scumbags'. In fact, one of the nice scumbags, who shall remain nameless, in correspondence with me would often sign his name as 'scummy (nice)', which has remained a standing joke with me and this individual to this day.

But on a more serious note, sometimes the demands weren't just excessive, they were illegal. There has been a lot of coverage in the press and on TV about so-called 'bungs' in football, but so far no one has really got to grips with it. In my experience, many agents were looking for a bung, and it wasn't simply in a way that was immoral, or against some obscure FA ruling; what they asked for was illegal.

Usually this came about when an agent would ask the club, rather than the player, to pay his commission on a contract or transfer negotiation. This type of arrangement throws up several serious concerns. The most obvious one is the danger of there being a conflict of interest: the club and the agent might agree to a lower wage for the player if the agent got a bigger commission. The second objection, partly because of this fear, is that FA rules quite clearly say that an agent can only act and accept fees from the principal, i.e. the player or club, not both. But the third objection is the most important one of all: by doing this, you have just participated in a scam to defraud the Inland Revenue of tax which would otherwise be due to them, because the fee the club pays to the agent should obviously have been paid by the player.

Let's say, for example, the agent's commission is £100,000 for a few hours' work. If the club has just paid that sum, which should have been paid by the player who is the person he is representing, it is effectively a benefit. This means that the player should pay tax at the higher rate (i.e. 40 per cent) of earnings on the £100,000, in other words £40,000. Instead, because the club has paid the fee and treated it as a cost to the club and not declared it as a benefit to the player, the club gets tax relief on the sum as an expense and the player has no liability.

This is highly illegal, but I was told by many agents when I arrived in the professional game that this was quite normal and that I should get used to it. It did not matter how many times I had the conversation with agents. I was not having it, and this made me very unpopular with them. Sometimes it even upset our own players, who would rarely be given the full story by their agent, and they ended up thinking that I was being penny-pinching and not appreciative of their talents, work and position in the team. They couldn't have been more wrong. I just did not want to break the law and end up getting to know the agent and the player better by virtue of sharing a prison cell.

I was very fortunate with all my managers as they were completely honest and straight. But to be fair to many in the business who get caught up in an agent's demands, it may be that they get confused by what is going on and don't understand the ramifications. Because I was always closely involved in our contract and transfer negotiations, I could make sure we never came a cropper. There was, however, one occasion where we nearly did. I was eventually able to sort things out, but at a price.

It happened when a representative of a football agency was negotiating the contract of one of our better players. This agent had latched on to this player at an early stage, and it was in the best interest of the player and the club that we review his contract regularly so it was in keeping with his rising status in the team. On this occasion, the agent had called with his demands for a new contract for his client. In our conversation, he managed to get up my nose even more than normal for an agent, and by the end of it we agreed to meet the following day.

He proved to be no less obnoxious in the flesh than he was on the phone. After a lengthy discussion and negotiation, I had had enough and left him with a take-it-or-leave-it offer followed by a near-physical removal from the stadium, since he seemed to have made himself very comfortable and acted as if he owned the joint. This was taking confidence a step too far, but for some reason he seemed to feel he had the upper hand because of the not-so-veiled threat that he would move the player to another club that would pay him the money he thought the player was worth. We both also knew that the agent could expect to be rewarded handsomely for bringing the player to the new club, whereas he would receive less for simply renegotiating his contract to stay with Millwall.

During the negotiation, I had made it clear that we would not be paying the agent a fee, since he was acting for the player and was thus employed by the player, who was responsible for paying his fee. He took serious umbrage to this, because he had previously told the player during his pitch to represent him that the club would pay all the agent's fees. He knew it would be very difficult to go back and demand payment from the player, especially as he would have to disclose to the player the outrageous and unjustifiable fees that he was demanding for his services, which seemed to consist of little more than a few hours' work.

He knew that it was always easier to get payment from the club than the player. Clubs tend to have a bigger cheque book, and their client had no need to know how much his agent received from the club. (In fairness, in most cases the player did not want to know how much the agent received as long as he did not have to put his hand in his pocket.)

I left for a holiday shortly after this meeting and delegated the final negotiations to my manager on the terms I indicated to the agent. I was not surprised to receive a call while lying by the pool from the manager to say that he was struggling to conclude the contract on those terms and could he have a little latitude with which to sweeten the deal, and persuade the player and agent to put pen to paper. I agreed to this small change.

On my return, I was informed that the player had signed the new contract on near-identical terms to the ones I had offered, and after all the stress, it seemed all's well that ends well. Or maybe not. There was a sting in the tail which taught me a very valuable lesson. From that day onwards, I made sure I took a very healthy interest in all transactions right till the end, much to the annoyance of many individuals.

What happened was this: some time after the deal had been signed, I received a call from a senior official at the football club stating that this particular agent was chasing payment of an invoice. During the manager's negotiations with him, the agent had somehow assumed that we would pay his fees and when the point was subsequently clarified by my colleague that we would not, he went straight back to the player and told him we had reneged on what was agreed and that the player would have to pay his fee. He claimed this showed we did not value his player, who was now unsettled, and went to the manager complaining that he had been treated badly by the chairman and the club and that he was thinking of putting in a transfer request.

I asked the official to make a file note of what they discussed and send it to me prior to calling the agent myself. Thus began the most bizarre and worrying conversation I ever had in the world of football. Nothing had prepared me for what followed, but given the sensitivity of what I thought was likely to crop up, I decided to keep a record of it before we got started. For those who have ever wondered how these people operate, I hope the following will prove enlightening.

The agent began by claiming, 'We have a one-page agreement with you where you basically instruct us to give you European or international scouting information, so we are employed by you to give you that information and we charge you a fee, so it will be in this case twenty-eight grand.'

I knew he had done no such work for the club, and in fact this was the sum the player owed him in commission, which we could not pay him. He replied that it was being done like this so the player did 'not have to pay the tax . . . we put it through as a sort of consulting bill, either for scouting information or to consult on a new stadium or anything really' because in this way 'who is gonna be aware that it's anything to do with' him? I pointed out that this would be breaking the law, as what he was suggesting was tax evasion.

We circled round the topic for a while, and I admitted that if we had agreed to pay the agent's commission on behalf of the player (which can sometimes happen), we would have done it in the proper way, via the Football League, and so the player would have had to pay tax on this benefit. But that clearly wasn't what he was suggesting here. I was intrigued to find out if he had done anything like this before. He mentioned one or two international deals he'd been involved in, but I was more interested to hear about UK deals, as foreign tax set-ups might be different to ours. He then told me about some Premier

League clubs where he'd had this arrangement, both for transfer deals and for contract renegotiations.

He claimed that the FA rules had been set up merely to prevent both players and the club paying an agent during negotiations, and so 'what we're talking about here is flouting the rules.' If a small-time agent had put in an invoice saying that they could provide scouting information 'it looks dodgy, whereas we can legitimately produce information for you that you won't be able to get yourself, [so to the] naked eye it's a . . . legitimate deal.'

I tried to return him to the subject of whether he'd done something similar with any of the top clubs, and he told me not only about some very big deals, but also with teams smaller than us, all done on a similar basis with scouting fees being used to cover it all up.

In the end, we had to reach a deal whereby we loaned the player a sum of £28,000, cleared it with the league and he had to pay tax on the benefit of the loan. Then on renewal of his contract, gave him a payrise of a gross figure which netted down to £28,000, which he then used to repay the loan; in effect it cost us nearly double what it would have had we paid the agent in the illegal way he had originally suggested. But in this way, we had kept our noses clean, the player was happy and no worse off than his agent had promised, and the agent got his money after all. So for anyone who thinks that I've spoken harshly about agents when I described them as 'scumbags', I hope this ensures you'll understand why.

Chapter Nineteen

Meeting the Dragons

Towards the end of my tenure at Millwall, I became involved with *Dragons' Den*. Prior to becoming a Dragon, I had a bit of television experience in my role at Millwall and had given scores of interviews about the club. I was always able to give a quote on all things football and because I had risen through the ranks from Walton and Hersham via Millwall to being on the Football League and the Football Association, I was much in demand.

During my early days at the New Den, BBC TV even followed me around for a week for a one-hour special called *Back to the Floor*. This programme went out on BBC2 and lived up to its label – it put bosses back on the shop floor to see how they fared doing menial tasks. I did everything, working in the club shop, cleaning up the terraces and helping out at the training ground, where I served the players in the canteen, much to their amusement. I cut the grass on the pitch in the pouring rain and took abuse from away fans serving pie and chips in the kiosks at the ground one match day. I even had to get up on a ladder and change a light bulb, despite my protests that I suffered from an acute form of vertigo.

So although I was surprised when I was approached by the *Dragons' Den* production team, I did have a bit of 'previous' and I

222

suppose the BBC must have seen some potential in me. I did, however, have serious misgivings about doing the programme, even though it was potentially a major breakthrough for me. The way the BBC went about recruiting me was unconventional – and did nothing to allay my fears that the show wasn't right for me.

The BBC persuaded me to go down to Television Centre to discuss joining *Dragons' Den*. To my surprise, when I got there, they had some people there to pitch to me. In effect, it was a screen test. One of the ideas pitched to me was absolute rubbish, while the other was actually very good, but neither needed money.

I told the guys with the good idea that I wouldn't invest in them because they didn't need the money, but that I thought they had a great product and that they should contact me if I could do anything to help them. They had developed a language tutorial on CD, all set to music. The pair liked languages and liked music and had developed a way in which you could learn to speak a language by singing songs.

When the 'interview' (screen test) was over, they told me they wanted me for the show, and after some negotiation I left and continued on my way into London. On the way, I recalled the boys' demonstration and realised I could remember all the words they had taught me during their three-minute pitch. If it could work on me, a dyslexic, it was bound to work on others. So when they got in touch, I was really pleased to hear from them. They called their product Earworms and produced a marketing plan. In fact, they even had an offer from the *Sun* to do a giveaway deal, which they decided against because they would have killed their market and it was also very expensive.

It can now be downloaded on iTunes and we are selling it at Ryman, where it's been a huge success for us and for them. They have done incredibly well with it – and it never appeared on *Dragons' Den*, only in my casting session.

There is nothing fake about *Dragons' Den* – it's real in every sense of the word. We haven't a clue who – or what – might be coming up those stairs. People think we're primed about the people and products in each programme, but we're not. So, in that sense, my casting session was exactly like the real thing. Maybe that was the purpose of the subtefuge. The producers have their own idea whether something might be worth investing in or not, but actually they haven't got a clue. Their skills are in the world of television, not in the world of business.

When I joined *Dragons' Den*, my fellow Dragons were Peter Jones, Doug Richard, Duncan Bannatyne and Rachel Elnaugh. I was replacing Yo! Sushi founder Simon Woodroffe, who was dropped after Series One. I remember I was in Barbados for our company conference when I got a call from Peter, which woke me up because of the time difference. He wanted to congratulate me after being told I was going to be joining the programme. I had met Peter a couple of times before because he was in mobile phones and at one time his company, Phones International, had supplied us with mobiles. I found him a nice enough guy, but we never were close friends. We were just acquaintances.

I had seen bits of the show but had never watched an entire episode, so I asked the BBC to send me the first series on DVD. I watched it in the car, which is often the only place where I have the time to watch things – my chauffeur, of course, was behind the wheel. Having watched the DVD, I was a little concerned that I had agreed to do it. But there was no going back now. I have a fun outlook on life and business, and felt the show was way too serious. It appeared to be aimed at an audience of accountants, solicitors and business people. I thought it had no appeal for the ordinary man or woman in the street. How wrong can you be?

I turned up on my first day at a big old warehouse, just off

Commercial Road, and was given a seat between Peter and Doug, who were perfectly charming and polite, but seemed very full of their own importance. Doug, who is a prolific investor in high-tech companies, certainly knew his stuff. He's a very analytical guy and very intellectual, but not the sort of person I would normally be rubbing shoulders with. He frightened me!

Peter is very charismatic, but that didn't come across on the show because I think he had adopted the demeanour of everybody else. Later he was to become my closest ally in the Den and one of my dearest friends, once he had lightened up a little, for which I take full credit. Then, of course, there was Duncan, who is your archetypal Scotsman and who plays the part very well. He is, after all, the only Equity card-holder among the Dragons and he had been taking acting lessons, though *Dragons' Den* probably wasn't in his mind when he started them. He's a very good businessman but you got the feeling that he was looking for his own space and hadn't quite found it.

And then there was Rachel. Well, what can I say about Rachel? With all the other Dragons, whatever their good points and bad points, you knew that they were hugely successful entrepreneurs. Indeed, some of the girls working within my own businesses were and are far more impressive. Her PR image was that she was successful and incredibly wealthy, but I couldn't see where this wealth and success was. I hadn't bothered to analyse her wealth because it was none of my business, although as the shows continued I became more and more intrigued by her.

She didn't exactly welcome me with open arms, quite the reverse. She was very cold towards me, although she gave me one piece of advice for which I will always remain grateful. The BBC felt, like me, that the show was a bit flat and told me to bring in a selection of suits. I made the mistake of taking a light-coloured one with me, which they thought was exactly what I should be wearing because it would break up the greyness of everybody else.

But when I saw the stills I looked like a cross between a pretzel salesman and John Travolta in *Saturday Night Fever*. I think Rachel had more idea about fashion than all the other Dragons put together and she just looked at me and shook her head. That shake of the head said something like, 'If you wear that on television, you're going to look a right plonker.' I quickly went back to wardrobe and put on a black suit with a black shirt and I've stuck with that colour scheme ever since.

I was nervous when I started in the Den, but I was amazed at how quickly I took to it. Mind you, I had spent most of my working life interviewing people who had come to me with their business proposals – precisely what we had to do on every programme. That part wasn't difficult; what I did find hard was all the hanging around between pitches and having those studio lights shining on you, especially during the height of the summer.

Series Two wasn't shot in the same place as Series One because that particular warehouse wasn't available. The Beeb found another warehouse, but they wanted to replicate the first. So what did they do? They built a set that looked like the first warehouse inside the second warehouse! I never could get my head round that.

On our first day, shooting started early in the morning, but it wasn't long before the director called cut, saying he wasn't happy with the set, which meant a visit from the BBC's bigwigs in the afternoon. There were a lot of comings and goings, and a lot of hanging around for everyone else. There was even talk that the show was going to be scrapped altogether because they didn't feel the set looked authentic enough. In the end the powers-that-be decided they could live with it, but we wasted a whole day.

The hanging around was getting to me. You would build yourself up to listen to a pitch that might go on for hours, even though most of it would end up on the cutting room floor, and the public would only see a few minutes of it on the box. So when people see you get bad-tempered or take a hard line with somebody, they think it's unfair. But if they'd sat there in the sweltering heat for hours, listening to someone who's a bit over-confident talking absolute rubbish, they'd react too.

It didn't happen immediately, but things came to a head for me when a guy who was running what he described as an 'ambient advertising agency' had been on set for several hours. He had really pissed me off, because I knew something about the marketing, sponsorship and advertising business through Movie and Media Sports where we advertised around sports grounds. I knew the audience, I knew how much we paid staff, what the rates were, and this guy was talking nonsense. Every time I questioned him about some of his numbers he'd attack me as if I didn't know what I was on about. In the end I had to put him right because he needed to be straightened out. But he still wouldn't accept what I was saying. I think in the end I said something like 'I'd rather stick pins in my eyes than invest in you.'

It wasn't the sort of thing that had been said in the previous series and when we went off set the other Dragons assured me it would be taken out in the final edit. The fact that my more cutting remarks could – and probably would – be edited out comforted me. I thought I could be myself and leave the show's producers and editors to decide what was and wasn't suitable for a BBC2 audience. I could just get on with giving a proper investment critique without worrying that it might upset some of the viewers. So I proceeded, during the course of the series, to say things like 'The wheel's going round but the hamster died a long time ago' or 'I'd rather pass a kidney stone than invest in this', safe in the knowledge that it was never going to be aired.

You can imagine my shock when the series had been edited and part of the promotional trailer contained the phrase 'I'd rather stick pins in my eyes than invest in this.' The producers had decided comments like this would make the programme appeal to a wider audience and that my involvement brought a different dimension, a down-to-earth and simplistic approach to business. I have always believed that business is very simple, it's the people involved in business that make it complicated.

The people at the Beeb were proved right again and the audience figures were double that of the previous series, which was a tremendous achievement. And not only did the audience double, it changed dramatically. There might have been a few more bank managers and accountants tuning in, but even they couldn't account for the huge increase. That was made up of a much wider cross section of the viewing public, including schoolchildren, students and housewives. In fact, everyone seemed to be watching *Dragons' Den*.

I often quote Napoleon who said the British were a nation of shopkeepers. Well, a shopkeeper is a small business person and that's what we are. He was dead right. The fact that anyone can run his or her own business is attractive to the British public. Everyone feels they can be successful and that's why *Dragons' Den* was becoming so popular: here was an investment programme that you didn't need a degree in business studies to understand. It wasn't like *The Money Programme* on the same channel; *Dragons' Den* appealed to everyone out there, and proved that business could be made simple.

But not far from the successful surface of the show, business problems were beginning to crowd in on Rachel. It became apparent during the recording of the series that Rachel was under huge pressure, and not only because she was pregnant, which couldn't have helped. Red Letter Days, the company on which she had built her whole reputation, was in big, big trouble. Yet here she was, week after week, handing out business advice to complete strangers when she should have been back at the office trying to sort out the mess. I couldn't understand her. One day she got so upset about something that she didn't come back in the afternoon and that put an end to filming for the day, which annoyed the producers.

Because of her problems and her pregnancy, the BBC had Richard Farleigh there as a reserve, just in case things went wrong with Rachel again. While Richard was sitting on the substitutes' bench I got to meet him for the first time.

I could see it from the BBC's point of view, because they had only limited time to get the filming done, which was an expensive operation, and you can't have someone disappear off the set. However, I still can't understand how they could let her carry on in the show when it was obvious that her pregnancy, coupled with her other issues, was beginning to take its toll. If I had had such problems – and I don't mean being pregnant – I wouldn't have been within a million miles of a television programme freely dispensing business advice.

We did manage to finish the series together, although the other Dragons' relationships with Rachel became a bit strained. I think the four guys got on reasonably OK. Peter made me quite welcome and was helpful, while Doug is a lovely guy as long as you stay at his level! If you sat down with a pint of bitter and talked about football, his eyes would glaze over. You could see he was trying to understand what we were talking about but he didn't have a bloody clue. You can't really analyse football to the nth degree in the way that Doug does his business life. Duncan was quite good fun too. The minute you came off set he would be a bit more relaxed. It became clear that on set he took on a different persona and, armed with that knowledge, I was able to understand him.

When we finally finished filming the series the news broke that Rachel's business had gone into administration. It attracted masses of publicity. Earlier on in the year, I discovered Peter had tried to help her out, and for my part I sent Rachel a text message saying I was sorry to hear what she was going through and that she shouldn't hesitate to contact me if she needed my help, but I didn't speak directly to her.

It was clear the company wasn't paying their bills, and suppliers and staff were complaining. There were lots of leaks coming out of the organisation that the company was on the verge of bankruptcy. Even though my relationship with Rachel wasn't great, I did think there had been a lot of unwarranted and bitter personal attacks on her in the papers. Of course, she had lived by the sword of PR and I'm afraid she was dying, very painfully, by the sword of the media. She'd built up her whole profile on the back of the media through Red Letter Days and *Dragons' Den* and now that self-same media, which had bigged her up, was gleefully knocking her down.

Then one afternoon, only a few days after she'd had her baby, I was surprised to hear from her on my mobile. She was following up on my message and wanted to talk. We agreed to meet her at Peter's office, which was halfway between us. While the baby was outside with a nanny or an au pair, Rachel told Peter and I what the issues were. We analysed the business, but couldn't see how we could bail it out. It could only go bust. There were too many problems and too many debts for it to survive. She had taken various steps to try to salvage what remained of the business over the last twelve months, but these measures hadn't worked and had created more liabilities.

Soon after, I got a phone call from the receiver, who said he had been informed I might be interested in buying the business and that Peter and I had looked at it. In fact, that wasn't really the case at all – we'd just had a chat with Rachel.

Despite that, I decided to send Kypros, my invaluable number two, who didn't live far from Red Letter Days' headquarters in Muswell Hill, to go and carry out a review of the business. If that proved positive, Peter and I would try to negotiate a deal. So we went through the business and eventually agreed a price with the receiver. Before we knew it, Peter and I were the joint owners of Red Letter Days.

Why did we do it? There is always the satisfaction of doing a deal, but I've never done a deal just for the sake of it. I've turned down enough businesses not to fall for that one. Having done the deal, Red Letter Days would survive, and *Dragons' Den* Series Two could be broadcast. There was a danger that the bad publicity would mean that the show would never air, and having spent four weeks filming, I certainly didn't want all that to go to waste. But those factors alone weren't a good enough reason to buy the business. We believed that buying the business was a good investment and the fact it saved the show was an added bonus.

The company had gone bust in a very public way and ITV's *Tonight with Trevor McDonald* programme was doing a special half-hour on Red Letter Days. We felt it was bound to be a hatchet job, concentrating on all the company's problems and how it had let customers down. There was no doubt the brand was damaged and Rachel had been damaged as well, which meant that *Dragons' Den* would also suffer in the fall-out.

Red Letter Days had seen better days – it was in a terrible state. It was undoubtedly the worst-run business I had ever come across and I had encountered quite a few bad ones in my business career. I think the company had been sick for a long time and I'm surprised it survived for as long as it did.

So *Dragons' Den* went ahead and, in fairness to the BBC, they worked hard trying to make Rachel look good because I don't think she performed well in that series. She even invested in one or two businesses, but I can't remember what actually happened to them afterwards.

I wasn't sure I would be asked back for Series Three. I'm hugely self-critical but I was told by friends that I had done all right. When I was asked to go back for Series Three, it wasn't much of a shock to learn that they were replacing Rachel, but I was quite surprised to hear that Doug had been dropped as well. One of Doug's problems was that he very rarely invested in anything, which was a bit of a drawback considering the format of the show. He was so analytical that he presumably felt that nothing was good enough for him to risk his money on.

We were told that the two new Dragons would be Richard Farleigh – he must have made a big impression as a substitute – and Deborah Meaden. I didn't know what to expect from the two new Dragons, but what soon became clear was that I had been moved away from Peter because it was felt that we were being disruptive – it was a bit like being in school. Peter and I had built up quite a friendship during the second series and we made all sorts of jokes as the show went through its metamorphosis into what I felt was a much more light-hearted programme. So the Beeb, in their infinite wisdom, thought they should break up our little cartel and they put Deborah between us.

I didn't know much about Deborah and even did a Google search on her while I was on holiday shortly after she was announced as one of the new Dragons. I could see what she had done and that she had holiday parks throughout the UK. What little PR there was on her suggested that she was a serious and successful lady. But at first, as far as Peter and I were concerned, she was a wedge in the middle of a rolling wheel.

Richard, on the other hand, is a very quiet person and it didn't help that they sat him right at the end. He was affectionately known as Charley Farley, the character made famous by

Ronnie Corbett in *The Two Ronnies*. Richard had never really run a business or got his hands dirty in a business sense, but was an investment fund manager and had invested in plenty of businesses. I suppose he was a direct replacement for the analytical approach of Doug, while Deborah ensured there was a continued female presence among the Dragons.

On first meeting her, it seemed she had been born without a sense of humour and one look from her could turn you to stone. But Deborah's serious demeanour didn't stop Peter and me from pulling funny faces at each other and cracking gags between pitches. I think the poor lady realised very early on that she would either have to join in with this adolescent behaviour or she might well lose the will to live. Slowly but surely Deborah joined in with our antics and we found that first impressions can sometimes be completely wrong. Deborah became one of the boys and I am sure she won't mind me saying that.

Unfortunately, her sense of humour didn't translate easily to the screen and she came across in Series Three as being very stern. I cannot tell you how many times I have found myself defending Deborah at dinner parties and having to explain that she is one of the nicest, most capable business people I've had the pleasure to meet. Because of the way the programme was edited, the real Deborah doesn't begin to surface until Series Four.

While on the subject of Deborah, I'll let you into a secret about the high heels she wears on the show. She can barely walk in those heels without toppling over and only wears them when she's sitting down during filming. She has a pair of flat shoes for walking around in. Sometimes, just to wind her up, I sit in her chair and hide her shoes.

We do all sorts of things to break up the monotony and annoy the producers. We normally film the series in four blocks and then they mix them up to make the individual programmes, because they like to have at least one investment in each show. So continuity with clothing and the piles of money on the tables in front of us is important. Many a time I've nicked some of Peter's money so we'll start filming with Peter's pile about £30,000 short of what it should be.

We all have microphone packs that we leave on the table at the end of a pitch when we get up to stretch our legs. Sometimes I'll switch Peter's microphone off, so that when we start filming again he can't be heard. Alternatively, when we come back into the studio after one of our breaks, I get in first and empty half of Peter's water on to his chair so he ends up listening to the whole pitch with a wet bum. We are a bit like naughty schoolboys sometimes.

The same five Dragons returned for Series Four, but by then cracks were starting to appear. There were certainly fault lines appearing in Duncan's relationship with Peter and me, and little cliques began to form.

We film in a dusty, old warehouse and in the compound there's a Winnebago, half of which is used for make-up and for non-smokers, and the other half for smokers. Peter and I were smokers and we'd go into the one half, while Richard and Duncan would sit in the other section. Deborah would always play it straight down the middle – literally! She would spend one part of the break in one half of the Winnebago and the other part in the other half. It can get quite competitive in the Den, however, and for the first time that competitiveness spilled over into the breaks. It definitely became a bit of me and Peter against Charley Farley and Duncan.

About this time, something really weird happened – Duncan underwent some form of personality transplant. He won't admit it, and we have agreed to disagree on the subject, but I am convinced his personality altered dramatically and I think it was difficult for the Dragons to take on board. If Duncan wanted to change the way he was that was down to him and was fine by me. He had got married and started being uncharacteristically moralistic about things. I don't have a problem with that, either, unless it was ridiculously directed at me. Then I would respond and Peter did likewise. Charley Farley was slightly different because he didn't know the previous Duncan.

We did manage to get through to the end of the series but there was a sense of increasing tension. It didn't help that we all spent a lot of time mocking each other publicly. It was fun at first, but there is always an element of truth in humour, and because of the prevailing atmosphere, whoever was the target of the mockery sometimes got upset. A bit too sensitive, I would say.

We had gone from Dragons to demons. We'd become luvvies and were no longer successful business people who happened to be making a TV show, but were also TV celebs. All of a sudden some of the Dragons, who shall remain nameless, were more interested in the image than the reality. They thought that having a laugh at someone else's expense was no longer acceptable because it might reflect badly on their public persona. Now I couldn't handle that because I say what I feel and that's the end of it. And I like to have a laugh. And if people can't handle it, they shouldn't be on the show. Once a Dragon starts worrying about his image, then it can get in the way of the decisions he takes.

However, there was no doubt the tension between the Dragons was good for business because viewing figures were up again and the fourth series proved an even bigger success than the previous three. When I was asked to do Series Five I was told there would be one change to the team and I was really surprised when I was told Charley Farley had been dropped. I don't know why Richard was left out but it saddened me. I was told Richard's place would go to James Caan.

I didn't feel happy about the idea of doing another series with the same tensions that we'd had in Series Four. I didn't want to spend four or five weeks of my life filming, cooped up in a caravan for a lot of the time, and being miserable. Peter and I had a long chat about it and we discussed it with the BBC. We explained that there wasn't animosity but that we weren't happy. In the end, despite our misgivings, we decided to go ahead with it.

Because of building work near our old set, the Beeb recreated the whole thing at Pinewood Studios, where there are lots of recreational facilities, which we thought would help the atmosphere. In fact, the first two days of filming were diabolical. Duncan and I seemed to be treading on eggshells and it looked as if neither me, Peter nor Duncan would comment on what the other was saying in case it blew up into a disagreement.

But these responses to each other's input had been part of the ebb and flow that had made *Dragons' Den* so successful, so it couldn't go on. I spoke to Helen Bullough, the executive series director, and told her we needed to sort it out. Duncan and I got together in what had become known as the 'naughty room', a spare room at Pinewood where people spent a lot of time apologising to each other if things had gone wrong on set. We were in there for forty-five minutes and had it out about the issues that had festered from the previous series and that were now badly affecting this new series.

We both knew it couldn't go on – if it did, the show would go down the pan. After quite a heated exchange of views, as they say in political circles, we decided to put our personal feelings behind us and get on with making a good television show. We got up, shook hands, had a cuddle and walked out of the 'naughty room' with smiles on our faces and I could see that made Helen feel a million times better. I firmly believe that once we had got over these teething problems we proceeded to make

the best-ever series of *Dragons' Den*. I think it had everything –
plenty of dialogue between the Dragons, who were still as
competitive as ever, and plenty of good investments. The
bottom line was that it was damn good television.

We had lots of fun doing Series Five and James Caan, who is
quite happy to laugh at himself, was a great addition to the Den.
He built up a very successful recruitment business, called
Alexander Mann, which he sold in 2002, and now he runs a
small private equity fund using his own money to invest in
businesses. In many ways he is the perfect Dragon, but there is
one drawback with James – he has no dress sense whatsoever.

His other problem was making that first investment as a new
Dragon. He had been knocked back four times before he finally
got to put some money into a business, but he should have
waited a little bit longer. James decided to invest in a dog
treadmill and in my opinion, and that of the other Dragons, it
was never an investment. But he had to get off the mark. Like a
batsman who has been at the crease for several overs, he was
glad to nick one through the slips.

We'll never let him forget his dog's dinner of an investment
though. One of my favourite lines from the last series went like
this: 'I know three Dragons are out and we've absolutely
destroyed your business plan, so I'm out as well, but don't be
disheartened, because there's still James. And while there's
still James, there's still hope. You are looking at a man who
invested in a doggy treadmill, so you've got a chance!' He
never took it personally and that's one of the things I really
like about James.

Boys will be boys, especially when it comes to boys' toys – and
we had a lot of fun playing with our own somewhat expensive
toys during this series. I'm not shy to admit I have a rather nice
car, a Maybach. Peter had some old Bentley and, as he copies
almost everything I do, he went out and bought an identical car

but unfortunately in Jewish racing gold – if he wasn't so tall he would probably copy my dress sense as well! The Maybach competes with the Rolls-Royce Phantom, which is what James drives. Unfortunately, his vehicle is black and every week when he turned up in his 'hearse' we really slaughtered him.

Just for a laugh – and I know it's really childish but there were times when we were going stir crazy and needed to relieve the boredom – we would push down the silver lady on the bonnet. That pissed him off so he would turn up in his other vehicle, which was an antiquated Aston Martin convertible. Peter thought he would counter that by leaving his Maybach at home and driving to the studio in his Ferrari – although I didn't believe they made Ferraris big enough for Peter to squeeze his large frame into.

So one day James turned up in his Aston Martin with the number plate JC – Jesus Christ – and Peter arrived in his Ferrari, although it delayed filming for an hour while the crew extricated him from the car. In fact, his exit was so painful he had to have a back massage before he could sit down properly.

I then turned up in my chauffeur-driven Maybach and was upstairs changing, in the green room, and chatting with Deborah, when she said, 'Look at them, like little boys, squabbling down in the car park about who has the better car.'

I said, 'They're clueless, both of them. Neither of them knows anything about cars.'

As we went in to start filming, I organised for my driver, Michael Brown, better known as Kato, to go back to my home and get my Harley Davidson truck, a big black chromed-up vehicle with flashing blue lights. It's a real cruise mobile with blacked-out windows, fluffy dice and a fluffy steering wheel as well as a six-litre engine that would easily drown out any Ferrari or similar super sports car.

I also told Kato to go into my son's bedroom and get a set of number plates that I'd bought him for his birthday. He'd never put them on his car because he thought he would look like a tosser, mainly because the number plate was W411KER, with a judiciously placed spot on the plates between the two figure ones, spelling it out! The plan was to put these 'wanker' plates on Peter's Ferrari.

Kato carried out my instructions to the letter and as we came out I said, 'Boys, why don't you stop talking about your little cars? If you want to see a proper car . . .' and Kato came blasting round the block in this beast of a truck with the engine roaring, the fluffy dice bobbing up and down, the blue lights flashing and the music blaring. Everybody started laughing.

Peter wasn't really impressed and questioned how my truck could ever be compared with his Ferrari. As they turned to look at Peter's Ferrari everyone burst out laughing at its new 'wanker' number plate! Peter didn't spot it at first, but as soon as he did he started chasing me around the car park. Eventually he caught hold of me and, wearing our suits, we start grappling on the floor. The BBC filmed the incident for their website to show what goes on behind the scenes, but given the amount of industrial language, I suspect it will never get aired. This sort of fun and frolics helped ease all the tension and made Series Five great television and far more fun to do than it initially seemed.

Chapter Twenty

Beware the angry Dragon

As I've said, *Dragons' Den* is real. Our money is real and we have no idea whether it's a man or a woman, an orangutan or a herd of elephants coming up those stairs. The first time we know anything about the pitch is when he, she or they start talking.

That's not to say we don't have any preconceived ideas from the minute they come into view. Many a time you'll see me slump into my seat at the sight of another board game, or internet site, or cooking utensil that's going to change the world, or idea that's going to save the planet from global warming.

There have certainly been some odd ideas and people. On my first series, a guy came up and put some trophies down on the table next to him. For a moment, I was intrigued until he opened his plastic bag and took out a pair of roller skates for his knees. He then crouched down and started racing round the Den. He was six-foot-plus, rather gangly and Eastern European so he spoke with a very KGB accent. It was pure farce – and the reason behind this 'invention' was so that parents could get down to the level of their children and their kids could climb on top of them and go for rides. He was totally and utterly nuts, and, in fact, when it appeared on the programme it looked even worse than it had during filming.

Bringing things right up to date, there was an Asian lady in the fifth series who came up the stairs and stood next to a prop covered in a black cloak. Nothing unusual there, props are usually covered up so we can't sneak a look at them, although Peter and I always try to take a peek. (The BBC now employs a security guard to stop us in our tracks – he's better known as the floor manager.)

Occasionally, there's just a tripod standing there ready for someone to place a graphic on. I've often gone and adjusted its height when the floor manager isn't looking so that it is lopsided when filming begins and they have to stop to straighten it up again. It's my way of getting even with the floor manager.

Anyway, we couldn't work out what was under the cloak as she started talking about her hatred of ironing, something Mrs P and lots of the viewers can relate to. I thought that if she had the solution to this age-old problem she could make a fortune and we would end up fighting over her as a sure-fire investment. But it all started to go wrong when she pulled off the cloak and revealed the box, which looked more MFI than Ikea. It was the archetypal flat-pack, put together in a hurry and rather badly.

She opened various parts of it to expose the front end of an ironing board. She hadn't invented a solution to ironing at all, she had just reinvented the ironing board in a worse way than ever before. The idea was that you kept this monstrosity in the box and if you pulled all the right flaps and levers, you'd end up with something that looked a little bit like an ironing board. And then she said those immortal words 'Everybody I've shown it to loves it.' I think she'd shown it to the three Fs – family, friends and fools. We were flabbergasted; it was horrendous. If *Blue Peter* had put it together out of sticky-back plastic it would have looked a whole lot better. But she was deadly serious and was determined to patent the 'idea'. Needless to say she was out of the Den sharpish – without a penny.

Then there was the very well-spoken woman who arrived seeking a six-figure sum to develop a product that she felt was going to revolutionise the world of travel. She had no props, only a little bag – and she immediately grabbed our attention. We all wanted to know what was in the bag.

Dramatically, she put her hand in the bag and brought out a box, which was only six inches square, and opened it up. It contained a piece of plastic with four suction pads at the back and a holder for a shower head. There was a stunned, almost disbelieving, silence. I slouched down in my chair with my arms hanging either side of me. I'd rather have gone and helped Mrs P with the ironing. What was I doing there?

But she ploughed on, telling us she had spent over £100,000 of her own money trying to alleviate a problem she often encountered when staying in hotels – the lack of a decent shower. Sometimes, she said, there was a shower head at the end of the bath, but nothing to hold it up so she had to hold the shower with one hand while washing with the other. So she'd spent all this money developing this piece of plastic, which she'd patented worldwide, in order to overcome the problem.

Of course, she could have spent a fraction of the money staying in better-class hotels that did provide proper showers in their bathrooms, but that hadn't dawned on her. She might also have spent less by seeking psychiatric help. We pointed out the obvious, that usually when there was no shower head it was because there were no tiles, which would mean there would be nowhere to attach her suction pads. Furthermore, if the bathroom was set up that way, there wouldn't be a curtain and she would probably end up flooding the floor below.

Ignoring all of this, she said she already had an investor who was a 50 per cent shareholder and had put up £100,000 alongside her £100,000. I couldn't believe she had actually managed to persuade someone to part with £100,000 to invest in this piece of plastic, and I wasn't surprised that he wanted to remain anonymous. He was probably worried people would realise he was barking mad.

Another woman came along and told us she had written a book with the intriguing title of *Dance of the Goblins* and wanted to make a low-budget film of the book for £1.5 million. She needed us to provide some of the money. Apparently everybody loved the book and was willing to work on the film for nothing. Then one of the Dragons asked her when the book came out and how many she had sold. It turned out that her first print run of 2,000 copies had still not sold out, for which she blamed the publisher – on the basis that he only had two titles in his catalogue and the other one was written by himself. She had self-published the book – in other words she had paid to bring it out – but insisted she knew all about films.

Then I asked her what she was going to do with the money if we did invest. She told us she had a top-notch Hollywood actor who was prepared to star in the film, and she would be paying him a million pounds for his services, but she refused to divulge the name of the actor. For a million quid I think all the Dragons would have danced with the Goblins – I know I certainly would have done! The bottom line was that she wanted us to give her money to make a film with an undisclosed actor based on an unknown book and was shocked when we didn't cough up the cash. Afterwards when she was interviewed by Evan Davis, she was defiant, saying, 'I'm going to make it happen.' I'd concentrate on selling the book first, love.

I'm often asked about the ones that got away, but in my first four series there hasn't been one that I've kicked myself for not investing in. I suppose that's because if a pitch totally and utterly captivates me, then I'm going to invest. I wouldn't let anyone else beat me to a good investment. But there are some pitches that strike me as being 'take it or leave it' sort of ideas.

So far there hasn't been a pitch that has been turned down by all the Dragons and gone on to make a mint. There's been nothing along the lines of the record company that turned down the Beatles or the publishers who rejected J. K. Rowling. I don't think that's going to happen because what you have in the Den are five very experienced people and it would be highly unlikely that we'd all fail to spot an idea's potential.

I did invest in something in the last series that isn't going to happen. Peter and I gave this guy all the money he wanted, but he was really after advertising and not investment, as he simply didn't need the money so the deal didn't go through. He was just looking for cheap – actually free – advertising on prime-time television. But mark my words, the product, called Waterbuoy, which is a tiny inflatable key ring, will be a success. You attach it to any item of value on a boat, such as your satellite navigation system, your binoculars or your keys, and you know you're never going to lose them if they fall overboard. If it falls into water it inflates into a balloon that can carry up to two kilogrammes and keep the object floating in the water.

For me, though, the main interest was not so much the key ring but the trigger mechanism that he'd developed. It does the same job as the automatic trigger in life jackets but it's a lot cheaper to produce and more robust, and I think that this is the product that's going to make him the real money.

Then, at the end of Series Four, I came across iTeddy. It was a tiring day and our last of filming and we were demob happy. As we came into the Den there was a big, black cloak in front of us – about seven foot, even taller than Jonesy. We all wondered what was underneath it.

Imran Hakim, from Bolton, introduced himself and started to tell us about his invention. We all wanted to get it over with and go home, we didn't want to hear about Imran's teddy bear. But our interest was rekindled slightly when he pulled away the cloak and revealed someone in a teddy suit with a laptop attached to his belly. The teddy proceeded to give Imran a big hug.

I had still switched off though, and was only half listening to his pitch when he said something that intrigued me. He'd made a prototype, which he brought out of his bag, and which he said had been produced in the Far East in four or five weeks. Well, I manufacture stuff in the Far East and I didn't see how he could have done it so fast, so I decided to expose him. I was ready to pounce and ask him about the manufacturing process when he started to demonstrate the software on the big teddy's stomach. He showed how people could log their teddies on to the website and download products. It was rough and ready but it was functional and you could see clearly what he was trying to do.

He had my full attention. I was interested in the download concept, which could produce a secondary income in addition to selling the teddy in the first place. I began to warm to the man, particularly when he explained how he'd got on a plane and gone to China and sat there in a factory while they developed the product. He didn't just send drawings backwards and forwards but had done it all face to face with the manufacturers. He was a doer and not a talker and I like doers.

He had credible answers to all my questions bar one, about patenting the product. I couldn't see how he could do it in the time frame he had given himself. Registering a patent sometimes takes years and he admitted he had only just filed an application for a patent. Nevertheless, I was seriously impressed with Imran, with his knowledge, drive and ability.

I also liked the idea of this teddy bear, which a child can take anywhere, with a media player in its tummy that played feature films and cartoons. Parents could even download a story on to the teddy bear so that if they weren't at home for any reason the child could still see and hear mum or dad reading a story. It could even smell like mum, using her perfume.

I liked him so much I offered him the money. Peter also offered him the money, so we did a bit of haggling and in the end we invested jointly. Initially, we agreed to put in £70,000 each, £140,000 for 40 per cent of the business. But there was a lot of work to do and the business took on a life of its own and grew and grew and grew. In fact, it expanded so rapidly that following the pitch in January, we had made our first delivery to Argos in July of the same year. It was absolutely unbelievable. We signed an exclusive deal with Argos to sell them 35,000 iTeddys for Christmas and it was a phenomenal success. We launched the product at Bear Mountain in London Zoo where Jonesy and I dressed up as teddy bears.

Peter wasn't happy with the dressing up; he felt uncomfortable. But it was his 'forfeit' as he wasn't spending much time on the new venture while starting up his own show on ITV called *Tycoon*. He said he'd catch up with iTeddy when he got his breath back and in the meantime it was down to me, but I explained that it all rested on him dressing up as a teddy bear.

Imran ended up needing considerably more than the £140,000 we put up, but it was all down to iTeddy being a product that everyone seemed to want. It has been an incredible success story so far but we did have to pay for all the stock to come over from China, as Argos don't settle up until much later in the process. In December 2007, we signed an exclusive worldwide license deal with Vivid Toys, which allows them to manufacture and distribute iTeddy for a handsome royalty, meaning that we no longer need to do anything other than sit back and watch the cash roll in. Young Imran is probably the first *Dragons' Den* millionaire – apart from the five of us, that is!

Another presentation that impressed me came from Exeter-based Ian Chamings, a Richard Hammond look-alike with a product called mixalbum.com, which he said would make DJs redundant. He'd developed a software program that allowed two dance songs to mix together perfectly. He gave us a demo and it appeared to be seamless. There was no way you could see the join, as Eric Morecambe used to tell Ernie Wise. No DJ in the world could have made it work any better.

He needed money to develop his website and do a deal with the record companies to have their music on the site. Deborah and I invested and we did a deal with Sony, EMI and the Ministry of Sound. Now we've got their music on Ian's website and it's been coded so you can download it from mixalbum.com ready to be mixed. We're in the process of doing licensing deals with some of the record labels to have the codings built into their songs as they're released. If it goes through we will be receiving pennies in royalties but, you know what they say, look after the pennies and the pounds will take care of themselves!

But it's not always about making money in the Den. Sometimes it's about backing your judgement and whether your life will be enriched by supporting a potential entrepreneur. A case in point was Max McMurdo. He works out of a barn in the Bedford area, running a company called Reestore, which does exactly what it says on the tin – it restores things. It re-uses and recycles unwanted products into something useful. So, for example, he might take an unwanted washing-machine drum and fashion it into a coffee table. I found it all quite fascinating and in my office today there is a sofa made out of a bathtub, a meeting table made out of a car gearbox and glass, four chairs which were originally shopping trolleys and a desk that started life as an aeroplane wing.

Deborah and I invested £25,000 each, which didn't seem like a lot of money to us, but it's a huge amount if you haven't got it. We wanted to support a man who, I believe, is making works of art out of waste. But they're works of art that are functional and not just good to look at. When am I going to get my money back? You could say I've already had a return in the office furniture I've got. The business plan is still in the making, but what we don't want to do is stifle Max's creativity with balance sheets and targets. At the end of the day, it's Max's artistry that will bring us a return.

So here I sit in my shopping trolley. You may remember from an earlier chapter that I spent the odd night in a shopping trolley in my formative years, being pushed down Bond Street after a good night out. I never imagined sitting in one in my office all these years later!

If you're planning on coming on *Dragons' Den* and want to know how to impress me and win my support, here are my key tips: first, I've got to like the person or the people making the pitch. If I don't like them, I don't want to be in business with them. They might have the best product or idea in the world, but if I don't like the look of them, I'm not going to invest.

The second key factor is the business proposal itself. Is it any good? If they've sweated and stuttered, got a few numbers wrong initially and then put them right later on after I've gently interrogated them, I don't think that's a reason not to invest. Equally, if they can make a fantastic pitch under the pressure of the television cameras, that's an added bonus. But, truth to tell, I've invested in lots of things where the pitch has been absolutely appalling, but that's usually because they're standing there in front of five people, with cameras stuck up their nostrils and lights glaring into their face.

I understand that people can get their pitch a little bit wrong but the presentation is not what it's about, it's more important that you know all the facts about your proposal. I'm sure that if I were doing a presentation, certainly in my earlier days, I'd have probably forgotten loads and loads. Once people started questioning me though, I would come up with the right answers. But if the Dragons ask questions and you don't know the answer that's usually curtains for any idea no matter how good it might appear.

What can you expect to do if you agree to go on *Dragons' Den*? You must turn up armed with bags of confidence and your three-minute pitch, which you've been practising for weeks. You know you will have to answer basic questions about your own business, which, of course, you know from top to bottom because you live it every minute of every day of every week. You then thank the Dragons, shake hands with the Dragon or Dragons who have agreed to give you the money you asked for and you can toddle off home with your arms full of cash and bask in five minutes of television fame. How hard can that be?

It must be very hard indeed, because I never cease to be amazed by the number of people who turn up and fail to deliver those basic requirements.

We may be dubbed Dragons but we don't actually breathe fire and I'm astonished at the fear many of our budding entrepreneurs show. Fear is an essential ingredient in every successful business. If you have no fear you will come a cropper since only fools rush in. Every top-class sportsman and woman has a built-in fear of failure. That's what makes them so damn good and so damn hard to beat. And it's no different in business.

The first lesson you learn on *Dragons' Den*, therefore, is to conquer your fears and deal with them. If you've done your homework and you know your business inside out, there is absolutely nothing that is going to come up in the Den that you can't deal with.

Standing in the glare of those unforgiving lights with the cameras rolling can be a little bit off-putting. But I promise you it's no more off-putting than when you go to see your bank manager wearing his expensive suit in his expansive office – and he looks at you rather disdainfully over his half-rimmed glasses.

He will ask the same questions as the Dragons will be asking. There's only one difference – it's not his money he's putting at risk. It's the bank's cash. Don't ever forget that banks are faceless institutions that run television adverts full of people singing and dancing which attempt to convince you that the only thing you have to do is turn up and they will solve all your financial problems.

This is not how it is done in the Den. An investment in *Dragons' Den* is exactly that – it's an investment like any other. We invest and, not unreasonably, we are looking for a return on our investment. We are not looking to run your business for you. Nor are we looking to enter into a lifelong relationship with you. We're just putting up our hard-earned. And because it's our money and we all understand timing and the cyclical nature of business, we rarely expect to see a return in the short term.

We're there to support the fledgling entrepreneur for as long as it takes – as long as, of course, we have faith.

Electrical

Tel: 020 8559 7000
Fax: 020 8559 7007

Design, Manufacture & Distribution

Big or small, we've got it Al'

Chapter Twenty-one

My twelve rules for business success

If you're looking for 'normal' business advice, pop down to your local bank and ask to see the manager. I don't give 'normal' advice; I don't do business like anyone else. I'm not 'normal' – and that's precisely why I'm so successful.

I don't subscribe to what might be called normal business philosophies of 'We're the bosses, we sit in our ivory towers and we let the numbers do the talking.' My way of running a business is being on the shop floor, allowing people to make decisions, listening to junior members of staff, as well as the people at head office, and taking on board what they've got to say. I think it's important to drive the business in a hands-on way, as opposed to expecting it to function just because there's a hierarchy or a structure in place that says it should, or because some accountant or somebody who's got a university degree has read some theoretical book that says if you do this and this, the outcome will be that. It doesn't work like that as far as I'm concerned and as far as my businesses are concerned.

Anyway, if everyone did business in exactly the same 'normal' way no one would make any more – or any less – than anyone else. That's not the way I want to play the game. Daring to be different, daring to make more money than anyone else – that's how I want to play it.

Our lives are ruled by rules. If you want to play the game – whether it's football, cricket or even bridge – you have to learn the rules and play by them. If you don't, you're liable to be yellow-carded or even red-carded – and then you're off. Even war has rules, so it's no surprise that business has rules too. In my business life I have followed my own rules and here's your chance to find out exactly what those rules are and why they've been so phenomenally successful for me. I'm giving you a unique opportunity to run the rule over my rules and see if they can work for you just as they've worked for me.

Rule One: Reduce the risk

I have only three reasons for going to work: one, to make money; two, to have fun; and three, not to forget to make money. I'm a great believer that the risk should reflect the reward. If it's a high-risk strategy, then I want a high reward. It's a far better policy than 'high risk, low reward', that's for sure. My whole business philosophy is based on a risk-reward ratio. But it's got to stack up. If it doesn't, don't do it. You might as well go to a casino. You might strike it lucky, but in the end, you'll lose the lot. That's guaranteed.

The world is awash with business – everybody seems to have a money-making scheme, but will they end up as successful businesses? If you think you've come up with the business idea to end all business ideas, there's just two things you've got to ask yourself: what are the risks, and what are the rewards?

Businessmen and women don't become successful by taking unnecessary risks. They become successful by taking calculated risks. People often say to me that I take huge risks. But I don't. They are absolutely wrong. I never take ridiculous risks. I am the most conservative person you will ever come across, and that's because I'm good at reducing risks while leaving the potential rewards high.

The trick is in how to lower the risk factor. When you have a proposition in front of you, that's when you have to weigh up the risk-reward ratio. Then you look at how you can stack the cards in your favour. Do that in a casino and you get barred. But in business, it's not called cheating, it's called good business.

You've got to make sure you've got all the information and you know more about what's happening than the next guy. If you use inside information when you're dealing in stocks and shares, you go to prison. If you know more about a business than anyone else because you've done a lot more research, then you don't go to prison – you make money. So it's about knowing the business and making sure that when you get involved you have done your homework and know exactly how you intend to turn it round. Of course, you don't want to share that knowledge with anyone else until you have control.

The way you buy a business can also give you an advantage. One of the reasons I've often bought businesses out of receivership is because you can automatically dispense with a lot of overheads – the loss-making activities that eventually pushed the business over the edge. If you buy a business before it goes into receivership, you have to take on all its assets, all its liabilities, all its loss-making and then it's very difficult to turn it around. You've got a lot more room to manoeuvre when you're buying a company from receivership because all you buy are the assets, the goodwill and the equipment to carry on the business; you don't take on the liabilities.

Things are automatically in your favour because the previous guy who was trying to turn that business round had all the liabilities. He couldn't shut down forty loss-making stores. Try shutting down forty stores when you own a business and it's a nightmare. For a start, you've got all the leases that you're committed to for up to twenty-five years. If you buy a company out of receivership you can leave the loss-making stores behind without any cost to you. Once you've done that, as long as you make sure you buy at the right price, and you've done your research, the risks should be much lower.

Rule Two: Don't fool yourself

You are the easiest person to fool. You can always fool yourself.

I spend lots of time in the bathroom. It's my thinking time. If a project has gone wrong I have to look at myself in the shaving mirror and say, 'I did my best but it didn't work out.' If I know I didn't do my best, took silly risks, didn't work hard enough or let my heart rule my head then I give myself a good kicking. I blame myself. No matter who's involved with you in the project, in the end it's down to you.

What makes *Dragons' Den* so good is that people really want it. They have nowhere else to go. The Dragons can relate to that as we are passionate too. When the people doing their pitch get worked up and emotional, we warm to them. In one case I asked two people who had been seeking our support to come and see me when we'd finished recording. I was so taken aback by their passion. It was a tear-jerking story. I couldn't invest, but I thought I could help. Within minutes I had got them a major order from La Senza – the buying manager placed an order there and then. It has changed their business life. On the show, my heart was saying invest, but my business brain was saying no. But that is not what the show is about. So I didn't do it on air.

If you have a business idea, honesty is very important. I'm fed up hearing wannabe entrepreneurs say, 'Everybody I have asked thinks my idea is fantastic.' Well, if I think your idea is crap, you can never say that again. Obviously you have no friends. At least one of them would have told you it was crap.

People say they believe in their ideas. That's because they have conditioned themselves to believe in them. Actually, someone needs to be brave and say the idea's rubbish. You have got to be honest with yourself about what you are doing.

Then you must ask yourself how commercial it is. It might be a good idea, a fantastic idea, but you have to work out how you are going to make money from it. 'Everyone is going to want one,' they tell me. Well, I don't want one, so not everyone wants one. 'I have given this to twenty people and they all said they would buy one.' How much did they pay you for it? 'Nothing.' That's why they took one. 'I have done my market research,' they say. No, you haven't, you've given things away.

Beware of all these ways in which people delude themselves.

Rule Three: Learn to let go

It's very difficult for an entrepreneur to let go. It's very hard to sell a successful business. People hold on and hold on until sometimes the business has no value at all. Sell it! It's the hardest thing to do, but it's the hallmark of a top-class entrepreneur.

You must be able to create something and then sell it at exactly the right time. That's really hard. I still find it hard. You've put so much of your life, your body and soul, into something you have created and nurtured – and then you have to let go, as I did with La Senza and Contessa. And there is always a right time to sell, because any business goes through ups and downs.

And for the people who come on *Dragons' Den*, if you really have faith in your idea but can't make it work on your own, realise that it's better to have 60 or 70 per cent of something than 100 per cent of nothing.

Rule Four: Know that cash is king

Cash flow is king. Profit is sanity. Turnover is vanity.

A lack of profit is like a cancer. If it carries on for a long time it will eventually kill you. But a lack of cash is like a heart attack. If you can't pay the rent you shut down just like you would if your heart packed up. You're finished. If you can't pay the wages, it's all over. Don't be without cash. You can live without profit, but not without cash. It's very basic and simple advice.

Rule Five: Embrace change

As I mentioned, I have recently sold two of my retail chains, La Senza and Contessa. Read into that what you want. The retail environment is changing very rapidly at the moment, partly because of the internet, which opens up a vast world at the touch of a button. Internet selling means that you don't need to pay vast high-street rents and employ lots of shop assistants. You can eBay trade. You can have a lock-up and keep your products there. It's fantastic – everyone can be a shopkeeper. And the consumer is now far better informed than previously. Because of this, I believed that to stand still was to go backwards, and I wasn't afraid to move on. If you don't adapt, your business will die, I can assure you. The high street is changing. The amount of business being done on the web now is shifting the balance of power. The internet has unshackled the business world.

Don't be scared of all this change, however. I have switched direction so many times and done so many different things. I am excited about what the next move is. I am not scared about what's out there. When I throw off the shackles of a particular business it frees me up to do something else, even if I'm not immediately clear what that will be; I know it's out there and I will find it.

There has never been a better time to make a success of business. Money is cheap; technology is cheap; knowledge is cheap. Consumers have got an insatiable appetite. And if you can satisfy that appetite, slake that thirst, you can make money. That's why the changes we are going through now make this the best time ever for anyone who wants to make a success of their life.

Rule Six: Use common sense

It might seem blindingly obvious, but business is all about common sense. In fact, business is 90 per cent common sense. To run a lingerie business you don't have to be a supermodel. To run a zoo you don't have to be a zebra. You just need to have a healthy dollop of common sense. I apply common sense in all my business dealings.

But common sense is not common. If it were, everyone would have it and everyone would be able to do what I do. And I wouldn't want that!

Rule Seven: Make decisions

The biggest problem for any business is when the people in charge are not running the business . . . they're running scared in case they make a decision and it turns out to be the wrong one. One of the things I preach to all my staff is never be frightened to make a decision. Of course, you'll get some wrong. But if you get more right than wrong then you're doing OK.

The only thing I ask my executives to do is to make decisions. If one of those decisions turns out to be wrong, then identify it quickly. Deal with it if you can. Stop the bleeding. Don't let that bad decision cause the business to bleed to death. And if you can't deal with it yourself, scream as loud as you can so that your colleagues can hear you and realise you're in trouble, and ride to your rescue. There's no shame in asking others to help you. The shame is in keeping quiet, trying to cover up your bad decision. Rest assured, it will come back to haunt you. Helping each other is what teamwork is all about. And that's a principle I stick to in every company I own.

Rule Eight: Weigh up the opposition – and yourself

In business, just like in football or any other sport for that matter, you must never underestimate the strength of the opposition. In training, you can prepare your eleven players to go out on the pitch with their tactics carefully mapped out. But there will be eleven other people out there trying to stop you winning. And that's exactly the same as in business. No matter how good it seems your organisation is doing, never underestimate the lengths to which other people will go to stop you being successful. And at some stage the competition will have the edge over you to such an extent that your business might go into reverse or even terminal decline.

You only have to look around the high street, where some of the biggest names – household names at one time – are no longer with us. One of the problems for these high-street giants is the nature of their tiered system of management, where strategy and communication often get misinterpreted and lost en route to their rightful recipient – a bit like Chinese whispers.

And that's why it's even more important for managers of businesses to question what they are doing. For a small entrepreneurial business, which is usually operated by the owner, it's a lot easier to apply the common sense principle without the hindrance of a corporate structure and all the inherent inefficiencies it brings with it.

In my opinion, internal communication is about people understanding what it is that you want in your business and understanding you. And in return you should be open with people working in the business and give them the whole picture, not half the picture. It's about explaining to people their part in the equation and explaining what the whole equation is and why their role is so important.

If people are doing things in isolation, it's very hard for them to understand why if they don't do something exactly as you want them to do it, it won't then all fit together. If you involve people in the whole process, there are always some gems of ideas that come from those on the shop floor. I work with some absolutely outstanding individuals who have risen to the top because I've allowed them to express themselves.

And technology has made that a lot easier. We have an intranet within my organisation that provides lots of information about the businesses. Sometimes people wonder why I'm giving that sort of information to shop assistants. It's because a shop assistant that's really interested in the business can actually take that on board, look at the wider picture, and it allows them, if they're driven and have ambition and ability, to progress within the organisation. They can get involved in things properly, outside their sphere or their responsibility.

I also communicate via email. Employees may send me an email and say, for example, that we're selling a particular product, but there's another one out there that's better and maybe in more demand. In the light of that information, we either stock that product or restructure our pricing on our own product to become more competitive. An employee might even suggest that we open a new store in such-and-such a place. There might be a very good reason why we haven't opened there, but it may be a town that the employee knows much more about than I do. I am willing to learn from those who work for me.

They might even ask why my shop is either open or not open on a Sunday. The employee might tell me that other shops are opening on Sundays when we're closed and it might be a good idea to take advantage of the extra customers coming into town on those days. It's this sort of information we take very seriously. It's all about keeping proper and regular lines of communication open, and looking at what you do and what everyone else does.

Rule Nine: Start small

If you're an entrepreneur and want to start a business, start small. You can start a business on your own or just with a partner or an assistant. It's only when you take on your first member of staff that you're more than likely to encounter other problems. All of a sudden you're managing the people as well the business.

But remember, just because you had a good business idea that looks like it's going to work, it doesn't mean you've suddenly acquired staff-management skills. Legislation is now so watertight – as well as being complicated and restrictive – that you have to consider everybody's feelings and requirements.

So how do you do this? Up until now you have been happily going along launching your business and product with a tight-knit group of people totally oblivious to working practice directives, trade discrimination laws, health and safety issues. They are other people's problems, aren't they? Wrong. They are your problems now. And they are only going to grow, along with your business. I suppose it's a bit like growing pains: necessary, but pretty painful at the time. But just like growing pains, they pass. In the case of business growing pains, though, you do have to do something about them before the pain becomes unbearable or even crippling.

It is imperative that man-management skills and knowledge of legislation are acquired pretty fast in your business cycle. Some of the more ridiculous EU directives, which have now been enshrined within UK legislation, can be neutralised by an understanding and appreciation of your staff and colleagues.

Basically, this means keeping them as happy and as motivated as you can. But you do have a head start – people want to belong. It's human nature.

Rule Ten: Get your staff on board

In any business I buy, the first thing I do is bring in as many of the staff as possible right down to the most junior managers for a get-together, presentation and overnight stay with an activity such as tenpin bowling – and plenty of free refreshments.

The first thing I ask our store managers when addressing them at such an event is who they think is the most important person in the business.

I'm never surprised by the answer, it's always the same – the customer. Not so, I say. Then they point to me. Wrong again, I say. Eventually, I have to tell them the answer – and I point to all of them, the workforce. They are the most important people in the business. My job is to make their working environment as stress-free as possible. I want them to look forward to coming in to work irrespective of any issues and problems they may have at home. I want them to feel they are valued and will be listened to. If I am able to achieve this I can guarantee the customer will get the best possible service and not a causal 'Have a nice day' as he or she exits the check-out.

Motivating staff is not just about making them feel wanted. Tangible rewards are equally as important if not more so. Incentives go a long way to help staff focus on the work they do. For instance, we always put in place weekly bonuses instead of the monthly ones that many companies have. Why? Very simply, if someone has a bad week in any particular month the motivational tool is transformed into a demotivational tool because they know it is going to be impossible to hit their monthly bonus. By having weekly bonus schemes you are allowing someone who has a bad week to start afresh the following week with the real possibility that they can still achieve their target – and their bonus. In addition, we look at longer-term incentives over two or three months – normally a week on a Caribbean island with yours truly – which resulted last year in me taking 130 of my store and head office staff to St Lucia and Mauritius for a holiday of a lifetime. The downside for the staff is that they have to spend a week with me – the upside for me is that I get to know them even better.

Rule Eleven: Capitalise on other people's ideas

I'll let you into a little secret – despite having made a fantastic living from my business ventures, I've never had an original idea in my life. But I have pinched a few from other people and made them work for me. Well, not exactly pinched, that's the wrong word. I've modified them, worked on them a little and adapted them.

I keep these ideas in my head and at the first opportunity or when I am able to find a bit of time, I consider them further. And if I still think the idea is a good one in the cold light of day, I start to plan how to capitalise on it. Normally I start by scribbling words and diagrams on a piece of paper and seeing if I can translate that idea into a money-making scheme.

Always remember that because something is innovative or uses leading-edge technology doesn't necessarily mean it's going to make pots of money. Many inventions that were thought to be technologically brilliant and ideas that seemed to have enormous merit never made their inventors a penny piece. A classic example of this was the videotape wars between Betamax and VHS, where the better product (Betamax) lost out to the one that was better organised.

Just as the road to hell is paved with good intentions, so the road to bankruptcy is paved with good ideas. There are many good ideas put to us on *Dragons' Den* that we don't invest in purely because they ain't going to make anyone any money. I'm often collared in the street by people asking why I didn't invest in such and such a project. I have to explain that while the idea was good it could not be translated into a money-making venture. There is always the danger in business of making ourselves into what I call 'busy fools' – taking a project, devoting time and resources to it, and ending up with no financial reward. But when I do find an idea – always someone else's – that I think will work, I get off my backside and do something about it. That's the difference between me and so many other people.

Rule Twelve: Turn your dreams into reality

There's not much difference between a fantasist and a visionary. We all have dreams and without dreams in business I don't believe you can be successful. The trick is to turn those dreams into reality. Obviously, the more success you have, the greater the resources available to you. And once you've made one idea come true, it's easier the next time. That's why people turn up on *Dragons' Den* to get the help they need to make that first dream come true.

And you have to have passion for that dream. It's got to be something you're going to enjoy, otherwise it's highly unlikely that you will achieve your goal.

You must not, however, fall into the trap of ignoring the facts and deficiencies in your idea. That's where a lot of people trip up – they lose sight of the bigger picture and ignore the failings of the idea. I've seen people persevere with a venture for ten or even twenty years, bring it to market and still refuse to accept the fact that it is not a viable business proposition – and never will be. There is absolutely nothing wrong with aborting a project when your analysis and market research show that it is not going to be the next big thing. Your first loss is your best loss. You take the hit and move on.

Making £100 million is easy. Making your first £1 million is the difficult part. You have got to be passionate about your idea. If you can go to the pub and bore your friends senseless about your dream you're halfway there. It is imperative that you have an idea you really believe in, and you also have to be absolutely determined you can make it work. But if you don't attempt to do it, it will never happen. Don't let your idea be the one that got away.

Index